COOK&
FREEZE

COOK & FREEZE

150 DELICIOUS DISHES
TO SERVE NOW AND LATER

DANA JACOBI

RODALE

To Joan and Serendipity

Rodale books may be purchased for business or promotional use or for special sales. For information, please write to:

Special Markets Department, Rodale Inc., 733 Third Avenue, New York, NY 10017
Printed in the United States of America

Rodale Inc. makes every effort to use acid-free ⊗, recycled paper ♲.

Recipe photo on front cover: Smoked Fish Cakes with Lemon Mayonnaise, page 87

Photographs by Kate Mathis
Book design by Christopher Rhoads

Library of Congress Cataloging-in-Publication Data

Jacobi, Dana.
    Cook & freeze : 150 delicious dishes to serve now and later / Dana Jacobi ; photographs by Kate Mathis.
        p.   cm.
    ISBN-13 978-1-60529-469-8   paperback
    ISBN-10 1-60529-469-1   paperback
    1. Frozen foods.   2. Cookery (Frozen foods)   I. Title.
TX610.J32   2010
641.6'153—dc22   2010019606

Distributed to the trade by Macmillan

2   4   6   8   10   9   7   5   3   1   paperback

We inspire and enable people to improve their lives and the world around them

contents

introduction

This is a book I did not expect to write. Single and living in a New York City apartment, I used my freezer primarily for storing nuts, exotic rices, vodka, and fruit for smoothies. Only those with a family to feed would, I assumed, fill it with prepared dishes, and that would require a real freezer, or at least a prestige-brand refrigerator with more freezer capacity than the modest compartment on top of my 15-year-old Magic Chef fridge.

Then I became a caregiver. Looking after aging parents soon had me cooking for three rather than just myself. After a chaotic few weeks of running back and forth to give them freshly prepared meals at least once a day, I started stocking my freezer with soups and one-dish meals in individual servings that I delivered to them once a week. This allowed my folks to heat up ready-to-eat meals every day on their own, and I got to control when I cooked. Using the freezer reduced stress and even made cooking time pleasant.

Still, I rarely thought to use the freezer for myself. Only while creating the recipes for a Mediterranean cookbook did I get interested in storing prepared food long term. Because I was cooking several delicious dishes a day, there was more than I could possibly eat. I gave some food away but began freezing the dishes I liked best. Weeks later, after the book was completed and I needed time off from cooking, I turned to my well-stocked freezer. What emerged was a revelation. Mostly, the soups and stews were fine, but the thawed rice in the paella was a mushy disaster, while other dishes turned watery. Gazpacho that went in tasting good was overpowered by garlic and full of soggy vegetables when defrosted.

These spectacularly varied results started a research phase during which I discovered what kind of recipes produced meals that were great both when freshly cooked *and* when defrosted. As I experimented with methods and ingredients, I developed a natural replacement that duplicates the canned condensed soups called for in casseroles and an apple pie you would never know came from the freezer. I also found out how to streamline the work of preparing several dishes during one afternoon or evening.

Now my freezer, which is less than 24 inches wide and only 11 $\frac{1}{2}$ inches high, holds several batches of soup, layers and frosting for a chocolate cake, a couple of stews, sloppy joes, lasagna, burritos, chocolate chip cookie dough, and rosemary-roasted almonds. Guests never know whether the dishes I serve them are freshly prepared or came from the freezer. Plus, when work deadlines have me on overload, I eat very well without ordering budget-busting takeout or buying frozen entrees. In fact, I shop the supermarket for specials and save money by packing the freezer.

A well-stocked freezer provides multiple benefits. It can help parents, professionals, students, singles, and older people with busy lives meet mealtime effortlessly. You will know the meals you serve your family, a partner, or yourself are good because you made them. You are certain they contain only the best fresh ingredients, were made safely, and meet any special dietary needs. Plus, cooking to freeze can do more than fit your budget—it can help you trim it while eating fabulously.

If this sounds good, I hope that using this book, you will join me in serving meals that prove convenience need not compromise quality. Drawing raves whether served freshly made or out of the freezer, the recipes in this book include dishes for casual dinners, quick hors d'oeuvres, sweet treats, hearty soups, and even elegant dishes to serve by candlelight.

everything you need to know

Serving dishes from the freezer saves time and money. Doing it successfully depends on what you make and how you store, defrost, and reheat it.

Not all dishes freeze equally well or should be handled the same way after freezing. I have experimented to find what works best. The result is dishes that win raves when you serve them immediately and are still delicious when you serve them from the freezer. To assure this, the recipes in this book include directions for each step—from freezing and defrosting to reheating—that are perfected for each dish. As a result, your Double Chocolate Layer Cake and other baked goods will remain moist when the freezer wants to dry them out. Soups and stews will have lively flavors, meats will stay tender, and vegetables will remain appealing when reheated.

This book also includes many casseroles, which are freezer favorites, in recipes that offer a unique choice. When condensed soup is called for, you have the option to replace it with a homemade and natural equivalent. These creamy "souper sauces" I have created also happen to be gluten-free.

how freezing works

As foods freeze, the water in the cells of vegetables, meats, and other foods turns to ice crystals. The ice preserves food by slowing down deterioration caused by microorganisms, including bacteria, that leads to decay. These microorganisms must have water to function. Turning the water to ice prevents them from growing and creating reactions that make food spoil. It is important to note that depriving microorganisms of water does not kill them. This means food must be kept solidly frozen at 0°F or lower to be safely preserved.

The more quickly foods freeze, the smaller the ice crystals that form. Compare serving grainy refrozen ice cream to the creamy original and you will see why the smallest crystals are desirable. Fine ice crystals maintain better flavor, as well, because they do not rupture cell walls. As food defrosts, the ruptured cells collapse and moisture flows out. Think of the watery collapse of a defrosted strawberry and you'll have a good picture of the effect of ruptured cells.

freeze fast

To store food properly, your freezer needs to be at 0°F, and even colder when you are adding food to be frozen. Most freezers have a thermostat dial you can turn down. Others have a "fast freeze" function to switch on when adding foods to freeze. Once the new items are frozen, you can return the freezer to around 0°F. A freezer thermometer helps you make sure the freezer is reaching and maintaining the proper temperature and costs $20 or less. I like Maverick's RF-02 digital refrigerator/freezer thermometer for a combination refrigerator/freezer or Taylor's thermometers for freezers.

air is the enemy

When air reaches frozen food, it causes freezer burn, gray patches that are hard and tough. Food with freezer burn is dry and off-tasting. The air can be from the outside or inside. Air pockets in a container of frozen soup, for example, allow big ice crystals to form and then evaporate, causing freezer burn. Sealing food airtight requires both the right packaging and good technique.

freezing is not forever

While freezing preserves foods, they still deteriorate over time. We have all heard about a roast that languished in the freezer for years. If it was not covered with freezer burn and was still edible, odds are it tasted like a defrosted ice cube.

Since flavors fade long before frozen food becomes inedible, the storage times I recommend are the result of checking dishes after different amounts of time in the freezer. Stored longer, they absolutely will be edible; however, they just will no longer have maximum flavor and optimum texture.

the right materials

Packaging should preserve food's moisture content while protecting its nutrition, color, and texture. Plastic freezer bags, plastic wrap made for freezing, and heavy-duty aluminum foil provide the easiest and most space-saving, effective protection. I am also in love with my Food Saver, a machine that vacuum seals food, but let's come back to that later.

Heavy-Duty Plastic Bags

PRO

Heavy-duty bags with a zipper seal made specifically for freezing in 1-quart and 1- and 2-gallon sizes are indispensable.

Excellent for storing any liquid and semiliquid, including soups, stews, sauces, and any dish that flows.

Also good for holding individually wrapped baked goods.

CON

Unwrapped foods like meatballs and cookies, and plastic-wrapped items such as cake layers or casseroles, can get icy and dry out inside a bag.

Plastic Freezer Wrap

PRO

Made to be airtight, freezer wrap is heavier, clings tighter than regular plastic wrap, and protects flavor while sealing in moisture better, I recommend pressing it directly onto the surface of sauces, casseroles, puddings, and other dishes. This is particularly helpful when the contents do not completely fill a baking dish or plastic container.

Wide width requires cutting for smaller items.

Press-and-seal type does not cling to dry foods such as burritos and cupcakes. It also makes eliminating all of the air difficult. However, for short-term freezing of individual chicken breasts, chops, and burgers, I recommend it highly.

Aluminum Foil and Pans

PRO

Using heavy-duty foil to over-wrap plastic-wrapped food assures it is well protected and helps keep its flavors fresh.

Use heavy-duty foil because freezing makes regular foil brittle.

Heavy-duty foil baking pans go easily from freezer to oven to table.

CON

Does not seal surface of foods as well as plastic wrap.

Folding required to seal is bulky.

Foil baking pans do not conduct heat as well as other materials.

Plastic Containers

PRO

Protect crushable foods, including pies, cupcakes, and cookies.

Allow a neatly organized freezer.

CON

Unless made to use for freezing, plastic containers are brittle at low temperatures, so do not use take-out containers or ordinary containers from packaged foods.

Look for the snowflake symbol, which indicates containers are appropriate for use in the freezer.

Take up more space than plastic bags for storing liquids.

Airspace at top allows freezer burn. To minimize this, be sure the sealing system is airtight and fill containers fully (see "Pack Like a Pro" on page 10).

Here's How: Ladle food into the container. Press plastic freezer wrap onto the surface of the food, then open-freeze to freeze the food quickly (see page 8). When the food is solid, seal the container, leaving the plastic freezer wrap beneath the cover if there is a gap between the top of the contents and the cover. Return the container to the freezer.

Glass and Ceramic

PRO

The most attractive choice.

Conduct heat well. Before using a dual-purpose dish made for both freezer and oven, always check with the manufacturer to make sure if it will tolerate the sudden temperature change of going directly from freezer to oven.

CON

Costly because freezing ties up multiple baking dishes.

Require the most room in the freezer unless frozen food is unmolded, wrapped, and then returned to its original dish for reheating.

More difficult to wrap with an airtight seal.

vacuum packing

A system using heavy plastic bags and an appliance that sucks out the air and then heat-seals the bag. This is the optimal way to freeze certain foods at home.

PRO

Removes all the air and makes an airtight seal. The best way of protecting flavor and avoiding freezer burn.

Ideal for many dry foods and already frozen dishes.

CON

Requires a special appliance that is costly and takes up room.

Bags are costly.

Foods containing liquid, including soups and skillet dishes with sauce, must be frozen and then sealed.

Pressure crushes even some frozen items, such as cupcakes and waffles, unless you buy special containers.

labels

Scotch tape, masking tape, and paper labels do not stick when cold, and any writing on them is not indelible.

I like Label Once Erasable Food Labels because they stick to any packaging and are indelibly waterproof. When you use a permanent marker and the special eraser in the starter kit, they are easily and truly erasable and reusable.

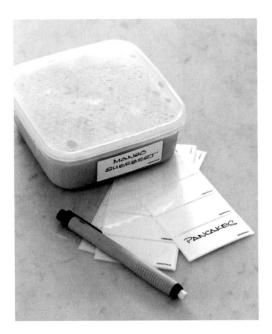

the big chill

Following a few rules is essential for good results in freezing. Here is the first and most important one.

Think Ahead, Think Small

Once most dishes are frozen, the entire amount must be defrosted. You cannot thaw one portion from a quart of soup or half a frozen lasagna. And thawed food cannot be refrozen, so forget about returning leftovers to the freezer. Instead, think ahead and consider freezing foods in one- or two-portion amounts. Even in a large household, this allows flexibility to suit changing schedules and individual preferences. Another benefit is that small amounts freeze, defrost, and reheat much faster.

SEVEN COMMANDMENTS FOR FREEZING

- Cool food to room temperature and then chill it in the refrigerator before freezing. This preserves the quality by helping foods freeze faster. (Baked goods are the exception. Most are frozen without chilling.) I recommend chilling dishes on a wire rack set on a plate on the bottom of your refrigerator—its the coldest area. This cools the food more rapidly while catching spills.

- Use wide, flat containers as much as possible. This exposes the greatest surface area of the food to cold air. Do not use plastic containers from take-out or commercially prepared foods, which may crack in the freezer.

- Use containers that are just large enough for the food you want to freeze. Headspace is necessary as foods expand in freezing, but empty space encourages freezer burn. With experience, you will know what is just right.

- Freeze foods on a baking sheet lined with baking parchment or wax paper. This prevents plastic bags and other containers from sticking. Chill the baking sheet before adding the food to speed freezing.

- Place only food that is already firmly frozen on wire racks in the freezer. Forget once and you will always remember prying off a bag of soup that sagged into the spaces of the rack.

- Allow space so cold air can circulate around food while it freezes. Once frozen, stacking packages tightly to save space is fine. (To protect baked goods from crushing, shelter them in plastic containers; see page 4.)

- Avoid UFOs (unidentified frozen objects) by labeling everything with the date, contents, amount, and directions for defrosting and reheating (see the opposite page for labels to use).

THREE MORE COMMANDMENTS

- Keep an inventory list on or near the freezer and *use* it. Include the date the dish was frozen.
- Place only plastic-covered racks in the freezer, as packaging can stick to cold metal.
- Group similar dishes together, such as main dishes, soups, or desserts. This speeds searching and avoids frozen fingers.

Three Methods for Freezing

Beyond these overall rules, some dishes are best frozen before and others after cooking. Some dishes should be wrapped before and others after freezing. In each recipe in this book, I'll tell you which method is best for that dish. Choosing the best way to freeze a dish also depends on how many portions you expect to defrost.

Open-Freezing

The most rapid method. This is ideal for freezing an entire casserole, individual portions of some dishes, and single pieces like meatballs, dumplings, and cookies.

Here's How: Foods that hold their shape, small or large, from meatballs and meatloaf to cookies, cupcakes, cheesecake, and pies, can be open-frozen on a baking sheet, then double wrapped or vacuum sealed.

Casseroles, lasagna, and other dishes that need help holding a shape are frozen in their baking dish, then unmolded and either double wrapped or vacuum sealed.

Liquid dishes like Sunday Red Sauce and Golden Cheese Sauce can be open-frozen in a container, then unmolded and wrapped or vacuum sealed.

Bagging It

Soups, stews, chili, sauces, and other liquid or semiliquid dishes freeze and store well in a plastic bag.

Here's How: To fill plastic bags easily, create a "stand." A cut-off half-gallon plastic milk bottle or empty coffee can works well. Fold the top of the bag out over the container and ladle in the food.

To seal the bag, zip it almost closed and then lay it flat on the counter. Stroke the bag from the bottom up, spreading the contents to fill the bag evenly up to the top and pushing out air bubbles, then seal the bag completely. Reopening and repeating this may be necessary to remove all of the air. The chunkier the food, the harder this is, and it may take a minute or two of repeated stroking. Sometimes, gently pushing a rolling pin over the bag from the bottom to the top is helpful.

When an amount does not fully fill the bag—perhaps 1 cup of chili, sauce, or soup—after the air is pressed out, folding the bag over further seals the empty part and reduces the risk of freezer burn.

To vacuum seal liquids such as soup or a dish with sauce, seal the bag with a clip until the food is frozen, then heat-seal it.

Double Wrapping

For secure protection, either wrap food first in plastic freezer wrap and then in heavy-duty foil or foil-wrap, then slip the wrapped food into a resealable freezer bag. I find plastic plus foil protects flavors better, although I store some individually plastic-wrapped desserts, including cupcakes and Almond Tortoni, together in a plastic bag.

Double wrapping can be used before freezing foods or after open-freezing. It protects food in a casserole or baking dish or on its own (see "Super Space Saver," on page 10).

Here's How: Center the food on a length of plastic wrap long enough to cover the top twice. Smooth the wrap tightly against the food from one side, then the other, pressing it onto the surface, particularly for casseroles, pasta, and other dishes. Press the plastic neatly down the sides and smooth the ends under the food.

Next, center the food on a length of foil long enough to bring two opposite sides up to meet over the top. Holding both sides together, make a 1-inch fold along the length of the foil, then roll down until you can press the foil tightly against the food. Mold the foil against the sides, then fold the ends up and over, flattening them to seal the package.

Cut foil to a smaller size for small items like a single portion of lasagna, a stuffed pepper, or a brownie.

Super Space Saver

To save room and not tie up baking dishes, pie plates, and other bulky or costly containers, freeze casseroles and other dishes, and then for storage, lift the food out of the original container. When ready to serve, drop the frozen dish back into its original container and defrost or reheat to bring it to the table.

Here's How: Coat the inside of the baking dish with nonstick spray.

Fill the baking dish with food. Depending on the recipe directions, either open-freeze immediately or cook, then cool and freeze.

Unmold the frozen food and double wrap in plastic freezer wrap, then foil, or vacuum seal, and return to the freezer. Before defrosting, unwrap and drop the food back into the original baking dish.

defrost with care

How you defrost food is as important as how you freeze it. The key is defrosting slowly, or at least gradually. This helps food hold on to moisture as it thaws and

pack like a pro
Pressing a piece of plastic freezer wrap directly onto food before freezing, the way chefs cover the surface of a sauce to prevent a skin from forming, prevents ice from forming on the surface of casseroles as well as sauces, dips, and sorbets. Doing this when storing foods in a plastic container, before double wrapping, or when open-freezing dishes keeps them in the best condition longer.

best preserves its texture. It means *never* thawing foods at room temperature, with the exception of some baked goods. Defrosting on the counter also invites bacteria to party as the outside warms above 40°F before the center de-ices.

Go Slow

Defrosting in the refrigerator is usually best. It definitely requires advance planning since an entire casserole or whole meatloaf takes 24 hours or more to fully defrost. Even frozen cookie dough bakes up better after it sits in the refrigerator for 24 hours. The recipes in this book show a range of time to take into account the size—single portions or a whole casserole. Defrosting time also depends on the temperature in your refrigerator.

Skipping defrosting is not the answer. Dishes taken directly from the freezer take twice as long to bake as when they are defrosted. During that time, the top and sides tend to dry out or get overdone before the center of the dish is fully hot. Overall, the quality you get is noticeably reduced.

This is where small is good. Eight slices of meatloaf transferred from the freezer to your refrigerator in the morning will be ready to serve for dinner.

When defrosting, set food on a plate to catch drips. Placing a wire rack on the plate helps the bottom of a dish thaw as quickly as the top.

Before defrosting, many dishes should be unwrapped and dropped back into their original container. Coating the original baking dish with nonstick spray before doing this eases release when serving the reheated food and speeds cleanup.

If food has been unwrapped, at least cover it loosely with plastic wrap so it does not dry out while thawing. Again, some baked goods are the exception, as their recipes indicate.

If your plans change, most defrosted dishes keep in the refrigerator for 2 to 3 days.

Really Good and Much Faster

A cold water bath, where it is suitable, speeds defrosting considerably. This easy method works for most liquid and semiliquid dishes—soups, sauces, and stews—reducing their defrosting time to as little as 15 minutes for some dishes in 1- or 2-cup servings, and rarely more than 60 minutes.

Here's How: Be sure the food is sealed in an airtight plastic bag or container.

Fill a large bowl with cold water, around 45°F. Place the bag or container into the water.

Change the water every 15 minutes until the food is defrosted, checking it regularly.

To speed the process, when soups or sauces are partly defrosted, bend the bag to break the contents into chunks.

What about Microwave Defrosting?

I use the microwave to reheat thawed food but do not recommend it for defrosting. Microwave defrosting often produces results with poorer texture than using a water bath, plus the food requires frequent attention as it thaws, so I do not recommend it, with exceptions such as Fully Loaded Breakfast Burritos and Deep Dark Chocolate Fondue.

To defrost in the microwave, use the directions that came with your oven or follow these steps:

Use not more than 30 percent power.

Use short bursts and let the food rest in between.

Keep scraping, stirring, or breaking up the food so the thawed parts do not cook.

hot stuff

Some thawed dishes, particularly soups and stews, are merely reheated, but others are best when you actually cook them after defrosting. Sometimes, how the dish was originally cooked is also the best way to reheat it. For others, including Pecan Chicken Paillards and Lamb Shanks with White Beans and Lemon, it is not. For each dish in this book, the recipe will guide you.

In the Oven

Before heating, bringing dishes to room temperature reduces oven time significantly. Usually you can do this by letting them sit on the counter while preheating the oven.

Most dishes reheat best at 350°F, but each recipe specifies what temperature to use.

For safety, heat food until an instant-read thermometer inserted into the center registers 160°F. If the dish will dry out or burn, cover it with foil until this temperature is reached. If it is not brown enough, slip the dish briefly under the broiler. If you do not have a thermometer, insert a knife into the center of the dish. The blade should feel hot to the touch.

When cooking or heating up only one or two servings, using a toaster oven saves energy and time. It is perfect for cooking Turkish Ground Beef Kebabs and California Meatloaf Burgers, and to warm up one or two servings of Johnny Appleseed French Toast, casseroles, and other dishes.

On the Stove

A heavy saucepan is the best way to reheat soups, sauces, stews, and some skillet dishes, including Shredded Orange Pork and Green Beans in Greek Tomato Sauce. Dishes that are watery after defrosting are best heated up uncovered so evaporation reconcentrates their flavors.

On the Grill

Freeze dishes like Salsa Fajitas and Moroccan Pork Satay in their marinade, and they are ready to toss on the grill or cook in a stove-top grill pan as soon as they are defrosted.

Pat foods dry before grilling them, using paper towels.

what freezes well and what doesn't

Not all foods freeze well. This includes eggs, cured meats, and fruits and vegetables with high water content, such as strawberries, tomatoes, summer squash, eggplant, mushrooms, and celery. In this book, I show the best ways to work with these foods. For example, mushrooms do best when cooked until most of their moisture evaporates. Vegetables cut into smaller pieces so they freeze more quickly also come out better. I avoid dishes made with egg whites, mayonnaise, or flour-based sauces, which can break when defrosted.

The recipes in this book all call for regular dairy products. Their fat helps keep ice crystals small by surrounding food cells and discouraging them from hooking up. Switching to low-fat dairy products is okay if you'll be serving the dish freshly made, but these products, including cheeses, sour cream, and milk, do not freeze well. Disregard this caveat, as did a friend who substituted reduced-fat ricotta cheese in Spinach and Pesto Lasagna, and you may get weeping or watery flavor when the dish is defrosted. I also believe a healthy diet has room to allow everything in moderation. For me, the time and money saved using the freezer balances out the amount of saturated fat in one serving of most dishes.

Some dishes freeze best when some of their ingredients are undercooked, particularly pasta. This is another reason why the recipes give specific directions to stop at an earlier point when freezing a dish than when serving it freshly prepared.

Finally, freezing can affect the flavor or texture of dishes. The outcome can be good, as when Freeze Please Fudge Brownies turn even creamier and defrosted soups taste even better. However, to avoid surprises, Freezer Notes alert you when the difference will be significant. I like to think this honesty sets this book apart from other freezer cookbooks. Always, you will find results so good that you will enjoy every dish, whether served now or later.

food safety

Bacteria love temperatures between 40°F and 140°F, so always store food below 40°F and heat it above 140°F. Cooling food before refrigerating, and chilling it before freezing, helps you keep your refrigerator and freezer safely cold. Using an instant-read thermometer when reheating helps you make sure the food reaches the safe zone.

Refreezing thawed food without first cooking it creates the risk of food poisoning. Exceptions include pie crust, cookie dough, and foods that are still at least partially icy and frozen.

In the freezer, if a bag tears and you do not want to consume its contents immediately, slip the bag, frozen food and all, into a new freezer bag.

Consuming perishable food stored at temperatures above 40°F is considered unsafe. If you accidentally forget food that is cooling at room temperature until it is warmer than this, generally longer than 60 minutes, heartbreaking as it is, throw it out. To ensure this does not happen, when food is cooling, I set a timer to remind me to move it to the refrigerator.

freezing as a lifestyle

Putting several dishes together during one kitchen session means you can draw from the freezer all week long or even for a longer period. It enables you to have dishes ready and waiting when you are entertaining. You can also prepare weeks of meals for someone who needs support to eat well.

As a lifestyle, freezing lets you take advantage of specials and allows you to buy well-priced quantities to turn into multiple dishes. Preparing multiple dishes at one session or multiplying a recipe requires organization and planning. To help you, Cooking to Fill Your Freezer (page 263) lists recipes that are easy to prepare during one cooking session.

If you are not used to cooking several dishes at one time, perhaps during one afternoon, here are helpful hints.

Make a master shopping list so you buy enough of every ingredient.

Take copies of all the recipes to be prepared with you when shopping.

If making more than two dishes, shopping one day and cooking the next may work best.

Group operations and ingredients. Before you start cooking, measure out the ingredients for every recipe and organize them by dish. For example, chop all the onions, then divide them into containers labeled for each recipe. Prepare the necessary pans. Assemble and label all the storage containers needed.

All the recipes in this book indicate whether they can be doubled. Doubling, in most cases, means preparing ingredients to make two meatloaves, two pans of Baked Four-Cheese Ziti, or two batches of Freeze Please Fudge Brownies. In some instances, cooking times remain the same as for a single recipe. If you decide to make the doubled recipe in a single, larger pan, you will need to adjust the cooking time accordingly. Likewise, when doubling a soup or stew recipe, it may need to simmer longer.

Make cooking pleasant. Pick out music you enjoy. Get a friend to help and make enough to share. Or make this quality alone time and savor it.

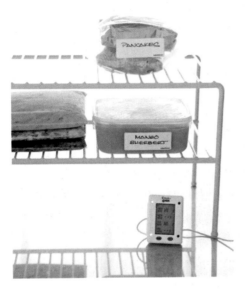

a cool benefit

When I started this book and learned the proper temperature at which to keep the freezer, I turned mine down to 0°F. This also made my refrigerator colder, 33° to 35°F, instead of around 40°F. This temperature difference has made foods keep fresh significantly longer. As a result, I now throw out milk and leftovers less often. Fresh meat and fish, dairy foods, vegetables, and deli products stay good longer, too. True, this uses more power, but with today's food costs, this benefit can be significant, especially for a smaller household where a barbecued chicken, quart of milk, or bunch of celery gets used up more slowly.

chapter 2

dips, nibbles, snacks, and small bites

Having these flavorful, light bites in the freezer is handy any-time—when a friend drops by to chat, if you need nibbles for a committee meeting, or to serve as hors d'oeuvres for formal entertaining. They also save you money. No need to buy an expensive wedge of cheese if you bake up Peppered Parmesan Crisps or to send out for hot wings when you have them ready to pop in the oven.

You can orchestrate a full party from this selection of cold and hot choices, many of them finger foods. Serve Roasted Rosemary Almonds for bar nibbles, Herbed Tapenade for bruschetta, Any-time Chicken Liver Mousse for canapés, and Parmesan-Crusted Chicken Tenders to please young guests. The more serious dishes can be a light meal, like Moroccan Pork Satay and Spanakopita with Mixed Greens and Feta.

Some dishes here do not need defrosting. Several make enough to both serve some now and also pack some in the freezer to have on hand for another time.

- all-american pimiento cheese
- herbed tapenade
- peppered parmesan crisps
- roasted pepper and eggplant spread
- anytime chicken liver mousse
- spanakopita with mixed greens and feta
- steamed vegetable dumplings, sichuan-style
- mexican mushrooms in won ton cups
- roasted rosemary almonds
- sizzling hot wings
- parmesan-crusted chicken tenders with honey mustard dip
- sweet and tangy bison balls
- moroccan pork satay

all-american pimiento cheese

▶ freeze for up
   to 4 weeks

▶ can be doubled

▶ quick fix

▶ feeds a crowd

Scoop up this tangy cheese with celery and carrot sticks, spread it on crackers for a snack, or use it in tea sandwiches. It also makes great grilled cheese sandwiches to serve with Tastes as Good as Canned Tomato Soup (page 52).

Makes 2 cups

3 ounces cream cheese, softened

2 cups (8 ounces) finely shredded extra-sharp Cheddar cheese

⅓ cup mayonnaise, regular or low-fat

1 teaspoon brown mustard

3 ounces (¾ jar) drained pimientos or Peppadew peppers

½ teaspoon salt

¼ teaspoon freshly ground pepper

to serve

¼ cup minced sweet onion or chopped green olives (optional)

side dish
For canapés, spread All-American Pimiento Cheese on warm toast triangles and garnish with a pimiento strip and finely chopped parsley.

cook smart
Pressing plastic wrap directly onto the surface protects against ice crystals that form on the surface when soft foods like this spread freeze.

In a food processor, whirl the cream cheese until fluffy, 30 seconds. Add the Cheddar, mayonnaise, mustard, pimientos or peppers, salt, and pepper and whirl until the mixture is finely flecked with pimiento and almost smooth, 90 seconds.

for serving now Pack the Pimiento Cheese into a 2-cup container and cover tightly. Refrigerate for 4 hours to allow the flavors to meld, or up to 1 week. Before serving, mix in the onion or olives, if using.

to freeze Pack the Pimiento Cheese into ½- or 1-cup plastic freezer containers, press plastic wrap onto the surface, cover tightly, and freeze.

to defrost and serve Transfer the frozen Pimiento Cheese to the refrigerator and thaw for 6 to 12 hours, depending on the amount.

Stir well and adjust the seasoning. Mix in the onion or olives, if using.

herbed tapenade

Spread this herbed French black olive puree on crusty bread for bruschetta, or serve it in a bowl surrounded by crudités as a dip. It also performs magic when you dot a spoonful on deviled eggs and is the perfect condiment to serve with grilled chicken.

Makes 1 ½ cups

1 ½ cups pitted kalamata olives

4 garlic cloves, chopped

1 tablespoon capers, rinsed and drained

1 teaspoon Dijon mustard

1 tablespoon fresh thyme leaves or 1 teaspoon dried

1 teaspoon finely chopped fresh rosemary

1 tablespoon brandy (optional)

2 tablespoons extra virgin olive oil plus additional for storing

Salt and freshly ground pepper

In a food processor, pulse the olives, garlic, and capers until coarsely chopped. Add the mustard, thyme, rosemary, and brandy (if using) and pulse until finely chopped. With the motor running, drizzle in 2 tablespoons of the oil. Season to taste with salt and pepper.

for serving now Scoop the tapenade into a serving bowl. Spoon over enough additional oil to seal the surface. Refrigerate for 1 hour to let the flavors meld. Covered with plastic wrap in the refrigerator, tapenade keeps for 3 days. Stir in the oil from the surface before serving.

to freeze Spoon the tapenade into one large or three ½-cup plastic containers, spoon on a thin coating of oil to seal the surface, cover, and freeze.

to defrost and serve Thaw the tapenade in the refrigerator for 8 to 24 hours, depending on the container size. Stir in the surface oil, adjust the seasoning, and spoon the tapenade into a serving bowl or use it as a condiment.

▶ freeze for up to 8 weeks

▶ can be doubled

▶ feeds a crowd

▶ quick fix

side dish

I sometimes whirl in 3 ounces of drained olive oil–packed light tuna along with the olives when making this tapenade. Do not freeze this version.

cook smart

Fleshy kalamata olives are a good alternative to the black niçoise olives, which are not available pitted, traditionally called for in tapenade.

peppered parmesan crisps

This savory shortbread is made with just cheese, flour, and butter, and putting them together takes only 10 minutes. A sprinkling of freshly ground pepper adds a nice kick to the rich Parmesan flavor in these coin-shaped nibbles.

Makes 3 dozen

½ cup (1 stick) unsalted butter, softened

1 cup shredded Parmesan cheese

½ teaspoon freshly ground pepper

Pinch of cayenne pepper

½ teaspoon salt

1 cup unbleached all-purpose flour

▶ freeze for up to 6 weeks

▶ can be doubled

▶ freeze now, cook later

▶ feeds a crowd

▶ elegant for entertaining

Preheat the oven to 350°F.

In a mixing bowl, work the butter and cheese together using the back of a wooden spoon. Mix in the pepper, cayenne, and salt. Add the flour and stir just until the mixture becomes a soft dough. Pinch off the dough in scant tablespoons and roll between your palms to form 1-inch marbles.

for serving now Flatten each ball of dough shaping it into a ¼-inch-thick round. Place the formed crisps on light-colored baking sheets, spacing them 1 inch apart. Top the crisps with a touch of the pepper.

Bake the crisps for 6 minutes. Reverse the position of the baking sheets, rotate them, and bake 2 to 3 minutes longer, until the crisps are lightly colored around the edges; they will remain pale on top. Transfer the crisps to a wire rack and cool. Peppered Parmesan Crisps keep for 1 week in an airtight container at room temperature.

to freeze Open-freeze the balls of dough, then pack them in a resealable 1-quart plastic freezer bag, or vacuum seal the frozen dough balls.

to defrost and serve Defrost the dough in the refrigerator for 24 hours. (The crisps can be baked as soon as the dough is soft enough to shape, but they will have better texture if the dough sits for 24 hours.)

Flatten the balls of dough between your thumb and flattened fingers, shaping them into ¼-inch-thick rounds. Place the formed crisps on light-colored baking sheets, spacing them 1 inch apart, and top with a light grinding of pepper. Bake as For Serving Now, above.

side dish
Serve Peppered Parmesan Crisps with a dry white wine, Merlot, or medium-dry sherry.

cook smart
Shredded Parmesan cheese gives these rounds a crisp texture, while using powdery grated Parmesan makes them more like a shortbread. If possible, splurge on genuine Parmigiano-Reggiano from Italy.

The drier the butter, the better the result. I recommend Whole Foods 365 brand or Cabot's.

roasted pepper and eggplant spread

▶ freeze for up
to 8 weeks

▶ feeds a crowd

One taste of this roasted sweet pepper, eggplant, and garlic combo reveals why it is eaten morning, noon, and night in Balkan countries, where it is called *ajvar* (pronounced *EYE*-var). Enjoy it as a chunky dip; spread it on bread for bruschetta; or serve it as a condiment with grilled seafood, poultry, or pork.

Makes 2¾ cups

2 teaspoons plus 3 tablespoons extra virgin olive oil

2 pounds sweet bell peppers, preferably a combination of red and orange

1 small eggplant, about 1 pound

2 garlic cloves, minced

Salt and freshly ground pepper

1 tablespoon red wine vinegar

Chopped flat leaf parsley, for garnish

side dish
Sprinkled with crumbled feta or topped with sliced hard-cooked egg, this spread becomes a light meal.

Preheat the oven to 450°F. Using 2 teaspoons of the oil, coat the baking sheets lightly.

Halve the peppers lengthwise and seed, then arrange the peppers cut side down on 1 of the prepared baking sheets. Place the eggplant on the second baking sheet and prick it all over with a fork. Roast the peppers and eggplant for 30 to 40 minutes, or until their skins are blistered and blackened. The eggplant should be soft but not collapsed. Using tongs, transfer the peppers to a large bowl, cover it with plastic wrap, and then set aside to steam for 20 minutes. Wrap the eggplant in the foil covering the baking sheet and set aside for 30 minutes.

With your fingers, peel the peppers. Cut their flesh into 2-inch chunks, place them in a food processor, and pulse 5 or 6 times to chop coarsely. Scoop the peppers into a mixing bowl. Scoop the flesh from the eggplant into the food processor. Add the garlic, 1 teaspoon salt, and the remaining 3 tablespoons of oil, and whirl to a smooth puree. Add the eggplant puree to the chopped peppers and mix to combine. Mix in the vinegar and season to taste with salt and pepper.

for serving now Let the spread sit for 1 hour at room temperature to allow the flavors to meld. This spread keeps, covered in the refrigerator, for 5 days.

to freeze Spoon the spread into ½-cup plastic containers and press plastic freezer wrap over the tops before covering, or pack 1 to 1½ cups into resealable 1-quart plastic freezer bags. Lay the bags flat and freeze on a baking sheet.

to defrost and serve Defrost on a plate in the refrigerator for 6 to 24 hours, depending on the amount. Or thaw in a bowl of cold water, changing the water every 15 minutes. Adjust the seasoning, including the vinegar, and serve at room temperature.

anytime chicken liver mousse

▶ freeze for up
   to 8 weeks

▶ can be doubled

▶ feeds a crowd

Chicken livers are inexpensive. Here, pureeing them with butter and herbs transforms them into a positively posh hors d'oeuvre. The mousse is slightly less silky after freezing, but this is a small trade-off for the convenience.

Makes 1¾ cups

1 tablespoon plus ½ cup (1 stick) unsalted butter, softened	1 garlic clove
1 tablespoon canola oil	1 tablespoon fresh lemon juice
1 pound chicken livers	Salt and freshly ground pepper
⅓ cup chopped shallots	¼ cup clarified butter, melted (see Cook Smart)
½ teaspoon dried thyme	Triangles of warm toast

cook smart

To clarify butter, melt it in a small, heavy saucepan over medium-low heat until the white solids fall to the bottom of the pan and turn dark brown, 15 to 20 minutes. Be sure to keep the heat low so the butter does not burn. Strain the clarified butter through a sieve lined with cheesecloth or a paper towel into a heatproof jar. Tightly covered, clarified butter keeps in the refrigerator for up to 6 months.

In a medium skillet, melt 1 tablespoon of the butter with the oil over medium heat. Add the chicken livers in 1 layer, then the shallots. Increase the heat to medium-high and cook until the livers are browned on all sides and slightly pink in the center, 10 minutes. Take care not to burn the shallots.

Scrape the contents of the skillet into the bowl of a food processor and whirl until smooth. Add the thyme, garlic, and lemon juice and whirl to combine. Cool the puree almost to room temperature.

Cut the softened butter into 16 pieces and add to the pureed livers. Whirl just until combined, stopping several times to scrape down the sides of the bowl. Season the mousse to taste with salt and pepper.

Pack the mousse into 1 or 2 containers. Rap the containers sharply on the counter to eliminate air bubbles. Smooth the top of the mousse with the back of a spoon. Spoon the clarified butter over the mousse to seal it. Cover tightly and refrigerate the mousse overnight to allow the flavors to meld. Before serving, let the mousse sit out for 20 minutes. Mix in the butter covering the top, then spoon the mousse into a serving bowl. Surround with toast triangles.

to freeze Transfer the containers of chilled mousse to the freezer.

to defrost and serve Defrost the mousse in the refrigerator for 12 to 18 hours, depending on the amount. Before serving, let the mousse sit out for 20 minutes. Mix in the butter covering the top, then spoon the mousse into a serving bowl. Surround with toast triangles and serve immediately.

spanakopita with mixed greens and feta

Once you taste these flaky phyllo rolls, you may always want to make them this way. A Greek friend gave me the recipe, which, along with spinach, uses arugula and broccoli raab because this trio tastes like the wild greens her family gathers. (See Cook Smart to use spinach alone.) I like these neat rolls even better baked after freezing than freshly made.

Makes 8 pieces

1 bag (5 ounces) wild or baby arugula

1 bag (10 ounces) spinach, stems removed

1 pound broccoli raab, coarse stems removed

8 tablespoons (1 stick) unsalted butter

¾ cup finely chopped onion

1 garlic clove

1 medium leek, white part only, halved lengthwise and sliced

8 ounces feta cheese, crumbled

¼ teaspoon freshly ground nutmeg

⅛ teaspoon freshly ground pepper

1 large egg

12 sheets (12 inches x 17 inches) phyllo dough

- freeze for up to 8 weeks
- can be doubled
- freeze now, cook later
- no defrosting

Bring a large pot of water to a boil. Add the arugula and cook for 30 seconds, just until it is wilted and bright green, then remove to a colander using a slotted spoon. Run cold water over the arugula to stop the cooking, then drain well. Add the spinach to the same water and cook until tender, 3 minutes. Add to the arugula then cool. Cook the broccoli raab in the same water for 5 minutes, or until tender. Add to the other greens and cool. (If using only spinach, you may have to cook it in 2 batches.) A handful at a time, squeeze as much moisture from the greens as possible. Chop them coarsely, place in a mixing bowl, and set aside.

Melt 1 tablespoon of the butter in a medium skillet over medium heat. Add the onion, garlic, and leek. Increase the heat to medium-high and cook until the onion and leek are tender but not colored, 5 minutes, stirring often. Pour into the mixing bowl with the greens, along with the cheese, nutmeg, pepper, and egg, and mix with a fork until the filling is well combined.

Melt the remaining 7 tablespoons butter in the microwave or a small pot over medium-low heat. Halve the phyllo sheets crosswise and stack them together. Place on a dish towel and cover with wrung-out paper towels. One sheet at a time, place the phyllo on your work surface with the short side toward you. Brush the phyllo lightly with melted butter, starting around the edges and brushing toward the center. Top with a second sheet and brush with butter, then repeat, adding

side dish

For a light meal, serve 1 or 2 of these rolls with a bowl of Tastes as Good as Canned Tomato Soup (page 52) or Arlene's Gazpacho (page 45).

cook smart

To use only spinach for the filling, use 2 more 10-ounce bags to replace the arugula and broccoli raab.

To get the greens as dry as possible, I squeeze them twice.

2 more sheets of phyllo. Spoon one-eighth of the filling across the edge closest to you, starting 2 inches above the bottom. Flatten the filling into a rectangle, leaving 1½ inches of dough exposed on either side. Lift up the bottom edge of the phyllo over the filling, fold in the sides, and roll away from you to enclose the filling, keeping the sides tucked in. The rolled pocket should resemble a wide, flattened egg roll. Brush the top and sides liberally with melted butter. Use the remaining phyllo and filling to make 7 more rolls.

for serving now Preheat the oven to 375°F.

Line a light-colored baking sheet with baking parchment paper.

Arrange the phyllo rolls on the prepared baking sheet and bake for 30 to 40 minutes, until the phyllo is deep golden brown. Cool on the baking sheet for 10 minutes, then use a wide pancake turner to transfer the rolls to a wire rack. Serve warm.

to freeze Wrap the unbaked rolls individually in plastic freezer wrap, then package in pairs in heavy-duty foil. Refrigerate on a plate until chilled, 6 to 12 hours. Transfer the chilled rolls to the freezer. If desired, store the frozen spanakopita together in a resealable plastic freezer bag.

to defrost and serve Preheat the oven to 375°F.

Line a light-colored baking sheet with baking parchment paper. Unwrap the frozen rolls and place on the baking sheet.

Bake for 30 to 40 minutes, until the phyllo is deep golden brown. Cool on the baking sheet for 10 minutes, then use a wide pancake turner to transfer the rolls to a wire rack. Serve warm.

To bake 1 or 2 of the rolls, a toaster oven works well.

steamed vegetable dumplings, sichuan-style

I find pleating and stuffing these plump half-moons pleasantly meditative. Steaming turns them into translucent gems that burst with the flavors of shiitake mushrooms and sweet napa cabbage, especially if you use Japanese gyoza wrappers, which are thinner than those made for Chinese pot stickers. These dumplings are perfect served with Sesame-Soy Dipping Sauce.

Makes 20 dumplings, 4 servings

1 large or 2 medium dried shiitake or Chinese black mushrooms (see Cook Smart)

1 small carrot, peeled and finely shredded

1 cup finely chopped napa cabbage or bok choy, including some of the leafy part

1 scallion, green and white parts, thinly sliced

1 tablespoon soy sauce

1 teaspoon sugar

½ teaspoon salt

¼ teaspoon freshly ground pepper

1 teaspoon toasted sesame oil

20 round gyoza or pot sticker wrappers

1–2 large romaine leaves

side dish

Also serve the steamed dumplings in a bowl of chicken soup flavored with the mushroom soaking liquid. Place 4 to 6 dumplings in a wide, shallow bowl of soup and serve with a small bowl of Sesame-Soy Dipping Sauce on the side.

cook smart

Steamed dumplings are healthier and cook more quickly than when fried, plus steaming avoids spattering your kitchen with a film of oil. Asian markets sell dried black or shiitake mushrooms. If you cannot find them, use large fresh ones and squeeze them together with the carrots.

Cover the mushrooms with hot water and soak until soft, 20 to 30 minutes. Remove the stems, squeeze the mushrooms dry, and chop finely. Place the chopped mushrooms in a mixing bowl. Save the soaking water in the refrigerator or freezer to use for flavoring a soup or stir-fry.

Place the carrot in a square of cheesecloth and squeeze dry, then add it to the mushrooms. Mix in the cabbage or bok choy, scallion, soy sauce, sugar, salt, and pepper. Then mix in the sesame oil.

Place a stack of the dumpling wrappers on a dish towel and cover with a paper towel that has been moistened and wrung out. Place a wrapper in the palm of 1 hand. Moisten the first 2 fingers of your other hand with water and wet a ½-inch ring around the edge of the wrapper. Pinch the edge of the wrapper to make a ½-inch pleat, then make 2 more pleats, spacing them ½-inch apart on 1 side of the dumpling wrapper; the pleated wrapper will be cupped into a little bowl. Spoon a heaping teaspoon of filling into the center of the wrapper and bring the side opposite the pleats up to close the dumpling. Press the moistened edges together firmly, flattening the pleats and sealing the dumpling into a half-moon with a flat bottom. Stand the dumpling on a plate. Repeat, making 20 dumplings.

for serving now Set a steamer rack in a large saucepan or deep skillet with a tight-fitting cover. Pour in water to just below the rack. Tear the romaine leaves to fit and arrange them to line the steamer. Cover the pan and bring the water to a boil. Add as many dumplings as desired. Cover tightly and steam until the dumplings are translucent and tender, about 15 minutes. Serve with Sesame-Soy Dipping Sauce.

to freeze Open-freeze the uncooked dumplings on a baking sheet covered with wax paper. Store the frozen dumplings in resealable 1-quart plastic freezer bags.

to serve Do *not* defrost the dumplings before steaming.

Set a steamer rack in a large saucepan or a deep skillet with a tight-fitting cover. Pour in water to just below the rack. Tear the romaine leaves to fit and arrange them to line the steamer. Cover the pan and bring the water to a boil. Add as many frozen dumplings as desired. Cover tightly and steam until the frozen dumplings are translucent and tender, 15 to 18 minutes. Serve with Sesame-Soy Dipping Sauce.

sesame-soy dipping sauce

3 tablespoons soy sauce

2 tablespoons rice vinegar

1 teaspoon sugar

1 teaspoon toasted sesame oil

¼ teaspoon hot chili oil (optional)

1 tablespoon finely chopped scallion, green and white parts

In a small bowl, combine the soy sauce, rice vinegar, and sugar. Mix in the sesame oil, chili oil (if using), and scallion. Serve with warm dumplings.

mexican mushrooms in won ton cups

▶ freeze for up
  to 8 weeks

▶ can be doubled

▶ elegant for
  entertaining

The contrast of the Mexican flavors in the creamy mushrooms and their crisp, baked won ton wrapper cups makes them a delicious and unexpected hors d'oeuvre. The cups are quick and easy to make. Since they turn from crunchy to hard when they cool, you need to fill and serve them promptly.

Makes 12

1 pound cremini mushrooms

1 tablespoon canola oil

2 garlic cloves, chopped

½ cup finely chopped poblano
   pepper

⅓ cup finely chopped walnuts

¼ cup dried currants

2 teaspoons dried oregano

1 teaspoon dried thyme

1 cup tomato sauce

Salt and freshly ground pepper

to serve

¼ cup sour cream

1 tablespoon milk

Salt and freshly ground pepper

12 square won ton skins

1 tablespoon canola oil

¼ cup pomegranate seeds or cilantro
   leaves (optional, for garnish)

side dish
The mushroom filling is good served over polenta for a main dish.

cook smart
Phyllo, triple-layered and cut in squares, can replace the won ton skins for cups.

In a food processor, pulse the mushrooms until finely chopped, taking care not to puree them.

In a large skillet, heat the oil over medium-high heat. Add the mushrooms, garlic, and poblano pepper and cook until the mushrooms are dry and very brown, about 15 minutes, stirring often. Mix in the walnuts, currants, oregano, and thyme. Add the tomato sauce and simmer until the filling is thick and clings together, 10 minutes. Season with salt and pepper.

for serving now Preheat the oven to 350°F.

In a small bowl, combine the sour cream and milk. Season to taste with salt and pepper and set aside.

Coat the cups of a mini-muffin tin with nonstick spray or oil and set aside. One at a time, brush the won ton skins lightly on both sides with the oil and gently ease them into the muffin tin cups with their points sticking up.

Bake until the edges and points are browned and crisp, about 10 minutes. Immediately remove the baked cups to a plate and fill with a generous tablespoon of the hot mushroom mixture.

Using a tablespoon, drizzle some of the sour cream sauce in a zigzag over the filling. Sprinkle on the pomegranate seeds or cilantro, if using. Serve immediately.

to freeze Cool the filling to room temperature, then transfer to a resealable 1-quart plastic freezer bag and refrigerate on a plate. Freeze the chilled filling flat on a baking sheet.

Freeze the won ton skins in their package or divide them into groups of 12 and wrap them in plastic freezer wrap, then in heavy-duty foil.

to defrost and serve Thaw the mushroom filling in the refrigerator for 8 to 12 hours. Defrost the won ton skins in the refrigerator for 6 to 24 hours, depending on the amount.

Heat the filling in a saucepan over medium heat, boiling off any excess liquid to return the flavor to its original intensity.

Preheat the oven to 350°F.

In a small bowl, combine the sour cream and milk. Season to taste with salt and pepper and set aside.

Coat the cups of a mini-muffin tin with nonstick spray or oil and set aside. One at a time, brush the won ton skins lightly on both sides with the oil and gently ease them into the muffin tin cups with their points sticking up.

Bake until the edges and points are browned and crisp, about 10 minutes. Immediately remove the baked cups to a plate and fill with a generous tablespoon of the hot mushroom mixture.

Using a tablespoon, drizzle some of the sour cream sauce in a zigzag over the filling. Sprinkle on the pomegranate seeds or cilantro, if using. Serve immediately.

roasted rosemary almonds

▶ freeze for up
  to 4 weeks

▶ can be doubled

side dish
Roasted Rosemary Almonds are perfect served with dry sherry as an aperitif.

cook smart
Using whole blanched almonds, which cost more and are harder to find, is a considerable time-saver, if needed. To skin the nuts, place them in a medium pot of boiling water for 60 seconds. Immediately drain the nuts in a colander. As soon as they are cool enough to handle, 1 nut at a time, squeeze the rounded end between your thumb and first finger and the almond will pop out of its skin at the pointed end. Spread the skinned nuts in 1 layer on a baking sheet and dry them for 24 hours, stirring occasionally. The more thoroughly the almonds are dried, the crunchier they will be, so stir the nuts frequently as they dry, and be patient.

Spanish Marcona almonds roasted with rosemary are a treat—a pricey one. Instead, I combine California almonds, which cost considerably less, with fresh rosemary and sea salt. They keep well in the freezer, so besides serving them to company, you can enjoy these irresistible nuts anytime. These aromatic almonds pair well with Peppered Parmesan Crisps (*shown right in photo and on page 21*) at cocktail time.

Makes 2 cups

2 cups whole raw almonds, blanched or with skin (see Cook Smart)

1 teaspoon extra virgin olive oil

½ teaspoon fine sea salt or 1 teaspoon kosher salt

2 teaspoons finely chopped fresh rosemary

Preheat the oven to 350°F.

Place the blanched almonds on a baking sheet and drizzle the oil over them, tossing to coat them with the oil. Bake for 5 minutes. Stir, then bake for 5 minutes longer. Repeat until the nuts are golden, 10 to 20 minutes longer, depending on how dry the nuts are.

Sprinkle the salt and rosemary over the hot almonds and allow to cool to room temperature.

for serving now Divide the nuts among 2 or more small bowls and serve.

to freeze Pack the nuts into 1 or more plastic freezer containers or a resealable 1-quart plastic freezer bag. Or vacuum seal the nuts.

to defrost and serve Defrost the nuts at room temperature for 1 to 2 hours, depending on the amount. Spreading them out on a plate speeds thawing. Divide the nuts among small bowls and serve.

sizzling hot wings

▶ freeze for up
  to 8 weeks

▶ can be doubled or
  halved

▶ feeds a crowd

Served immediately or reheated from the freezer, these wings can be a nibble, or—if you cannot stop munching—they make a spicy meal. Using mirin or sake in the marinade keeps these crisp wings tender and moist, while baking them means they have fewer calories than fried wings. Even with a hint of Asian flavor, they are delicious served with creamy Blue Cheese Dip.

Makes 24 pieces

¼ cup tomato sauce

2 tablespoons hot sauce, such as Tabasco

1 tablespoon mirin (see Cook Smart)

1 tablespoon reduced-sodium soy sauce

1 tablespoon Worcestershire sauce

1 teaspoon salt

½ teaspoon freshly ground pepper

1 tablespoon canola oil

2½ pounds chicken wings, tips removed, separated into 2 parts

cook smart

In place of mirin, you can use 2 teaspoons of sake and 1 teaspoon of sugar. For easy cleanup, coat the baking rack with nonstick spray.

Preheat the oven to 375°F.

In a large mixing bowl, combine the tomato sauce, hot sauce, mirin, soy sauce, Worcestershire sauce, salt, and pepper. Mix in the oil. Add the wings and toss to coat with the marinade.

Line a 9-inch x 13-inch baking dish with foil. Set a wire baking rack on or in the dish. Arrange the chicken wings in 1 layer on the rack, reserving the marinade in the mixing bowl.

Bake the wings for 10 minutes. Using tongs, turn the wings, brush with some of the reserved marinade, and bake for 10 minutes longer. Turn, baste again, and bake for another 10 minutes. Repeat turning and basting 1 more time. Continue baking until the wings are golden brown and crisp, about 10 minutes. Discard any remaining marinade.

for serving now Arrange the hot wings on a serving platter. Add a bowl filled with Blue Cheese Dip. Leftover wings keep for 3 days, covered in the refrigerator. Reheat as below.

to freeze Cool the baked wings to room temperature. Wrap them in plastic freezer wrap in groups of 2 to 4 pieces, place on a baking sheet, and refrigerate the wings to chill. Freeze the chilled wings, then pack them together in a resealable plastic freezer bag. Or chill the wings unwrapped, then vacuum seal them in 1 layer, 4 or 8 to a package, and freeze.

to defrost and serve Place packages of wings on a plate and thaw in the refrigerator, about 12 hours.

Preheat the oven to 350°F.

Separate the thawed wings and arrange in 1 layer on a wire rack set over a foil-lined pan and bake until the wings are hot and crisp, 25 to 30 minutes, without turning. Serve with Blue Cheese Dip.

blue cheese dip

If desired, use reduced-fat sour cream and yogurt.

▶ can be doubled

Makes 1 cup

¾ cup (3 ounces) crumbled blue cheese, at room temperature
1 cup sour cream
2 tablespoons Greek yogurt
Salt and freshly ground pepper

In a mini food processor or a blender, whirl the cheese, sour cream, and yogurt until combined and smooth. Season to taste with salt and pepper.

side dish
Use leftover Blue Cheese Dip as salad dressing.

parmesan-crusted chicken tenders with honey mustard dip

❱ freeze for up
   to 6 weeks

❱ can be doubled

❱ no defrosting

Rice flour makes the golden crust on these tenders amazingly crunchy, while Parmesan cheese adds irresistible flavor. To crisp the tenders, instead of deep-frying, I use only a moderate amount of oil. Frozen tenders are reheated without defrosting, making them quick to serve.

Makes 12 hors d'oeuvre servings or 4 main-dish servings

⅓ cup all-purpose flour

½ teaspoon dried oregano

½ teaspoon dried thyme

Generous pinch of cayenne pepper

¼ teaspoon salt

⅛ teaspoon freshly ground pepper

3 tablespoons grated Parmesan cheese

⅓ cup rice flour

1 large egg white

1 tablespoon milk

1 pound chicken tenders or boneless breast, cut in 1-inch strips

1 cup vegetable oil, for cooking

cook smart
Look for rice flour at natural food stores and in the Latin or gluten-free sections of supermarkets.

Line a baking sheet with wax paper or baking parchment paper and set aside.

In a wide, shallow bowl, combine the all-purpose flour, oregano, thyme, cayenne, salt, and pepper. In a second shallow bowl, whisk the cheese with the rice flour. In a small bowl, whisk the egg white with the milk until frothy.

Coat the chicken in the seasoned flour, then the egg mixture. Finally, roll them in the rice flour and cheese mixture, taking time to coat them well. Arrange in 1 layer on the prepared baking sheet. Discard any leftover coating.

Cover the tenders loosely with foil and refrigerate for 20 minutes to help the coating adhere.

In a cast-iron or other heavy skillet, heat the oil over medium-high heat until it registers 375°F on an instant-read thermometer. A few at a time, add the tenders to the skillet, avoiding crowding. Cook until the tenders are golden brown on both sides, about 4 minutes, turning them 2 or 3 times. When the chicken is white in the center at the thickest point, or an instant-read thermometer inserted into the thickest part registers 160°F, drain the tenders on brown paper.

for serving now Arrange the baked tenders on a serving platter. Add Honey Mustard Dip in a small bowl and serve immediately.

to freeze On a wire rack, cool the baked tenders to room temperature. Wrap individually in plastic freezer wrap or self-sealing freezer wrap and refrigerate the tenders. Transfer the chilled tenders to the freezer; when frozen, store them together in a resealable large plastic freezer bag. Or open-freeze the tenders, then vacuum seal in groups of 4 or 6 and return to the freezer.

to serve Preheat the oven to 375°F. Arrange the frozen tenders on a baking sheet and bake for 15 minutes. Turn and bake until the tenders are hot in the center, 10 to 15 minutes. The reheated tenders will not be crisp, but thanks to their savory crust, they will still be delicious. Serve with Honey Mustard Dip.

freezer note Defrosting makes the coated tenders rubbery, so always reheat the tenders without thawing.

honey mustard dip

This simple, tangy sauce, just right with the savory flavor of Parmesan-Crusted Chicken Tenders, is also amazing spread on salmon fillets before baking them.

Makes ½ cup

⅓ cup low-fat mayonnaise

¼ cup sour cream

2 teaspoons honey mustard

In a small bowl, whisk together the mayonnaise, sour cream, and honey mustard. This sauce keeps for 3 days, covered in the refrigerator.

side dish
Serving baby carrots and broccoli florets along with the tenders and dip encourages children to eat more vegetables.

sweet and tangy bison balls

▶ freeze for up to
   8 weeks

▶ can be doubled

▶ feeds a crowd

▶ elegant for
   entertaining

Cranberries added to this contemporary version of a retro favorite make this hot hors d'oeuvre an even bigger crowd-pleaser. Serving the meatballs from a wide, shallow bowl is fine, but presenting them in an old-fashioned silver chafing dish, if you can, puts this dish over the top as a conversation maker, too.

Makes 30 pieces, 10 servings

1 medium Granny Smith apple, peeled and shredded

1 pound ground bison

1 garlic clove, finely chopped

1 small onion, finely chopped

½ teaspoon salt

Freshly ground pepper

1 cup fresh or frozen cranberries, chopped

1 cup tomato sauce

1 jar (10 ounces) red currant preserves or jelly

½ cup ketchup

½ teaspoon ground ginger

cook smart

Ground bison is very lean and dense. It makes a firm, shaggy meatball.

Preheat the oven to 375°F.

Spread the shredded apple on a plate lined with paper towels and pat to remove excess moisture. Place the drained apple in a mixing bowl.

Add the bison, garlic, onion, and salt and pepper to taste to the apple, and use your hands or a fork to combine them. Add the cranberries and work them into the mixture until evenly distributed. Form the bison mixture into 1-inch meatballs and place on a baking sheet or other baking pan with shallow sides, setting them about 1 inch apart. Loosely cover the baking pan with foil.

Bake the meatballs for 12 minutes, or until browned, firm, and barely pink in the center. Set aside.

In a large saucepan, combine the tomato sauce, preserves or jelly, ketchup, ginger, and ¼ teaspoon ground pepper. If using jelly, chop it into roughly 1-inch pieces with a spoon. Bring the sauce to a boil over medium heat, stirring as needed to help the jelly dissolve.

When the sauce is smooth, add the meatballs and simmer until the sauce is thick enough to coat the meatballs, about 5 minutes.

for serving now Transfer the meatballs and sauce to a serving dish. Serve hot, accompanied by toothpicks.

to freeze Transfer the meatballs to a wide plate to cool, using a slotted spoon. Pour the sauce into a wide bowl and cool to room temperature.

Pack the cooled meatballs in a resealable 1-gallon plastic freezer bag or two 1-quart bags, including any liquid from the plate. Pour the sauce into a plastic container just large enough to hold it. Refrigerate the meatballs on a plate and the container of sauce to chill.

Freeze the chilled meatballs on a baking sheet lined with wax paper. Freeze the sauce in its container.

to defrost and serve Defrost the meatballs on a plate in the refrigerator for 12 to 18 hours, depending on the amount. Defrost the sauce in the refrigerator in its container for 8 hours.

To reheat, place the defrosted meatballs and all the liquid in the bag in a medium saucepan. Simmer over medium heat until the meatballs are heated through, 12 to 15 minutes. Transfer to a serving bowl. If not serving immediately, cover the bowl loosely with foil.

Place the sauce in a small saucepan and adjust the flavor with a pinch of ground ginger, if needed. Simmer over medium heat, uncovered, until thick enough to coat a meatball on a toothpick, about 5 minutes. Pour the sauce into a small bowl and serve warm, along with the meatballs and toothpicks.

moroccan pork satay

▶ freeze for up
   to 4 weeks

▶ freeze now, cook
   later

▶ feeds a crowd

Marinated with aromatic North African spices, these cook perfectly indoors on a grill pan or in a cast-iron skillet. Freezing them in the marinade keeps the meat succulent and tender. Boneless chicken breast can replace the pork, if you wish.

Makes 24 skewers

2 garlic cloves, minced

1 ½ teaspoons sweet paprika

1 teaspoon ground cumin

¼ teaspoon ground coriander

¼ teaspoon ground turmeric

½ teaspoon salt

¼ teaspoon freshly ground pepper

1 tablespoon fresh lemon juice

3 tablespoons extra virgin olive oil

1 pound pork tenderloin, trimmed of silver skin and cut in 1-inch cubes

24 6-inch metal or bamboo skewers (see Cook Smart)

side dish

Serve 6 skewers over cooked jasmine rice for a main course.

cook smart

Metal skewers conduct heat to help the kebabs cook better in the center. Bamboo skewers should be soaked in warm water for 20 to 30 minutes before using so they do not burn. If freezing the kebabs, you can skip this step because the bamboo soaks up moisture in the freezer.

In a large mixing bowl, combine the garlic, paprika, cumin, coriander, turmeric, salt, and pepper. Stir in the lemon juice, followed by the oil. Add the pork, mixing to coat the cubes. Cover with plastic wrap and marinate in the refrigerator for 1 to 24 hours.

Thread 3 cubes of pork onto each skewer, keeping them towards the tip.

for serving now Heat a stove-top grill pan or lightly oiled cast-iron skillet over high heat until drops of water ball up and dance on the surface. Use paper towels to blot the kebabs dry. Discard the marinade. Cook the skewers, turning them every 1 ½ minutes, until the meat is white in the center, about 6 minutes in all.

to freeze Place the uncooked skewers in a resealable 1-quart plastic freezer bag, packing them in tightly towards the bottom of the bag. Add the marinade, and squeeze out as much air as possible before sealing the bag. Refrigerate to chill, then freeze flat on a baking sheet. Or pack the skewered kebabs and marinade in vacuum bags, clip shut, chill, and freeze, then heat-seal.

to defrost and serve Defrost the packaged kebabs on a plate in the refrigerator for 6 to 18 hours, depending on the amount. Or thaw the kebabs in the sealed bag in a bowl of cold water, changing the water every 15 minutes. Discard the marinade and blot the kebabs dry with paper towels before cooking.

Cook the skewers on a preheated stove-top grill pan or lightly oiled cast-iron skillet over high heat, turning them every 1 ½ minutes, until the meat is white in the center, 6 minutes in all.

chapter 3

soups

A soup-stocked freezer means you are well on your way to a satisfying meal. It can be Spiced Butternut Squash and Carrot Soup or Zucchini Vichyssoise, good to open a meal, or Santa Fe Vegetable Chowder or Italian Wedding Soup, which are hearty enough to serve as a meal.

Soups freeze well and defrost quickly, especially when stored in single or double portions and thawed in cold water, a method that works in as little as 20 minutes. This lets you go from thinking about a steamy bowl of Tastes as Good as Canned Tomato Soup to setting it on the table in 30 minutes or less.

When you cook for one or two, freezing ends the monotony of the bottomless soup pot. Enjoy eating My Favorite Mushroom Barley Soup once or twice, then stash the rest in your freezer until you feel like having it again. Note, though, that some soups hold better if stored in larger amounts. Recipes indicate where this is recommended.

After a month of making soup once a week, your freezer can look like mine, packed with a variety of soups ready for quick lunches—handy even if you brown-bag—and sustaining suppers.

zucchini vichyssoise

▶ freeze for up
to 6 weeks

▶ can be doubled

Refined enough for summer dinner parties, this creamy soup is low in carbohydrates, compared with the classic vichyssoise made with potatoes. Using cream cheese in place of cream adds both body and a nice tang.

Makes 6 servings

3 medium zucchini, 1 ½ pounds

4 cups Quick Rich Chicken Broth (page 69) or canned chicken broth

1 cup chopped sweet onion

1 medium leek, white part only, chopped

6 ounces cream cheese, cut into 1-inch cubes

⅛ teaspoon ground white pepper

Pinch of cayenne pepper

Salt

to serve

⅓ cup snipped chives or chopped dill (garnish)

side dish

Glass bowls show off the delicate, cool green of this soup.

Halve each squash lengthwise. Using a teaspoon, scoop out the seeds. Shred the squash, using the coarsest side of a box grater; there should be 4 cups.

In a deep saucepan, bring the broth to a gentle boil over medium-high heat. Add the squash, onion, and leek. Reduce the heat and simmer, covered, until the vegetables are tender but not falling apart, 15 minutes. Uncover and cool the soup for 10 minutes.

With an immersion blender, whirl in the cream cheese a few cubes at a time, along with the white pepper and cayenne, stopping before the soup is completely smooth; it should still have some texture. Or puree the soup in a blender, dropping the cheese in through the top. This may require working in 2 batches. Season to taste with salt. Cool the soup to room temperature.

for serving now If serving now, refrigerate the soup, covered, until well chilled, 6 to 24 hours. Divide it among wide, shallow bowls and garnish with chives or dill.

to freeze Divide the soup among resealable 1-quart plastic freezer bags in 2-serving amounts and refrigerate to chill. Freeze the bags of chilled soup flat on a baking sheet lined with wax paper.

to defrost and serve Thaw the soup on a plate in the refrigerator. If the soup is grainy, whirl it briefly in a blender. Pour into wide, shallow soup bowls, garnish with chives or dill, and serve.

chilled green pea and watercress soup

▶ freeze for up
to 4 weeks

▶ can be doubled

On days so hot I want to stick my head in the freezer, this chilled 4-ingredient soup is a dish I crave. Refreshing and vibrant, it delivers garden-fresh flavor whether you serve this light soup now or from the freezer.

Makes 4 servings

2 cups freshly shelled peas or frozen baby green peas

⅓ cup finely chopped onion

1 ½ cups watercress sprigs, chopped

2 cups Quick Rich Chicken Broth (page 69), canned chicken broth, or water

Salt and freshly ground pepper

to serve

Chopped fresh mint (garnish)

side dish

I like this soup hot as much as when it is served cold. At winter dinner parties, garnished with sliced leek sautéed in olive oil until browned, it makes an elegant first course.

cook smart

Watercress usually costs considerably less at Asian markets.

In a medium Dutch oven or a large saucepan, place the peas, onion, watercress, and broth or water and set over medium-high heat. When the liquid boils, reduce the heat, cover, and simmer until the peas are tender, 10 minutes.

Puree the soup, using an immersion blender or in a blender (see page 51). Season to taste with salt and pepper. Cool the soup to room temperature.

for serving now Chill the soup, covered, in the refrigerator until very cold, 6 to 24 hours. Just before serving, adjust the seasoning and serve the soup in wide, shallow bowls, garnished with the mint.

to freeze Divide the cooled soup among resealable 1-quart plastic freezer bags in 2-serving amounts and refrigerate to chill. Freeze the bags of chilled soup flat on a baking sheet lined with wax paper.

to defrost and serve Defrost the soup on a plate in the refrigerator for 6 to 8 hours. Or thaw in a large bowl of cold water, changing the water every 15 minutes and breaking the soup into chunks as it defrosts. If the thawed soup is grainy, whirl it briefly in a blender. Pour the soup into bowls, garnish with mint, and serve.

arlene's gazpacho

For maximum flavor, make this soup when local tomatoes are at their peak, the vines overloaded with sun-warmed fruit coming ripe all at once. Freezing then lets you continue to enjoy their flavor weeks after the season has ended. The lavish amount of chopped vegetables added for garnish turns this soup into a spoonable salad.

▶ freeze for up to 4 weeks

▶ can be doubled

Makes 6 servings

- 4 ripe large beefsteak tomatoes, 2½–3 pounds, seeded and diced
- 2–3 large garlic cloves, quartered (see Freezer Note on page 47)
- 1 cup tomato juice
- 2 slices stale white bread, crusts removed, each torn into 4 pieces (see Cook Smart)
- 3 tablespoons red wine vinegar
- 2–3 tablespoons tomato paste
- 2 tablespoons extra virgin olive oil
- 3 generous dashes hot-pepper sauce
- 1 teaspoon salt
- Freshly ground pepper

to serve

- ⅔ cup finely diced cucumber
- ⅔ cup finely diced green bell pepper
- ⅔ cup finely diced tomato
- ⅔ cup finely diced raw zucchini
- ⅔ cup finely diced celery (optional)
- ⅔ cup finely diced red onion (optional)
- 6 tablespoons croutons (optional)

In a blender, whirl the tomatoes and garlic to a pulpy puree. Add the tomato juice and whirl to blend. Strain the soup into a bowl to remove all bits of skin, then return the strained soup to the blender.

Add the bread to the blender and whirl until the soup has a pulpy texture. Whirl in the vinegar, tomato paste, oil, hot pepper sauce, and salt. Season with pepper to taste.

for serving now Transfer the soup to a container, cover tightly, and chill for 3 to 4 hours or overnight.

Return the chilled soup to the blender and whirl until it is silky. Divide the soup among individual bowls and add a generous tablespoon each of the diced cucumber, bell pepper, tomato, and zucchini, plus the celery and onion, if using. Drop in 1 tablespoon of croutons, if you wish. Serve the chilled gazpacho immediately.

side dish

With roughly ⅓ cup of chopped vegetables in each serving, this gazpacho is a lovely contrast of creamy soup and salad-fresh crunch.

Gazpacho is usually refrigerated overnight before serving to allow the flavors to meld. However, if freezing, refrigerate the soup only until it is chilled. It will finish mellowing in the freezer.

cook smart

Arnold's white sandwich bread is best in this recipe because it is firm and disintegrates evenly into the gazpacho.

to freeze Divide the completed gazpacho among resealable plastic freezer bags in 2- or 3-serving amounts and refrigerate to chill. Freeze the bags of chilled soup flat on a baking sheet lined with wax paper.

to defrost and serve Defrost the bags of soup on a plate in the refrigerator for 4 to 12 hours, depending on the amount. Or thaw in a large bowl of cold water, changing the water every 15 minutes and breaking the soup into chunks as it defrosts. Whirl the defrosted gazpacho in a blender to smooth it out. Garnish with the chopped vegetables, as in For Serving Now, page 45 and serve.

freezer note Garlic's flavor grows more pungent over time in the freezer, so I recommend using a single clove when making this soup to freeze.

smoky black bean soup

Once you taste this hearty soup, you will be glad this recipe makes plenty to feed a crowd or to store for later. For smoky flavor, I use preservative-free bacon rather than a ham hock cured with nitrites. I strongly recommend starting with dried beans; canned ones just do not deliver the same flavor. Chopped tomatoes, add flavor-brightening acidity.

▶ freeze for up to 8 weeks

▶ feeds a crowd

Makes 10 servings

1 pound dried black beans, picked over and rinsed	3 garlic cloves, peeled and halved lengthwise
10 strips preservative-free bacon	1 large bay leaf
1 medium onion, chopped	Salt and freshly ground pepper
2 celery ribs, chopped	
1 large carrot, chopped	**to serve**
5 sprigs flat-leaf parsley	2 vine-ripe tomatoes, seeded and chopped for garnish

Place the beans in a large bowl and add enough water to cover by 2 inches. Soak for 6 to 8 hours or overnight.

Drain the beans and place in a large Dutch oven. Add 3 quarts of cold water and bring almost to a boil over medium-high heat. Reduce the heat and simmer gently for 30 minutes, skimming off any foam.

Meanwhile, in a large skillet, cook the bacon until crisp. Drain on paper towels and set aside. Pour all but 3 tablespoons of the bacon fat from the pan. Over medium-high heat, cook the onion, celery, and carrot in the bacon fat until the onion is soft, 6 minutes.

Scoop the contents of the skillet into the beans. Add the parsley, garlic, and bay leaf. Cook until the beans are soft, about 30 minutes. Remove and discard the parsley stems and bay leaf. If desired, puree half the soup in a blender, then return it to the pot. Season to taste with salt and pepper.

for serving now Ladle the soup into deep bowls. Crumble 1 strip of the bacon into each bowl and add a tablespoon of the chopped tomato.

to freeze Cool the soup to room temperature. Divide it among resealable 1-quart plastic freezer bags in 2-serving amounts, and refrigerate to chill. Freeze the bags of chilled soup flat on a baking sheet lined with wax paper. Seal the bacon in another freezer bag, squeezing out as much air as possible without crushing the bacon.

to defrost and serve Defrost the soup on a plate in the refrigerator for 12 to 24 hours. Or thaw in a large bowl of cold water, changing the water every 15 minutes and breaking the soup into chunks as it defrosts.

Reheat the soup in a saucepot, covered, over medium heat.

Recrisp the frozen bacon strips in a 350°F oven or a toaster oven, crumble, and add to the hot soup. Garnish with the chopped tomato.

lentil and swiss chard soup with pesto

Traveling in Tuscany during the winter, I discovered that the weather is miserably damp and cold. I also discovered this rustic soup, which is perfect for chasing away winter's chill. Even with chopping the chard, you can have its ingredients in the pot in 20 minutes. To save time, I recommend buying the pesto. Trader Joe's, Costco, and other stores sell good prepared ones that are well priced.

Makes 8 servings

2 tablespoons extra virgin olive oil

1 large leek, white part only, chopped

3 garlic cloves, chopped

2 cups lentils

4 cups chicken or vegetable broth

4-inch sprig fresh rosemary

2 cups or 1 can (14½ ounces) diced tomatoes

8 cups Swiss chard greens, lightly packed, cut into 3/4-inch strips (see Cook Smart)

Salt and freshly ground pepper

to serve

½ cup prepared pesto

In a large Dutch oven, heat the oil over medium-high heat. Add the leek and garlic and cook until the leek is tender, 5 minutes, stirring often.

Add the lentils, broth, rosemary, and 4 cups of water. When the liquid boils, reduce the heat and simmer, uncovered, for 20 minutes.

Add the tomatoes (with juice) and chard. Simmer, uncovered, until the lentils are soft and the chard is tender, 10 minutes. Remove the rosemary stem and season to taste with salt and pepper.

for serving now Divide the soup among deep bowls. Dollop 1 tablespoon of pesto into each bowl and serve.

to freeze Cool the soup to room temperature. Divide it among resealable 1-quart plastic freezer bags in 1- or 2-serving amounts. Refrigerate to chill. Freeze the bags of chilled soup flat on a baking sheet lined with wax paper.

to defrost and serve Defrost the soup on a plate in the refrigerator for 8 to 24 hours, depending on the amount. Or thaw in a large bowl of cold water, changing the water every 15 minutes and breaking the soup into chunks as it defrosts.

Reheat in a covered saucepan over medium heat. Divide among soup bowls and garnish with the pesto.

◗ **freeze for up to 4 weeks**

◗ **feeds a crowd**

side dish
Ordinary lentils are sometimes called green lentils, although they are actually greenish light brown.

cook smart
To remove their stems, lay chard leaves flat on a work surface. Run a small knife down both sides of the stem and lift it away. Stack 2 or 3 leaves and roll them into a long cigar, then cut the chard crosswise into strips. Chop or slice the stems and sauté them or braise in broth.

easy split pea soup

▶ freeze for up
   to 8 weeks

▶ can be doubled

Whether you like it thick as London fog or want to keep it more spoonable, this soup is always a favorite. It is also one of the simplest and least expensive dishes you can make. For smoky flavor, instead of a ham hock, which generally contains nitrites, I garnish each bowl with uncured turkey bacon. Vegetarians can add in the crisp "bacon bits," which are made of soy and taste quite good, for garnish.

Makes 4 servings

2 cups dried split green peas

1 large onion, chopped

2 celery ribs, chopped

1 medium leek, white and 2 inches pale green parts, chopped

4 cups chicken or vegetable broth (see Cook Smart)

Salt and freshly ground pepper

to serve

1 tablespoon olive oil

2 strips uncured turkey bacon

1 small onion, chopped

1 carrot, sliced

In a medium Dutch oven or large, heavy saucepan, combine the dried peas, onion, celery, leek, and broth. Bring to a boil over medium-high heat, reduce the heat, and simmer, covered, for 30 minutes. Check and add ½ to 1 cup of water if the soup is getting too thick. Cover and simmer until the peas and vegetables are falling apart, 15 to 20 minutes longer.

Stir the soup vigorously with a wooden spoon until pulpy. Or, if you prefer a very smooth soup, either use an immersion blender or transfer the soup to a blender and whirl to puree. Season to taste with salt and pepper.

for serving now Heat the oil in a skillet over medium-high heat, add the bacon and onion, and cook until browned, 6 minutes, stirring often. Scrape the bacon and onion into a small bowl and set aside. Add the carrot to the skillet, pour in ½ cup of water, and scrape up any browned bits on the bottom of the pan. Cover, reduce the heat, and simmer until the carrot is almost tender and the liquid has evaporated, about 5 minutes. Add the carrot to the bacon and onion.

Divide the hot soup among wide, shallow soup bowls and garnish with the bacon and vegetables.

to freeze Cool the soup to room temperature. Ladle the cooled soup into resealable 1-quart plastic freezer bags in 1- or 2-serving amounts and refrigerate. Freeze the chilled bags of soup flat on a baking sheet lined with wax paper.

to defrost and serve Defrost on a plate in the refrigerator for 8 to 24 hours, depending on the amount. Or thaw in a large bowl of cold water, changing the water every 15 minutes and breaking the soup into chunks as it defrosts.

Heat the oil in a skillet over medium-high heat, add the bacon and onion, and cook until browned, 6 minutes, stirring often. Scrape the bacon and onion into a small bowl and set aside. Add the carrot to the skillet, pour in ½ cup of water, and scrape up any browned bits on the bottom of the pan. Cover, reduce the heat, and simmer until the carrot is almost tender and the liquid has evaporated, about 5 minutes. Add the carrot to the bacon and onion.

Pour the defrosted soup in a saucepan, adding ⅓ cup of broth or water per serving. Reheat the soup over medium heat, uncovered, stirring often. Garnish with the bacon and vegetables and serve.

cook smart
Because the carrot in most commercially made vegetable broths gives this soup an unattractive orange tinge, I recommend using Garden Vegetable Broth (page 70) or your favorite homemade one.

When pureeing hot liquids, never fill the blender container more than halfway. Work in batches if necessary. Press a folded dish towel firmly down on the lid before turning on the blender so its contents do not splatter.

tastes as good as canned tomato soup

▶ freeze for up
  to 4 weeks

▶ can be doubled

If Campbell's tomato soup is your ideal, my version, made without corn syrup and an excess of sodium, is just as thick and intense. Its concentrated flavor comes from combining oven-roasted fresh tomatoes with sun-dried tomatoes and will make you very happy. So reach for the soda crackers and enjoy it now and anytime from your freezer.

Makes 4 servings

1 cup dehydrated sun-dried tomatoes

2 cups boiling water

2 pounds ripe plum tomatoes, halved lengthwise

2-inch sprig fresh rosemary

10 sprigs fresh thyme or 1 teaspoon dried

3 garlic cloves, smashed and peeled

3 tablespoons extra virgin olive oil

1 cup chopped red onion

2 cups Garden Vegetable Broth (page 70) or canned vegetable broth

1 teaspoon packed brown sugar

4 teaspoons rice flour

Salt and freshly ground pepper

cook smart

Dehydrated sun-dried tomatoes cost less and have fewer calories than those marinated in oil. Some are treated with sulfur dioxide to preserve their color, so read the label if you avoid sulfites.

If doubling the recipe, roast the plum tomatoes on 2 baking sheets.

Preheat the oven to 400°F.

Soak the sun-dried tomatoes in the boiling water until soft, about 30 minutes. Drain and finely chop the tomatoes, reserving their soaking water. Set both aside.

Place the plum tomatoes on a jelly-roll pan. Scatter needles plucked from the rosemary, the thyme sprigs, and the garlic over the tomatoes. Drizzle with 2 tablespoons of the oil. Toss to coat everything, then arrange the tomatoes in 1 layer, cut side down, with the herbs and garlic on top. Cover the pan with foil, sealing it well.

Roast the tomatoes for 45 minutes, or until soft. When the tomatoes are cool enough to handle, lift off and discard the skins, along with the thyme branches. On the pan, coarsely chop the tomatoes, garlic, and rosemary, then set aside.

In a large saucepan, heat the remaining 1 tablespoon oil over medium-high heat. Cook the onion until soft, 6 minutes, stirring often. Add the sun-dried tomatoes with their soaking water and the roasted tomatoes, along with their seasonings and pan juices. Add the broth and sugar, bring to a boil, reduce the heat, and simmer, covered, until the tomatoes are soft, about 20 minutes.

Puree the soup with an immersion blender or transfer it to a blender, pureeing it in 2 batches if necessary, then return the pureed soup to the saucepan.

In a small bowl, mix the rice flour with 2 tablespoons of water until combined, then add to the soup. Cook over medium heat, stirring often, until the soup has the thickness of canned tomato soup. Season to taste with salt and pepper.

for serving now Divide the soup among deep bowls.

to freeze Cool the soup to room temperature. Divide it among resealable 1-quart plastic freezer bags in 1- or 2-portion servings and refrigerate. Freeze the chilled soup flat on a baking sheet lined with wax paper.

to defrost and serve Defrost the soup on a plate in the refrigerator for 6 to 12 hours, depending on the amount. Or thaw in a large bowl of cold water, changing the water every 15 minutes and breaking the soup into chunks as it defrosts. If the defrosted soup is pulpy or separates, whirl it in a blender until smooth.

Heat the soup in a saucepan over medium heat, stirring often. Adjust the seasoning to taste before serving.

mississippi pepper pot

▶ freeze for up to 8 weeks

▶ can be doubled

As a gumbo lover, I wanted to include one in this book, but filé, the powdered okra that thickens it, does not stand up to freezing. Instead, pairing collard greens with the flavors of the Deep South, I composed this pleasantly spicy almost-gumbo. When you feel ecumenical, it is great accompanied by New England Corn Bread (page 191).

Makes 6 servings

4 cups chopped fresh collard greens (see Cook Smart)

2 tablespoons canola oil

1 cup finely chopped onion

1 cup thinly sliced celery

3 garlic cloves, finely chopped

1½ cups diced green bell pepper

1 cup diced red bell pepper

1 tablespoon chili powder

2 teaspoons dried thyme

1 can (14½ ounces) diced tomatoes

4 cups Garden Vegetable Broth (page 70) or canned vegetable broth

1–2 teaspoons sugar or agave syrup

Salt and freshly ground pepper

to serve

4 cups brown rice, cooked al dente (see Side Dish), or frozen brown rice

Bring a large pot of water to a boil. Add the collards and cook for 5 minutes. Drain in a colander and set aside until the greens are cool enough to handle. Squeeze out as much moisture as possible from the greens and set aside.

In a large Dutch oven, heat the oil over medium-high heat. Add the onion and celery and cook until the onion is translucent, 4 minutes, stirring occasionally. Add the garlic and bell peppers and cook until they soften, 5 minutes. Add the chili powder and thyme and cook, stirring, until they are fragrant, 1 minute.

Add the tomatoes, collard greens, and broth. Bring to a boil, reduce the heat, and simmer, covered, until the greens are almost tender, 20 minutes. Add the sugar or agave syrup and season to taste with salt and pepper.

for serving now Add the rice and cook until the greens are tender and the rice is fully cooked, 10 to 15 minutes. Divide the soup among 6 wide, shallow soup bowls.

to freeze Cool the soup with undercooked greens to room temperature. Ladle into 2 or 3 resealable 1-quart plastic freezer bags in 1- and 2-serving amounts and refrigerate to chill. Freeze the bags of chilled soup flat on a baking sheet lined with wax paper.

to defrost and serve Defrost the soup on a plate in the refrigerator for 8 to 18 hours, depending on the amount. Or thaw in a large bowl of cold water, changing the water every 15 minutes and breaking the soup into chunks as it defrosts.

In a saucepan, combine the soup with the rice. Heat, covered, over medium heat, simmering the soup until the rice is fully cooked. Ladle into bowls and serve.

side dish
If the rice is frozen in the soup, it turns gummy when thawed.

To undercook the rice, deduct 10 minutes from the time listed on the package directions.

cook smart
One-half pound of fresh collard greens equals roughly 4 lightly packed cups.

To chop collards, see directions for Swiss chard (page 49). You may substitute two 10-ounce packages of frozen collards, defrosted, but only if the soup will not be frozen.

persian red lentil and beet soup

❯ freeze for up
   to 8 weeks

❯ can be doubled

The red lentil soup at my favorite Persian restaurant is vegetarian and low in fat, although it tastes meaty and rich. Beets and pomegranate juice add deep, earthy flavor and give it a lovely color. Best of all, this protein-rich soup is ready to serve in 35 minutes when you use cooked beets sold at the supermarket.

Makes 4 servings

2 tablespoons olive oil

½ cup chopped onion

3 garlic cloves, chopped

2 teaspoons ground cumin

1 teaspoon ground allspice

4 cups Garden Vegetable Broth (page 70) or canned vegetable broth

1 cup dried red lentils, picked over, rinsed, and drained

1 package (8 ounces) cooked beets, chopped

Salt and freshly ground pepper

to serve

1 cup pomegranate juice

4 tablespoons chopped dill or cilantro (garnish)

cook smart

The cooked beets packaged in a plastic vacuum-sealed pouch have better flavor and texture than those sold in a jar.

To cook fresh beets, place them in a deep saucepan and cover to a depth of 2 inches with cold water. Bring to a boil and simmer until a knife inserted at the thickest point of the beets meets mild resistance, 25 to 50 minutes, depending on their size, then drain. When the beets are cool enough to handle, wrap a cutting board in plastic wrap. Wearing rubber gloves, use your fingers to slip the skins off the beets. Chop the beets on the covered board. Store the beets in a stainless steel or glass bowl.

In a large, heavy saucepan, heat the oil over medium-high heat. Add the onion and cook for 2 minutes, stirring occasionally. Add the garlic and cook until it is soft, 3 minutes. Stir in the cumin and allspice until fragrant, 1 minute. Add the broth, lentils, and beets. Bring the soup to a boil, reduce the heat, and simmer, covered, until the lentils are falling apart and the beets are very soft, about 25 minutes. Season to taste with salt and pepper.

for serving now Mix in the pomegranate juice. Divide the soup among deep soup bowls, garnish with the dill or cilantro, and serve.

to freeze Cool the soup to room temperature. Divide the soup among resealable 1-quart plastic freezer bags in 1-and 2-serving amounts and refrigerate. Freeze the bags of chilled soup flat on a baking sheet lined with wax paper.

to defrost and serve Defrost the soup on a plate in the refrigerator for 8 to 24 hours, depending on the amount. Or thaw in a large bowl of cold water, changing the water every 15 minutes and breaking the soup into chunks as it defrosts.

In a covered pot, heat the soup over medium heat, stirring occasionally. Mix in the pomegranate juice, adjust the seasoning, and serve garnished with the dill or cilantro.

my favorite mushroom barley soup

Feasting like a peasant makes me happy, and I can do it anytime when this meatless soup made with 2 kinds of mushrooms is tucked away in the freezer. Dried porcini mushrooms add intense flavor that justifies their cost. In fact, they make this a robust-tasting soup even if you use water in place of some or all of the broth.

▶ **freeze for up to 4 weeks**

▶ **feeds a crowd**

Makes 6 to 8 servings

1 cup pearl barley

½ ounce dried porcini mushrooms

2 tablespoons canola or olive oil

2 medium onions, chopped

2 garlic cloves, chopped

10 ounces white mushrooms, sliced

8 cups Quick Rich Chicken Broth (page 69), canned broth, or water

to serve

1 tablespoon canola or olive oil

1 large carrot, cut into ½-inch pieces

1 celery rib, cut into ½-inch pieces

1 small parsnip, cut into ½-inch pieces (optional)

Salt and freshly ground pepper

Chopped fresh dill (garnish)

In a large saucepan, combine the barley with 3 cups of water. Bring to a boil, reduce the heat, and simmer, covered, for 30 minutes. Drain and set the barley aside.

Meanwhile, in a small bowl, soak the dried mushrooms in 1 cup of warm water until soft, 15 to 30 minutes. Remove and discard the hard stems. Squeeze the excess moisture from the mushrooms back into the bowl and reserve. Chop the mushrooms and set aside in another bowl.

In a large Dutch oven, heat the 2 tablespoons oil over medium-high heat. Add half of the onions and the garlic and cook until the onions are soft, 6 minutes. Mix in the sliced mushrooms and cook until browned, with bits sticking to the pan, 12 minutes. Add the broth or water, barley, chopped porcini, and the strained soaking liquid. Bring to a gentle boil, cover, and simmer for 15 minutes.

for serving now Heat the 1 tablespoon oil in a medium skillet. Add the carrot, celery, and parsnip (if using) and cook until crisp-tender, stirring often. Add the vegetables to the soup and simmer until the barley is soft, 3 minutes. Season to taste with salt and pepper. Divide the soup among wide, shallow bowls, garnish with dill, and serve.

side dish
When I have leftover cooked chicken, I like mixing it into the soup just before serving.

cook smart
Frozen carrots and celery turn mushy when thawed. Adding them when reheating the defrosted soup avoids this.

to freeze Cool the soup to room temperature. Ladle the cooled soup into resealable 1-quart plastic freezer bags in 2- or 3-serving amounts and refrigerate. Freeze the chilled bags of soup flat on a baking sheet lined with wax paper.

to defrost and serve Defrost the soup in the refrigerator for 8 to 24 hours, depending on the amount.

In a saucepan, heat the 1 tablespoon oil in a medium skillet. Add the carrot, celery, and parsnip (if using) and cook until crisp-tender, stirring often. Add the defrosted soup and ½ cup water and simmer until the soup is hot. Adjust the seasoning with salt and pepper. Divide the soup among wide, shallow bowls, garnish with dill, and serve.

freezer note Barley sponges up liquid as it freezes, then turns soft when defrosted, so this soup is especially delicious but different in texture after freezing.

cheese soup with broccoli

Even reluctant vegetable-eaters usually accept broccoli when presented with it in this golden cream soup. It also gets a flavorful nutrition boost from carrots and onions. Thickened with rice flour, this soup is gluten-free, too.

▶ **freeze for up to 6 weeks**

Makes 4 servings

¾ cup finely chopped carrots

½ cup finely chopped onion

1¾ cups chicken or vegetable broth

2 cups milk

4 tablespoons (½ stick) unsalted butter

¼ cup rice or all-purpose wheat flour

2 teaspoons Worcestershire sauce

⅛ teaspoon cayenne pepper

Salt and freshly ground pepper

1 cup (4 ounces) shredded sharp Cheddar cheese

1 cup (4 ounces) shredded Gouda cheese

to serve

1½ cups steamed broccoli florets (see Cook Smart)

Smoked Spanish paprika (garnish)

In a medium saucepan, combine the carrots and onion with the broth, cover, bring to a boil, then lower the heat and simmer until the vegetables are soft, 10 to 12 minutes. Using an immersion blender, puree the vegetables and liquid in the saucepan, or puree them in a blender and then return the puree to the saucepan. Add the milk and heat until the mixture is almost boiling. Set aside.

In a small Dutch oven or large, heavy saucepan, melt the butter over medium heat. Add the flour and cook, whisking constantly until the mixture looks fluffy and smells buttery, 4 to 5 minutes; do not let it color. Add the vegetable and milk mixture, one-quarter at a time, whisking vigorously until smooth before making the next addition. Mix in the Worcestershire sauce and cayenne pepper. Remove from the heat. Season to taste with salt and pepper.

Add the cheeses, whisking until they have melted.

for serving now Mix in the steamed broccoli florets. Divide the hot soup among wide, shallow soup bowls and garnish with a sprinkling of Spanish paprika.

cook smart

Fresh broccoli adds more flavor than frozen florets. To make using it easy, I grab the broccoli for this soup from the salad bar. Steam the florets until crisp-tender, 3 minutes, then transfer to a bowl of cold water and chill to set the color. Drain well in a colander and set the broccoli aside.

Rice flour gives the soup a more attractive color, and its neutral flavor lets you really taste the cheese. It also makes this dish gluten-free.

to freeze Transfer the soup to a large mixing bowl and press plastic wrap onto the surface. Cool to room temperature, then divide the soup among resealable plastic freezer bags in 1- or 2-serving amounts and refrigerate. Freeze the chilled soup flat on a baking sheet lined with wax paper.

to defrost and serve Defrost the soup on a plate in the refrigerator for 6 to 12 hours, depending on the quantity. If the defrosted soup is grainy or separates, whirl it in a blender until smooth.

Place the defrosted soup in a heavy saucepan over medium heat and add the broccoli. Cook the soup uncovered, stirring often. Take care not to let it boil. Adjust the seasoning to taste, garnish with the paprika, and serve.

spiced butternut squash and carrot soup

▌ freeze for up
   to 6 weeks

▌ can be doubled

Assembling this colorful, spice-warmed soup is easy enough to invite beginners to make this their first homemade soup. Its combination of autumnal vegetables and tropical seasonings makes a lovely contrast, while coconut milk adds creamy, dairy-free richness.

Makes 6 servings

1 pound butternut squash, peeled and diced

2 medium carrots, cut in ½-inch slices

1 Granny Smith apple, peeled, cored, and diced

1 medium onion, sliced in crescents

1 teaspoon ground cinnamon

1 teaspoon curry powder

½ teaspoon ground ginger

4 cups chicken broth

Salt and freshly ground pepper

to serve

¾ cup unsweetened coconut milk

Chopped apple, dill, or cilantro (optional, for garnish)

In a large Dutch oven or deep saucepan, combine the squash, carrots, apple, onion, cinnamon, curry powder, ginger, and broth. Add 2 cups of water. Bring to a boil, reduce the heat, and simmer, covered, until the vegetables are soft, 30 minutes. Let the soup cool for 10 minutes.

Using an immersion blender, puree the soup in the pot, or puree it in a blender in batches until it is smooth. Season to taste with salt and pepper.

for serving now Mix in the coconut milk, divide the soup among deep bowls and serve, garnished with apple, dill, or cilantro, if desired.

to freeze Cool the soup to room temperature. Divide it among resealable 1-quart plastic freezer bags in 1- or 2-serving amounts and refrigerate. Freeze the chilled bags of soup flat on a baking sheet.

to defrost and serve Defrost the soup in the refrigerator for 12 to 24 hours, depending on the amount. Or thaw in a large bowl of cold water, changing the water every 15 minutes and breaking the soup into chunks as it defrosts. Reheat the soup in a saucepan, uncovered, over medium heat, stirring occasionally.

Mix 2 tablespoons of coconut milk into each serving and adjust the seasoning to taste. Garnish and serve as above.

freezer note In the freezer, the ginger flavor intensifies and cinnamon fades. To balance it, add a dash of cinnamon and a teaspoon of brown sugar when heating the thawed soup.

side dish

For variety, substitute orange sweet potatoes for the carrots.

Using vegetable broth instead of chicken broth gives this soup a darker, earthy color.

cook smart

If time matters more than cost, buying diced squash, baby carrots, and sliced apple eliminates nearly all preparation, but you will pay a premium for them.

santa fe vegetable chowder

❱ freeze for up
   to 8 weeks

❱ can be doubled

This chunky, mildly spicy soup is a celebration of American natives, including tomatoes, butternut squash, corn, quinoa, and black-eyed peas, plus poblano and ancho chiles. For a light meal, serve with an omelet or accompanied by New England Corn Bread (page 191).

Makes 6 servings

2 tablespoons canola oil

1 medium onion, chopped

2 garlic cloves, chopped

1 medium red bell pepper, cut into ¾-inch pieces

1 small poblano pepper, seeded and chopped

2 cups peeled and diced butternut squash

¼–½ teaspoon ground ancho chile

1 can (15 ounces) black-eyed peas, rinsed and drained, or 2 cups cooked

1 can (14½ ounces) diced tomatoes with chile peppers (see Cook Smart)

4 cups Garden Vegetable Broth (page 70) or canned vegetable broth

2 teaspoons dried oregano, preferably Mexican

Salt and freshly ground pepper

to serve

¾ cup frozen corn kernels

1 cup cooked quinoa, preferably red, cooked according to package directions

⅓ cup chopped cilantro

1 lime, cut into 6 wedges

cook smart

If you cannot find canned tomatoes with chile peppers, add a 4-ounce can of chopped green chiles.

In a large, heavy saucepan or Dutch oven, heat the oil over medium-high heat. Add the onion, garlic, and red and poblano peppers and cook until they soften, 6 minutes, stirring often. Add the squash and ground chile and stir until the chile is fragrant, 1 minute.

Add the black-eyed peas, tomatoes (juice) with broth, and oregano. When the liquid boils, reduce the heat and simmer, covered, until the vegetables are tender, 20 minutes.

for serving now Mix in the corn and quinoa, and simmer until the corn is heated, 8 minutes. Season to taste with salt and pepper. Divide the soup among deep bowls. Garnish with cilantro and a lime wedge.

to freeze Cool the soup to room temperature. Divide it among resealable 1-quart plastic freezer bags in 1- or 2-serving amounts and refrigerate. Add the frozen corn and freeze the chilled soup flat on a baking sheet lined with wax paper.

to defrost and serve Defrost the soup on a plate in the refrigerator for 8 to 12 hours, depending on the amount. Or thaw in a large bowl of cold water, changing the water every 15 minutes and breaking the soup into chunks as it defrosts. Place the soup in a saucepan, add the quinoa, then simmer gently over medium heat, stirring often. Adjust the seasoning, garnish as For Serving Now on page 62 and serve.

freezer note Including frozen corn just before freezing the soup, then adding cooked quinoa after thawing it, keeps the soup tasting just-cooked.

true vietnamese pho

▶ **freeze for up to 8 weeks**

▶ **can be doubled**

Every Vietnamese restaurant serves pho (pronounced *fuh*), so why bother to make this beef and noodle soup? Friends who have eaten homemade pho have assured me that it is far superior to what restaurants serve. So I prepared it and was amazed at the difference. Cooking the broth takes care, but the resulting flavor, the soul of this southeast Asian comfort food, and the fragrance it gives your house are truly worth it. Having the broth in the freezer, you can assemble just a bowl or two anytime.

Makes 4 servings

1 piece fresh ginger, about 3 ounces

1 large onion, papery outer skin removed

2½ pounds beef shin, cut into 2 slices

8 cups low-sodium beef broth

4 whole cloves

4 star anise

1 piece (2 inches) cinnamon stick

1 teaspoon black peppercorns

3 tablespoons fish sauce

to serve

½ pound beef eye of round

1 pound small or medium dried rice sticks

1½ cups mung bean sprouts

2 large shallots, very thinly sliced crosswise

2 red or Thai chiles or 1 serrano, thinly sliced

½ cup cilantro leaves

½ cup Thai or small sweet basil leaves

1 lime, quartered

Fish sauce and hot chili paste, for seasoning

Using tongs, turn the ginger over the open flame of a gas burner or place it directly on a medium-hot electric burner and turn until the skin is blackened, 3 to 4 minutes. Peel and discard the skin. Cut the ginger into 4 pieces and set aside. Place the onion in the flame or on the burner and turn until much of the surface is charred, 4 to 5 minutes. Pull off the charred skin and set aside.

Place the beef shin in a stockpot or other big, deep pot. Add cold water to cover by 2 inches. Bring to a boil over high heat and boil for 5 minutes. Drain and rinse the beef and clean out the pot.

Return the beef to the pot. Pour in the broth and 2 quarts of cold water. Stick the onion with the cloves and add it to the pot along with the ginger, star anise, cinnamon, peppercorns, and fish sauce. Bring to a gentle boil over high heat. Cook, uncovered, skimming the scum and foam that rise to the surface of the liquid. When the scum stops rising, after about 30 minutes, reduce the heat and simmer until the broth is reduced to 2 quarts, roughly 2 hours. Remove the beef and set aside. Strain the broth through a fine sieve into a bowl and discard the solids. Skim as much fat as possible from the broth. (This is easier if you chill the broth.)

for serving now Wrap the eye round in plastic and place in the freezer for 1 hour to firm it. Cut the meat crosswise into 4 slices. With a very sharp knife, cut each slice of meat crosswise into paper-thin slices. (The ideal is if you can almost see through them.) Set the meat aside.

Add the rice sticks to a large pot of boiling water and cook until just tender, 30 to 60 seconds. Drain in a colander, rinse under cold water, and set aside.

Bring the broth to a boil. Meanwhile, rinse 4 large bowls under hot water and dry. Divide the noodles and sliced meat among the bowls. Pour the boiling broth over the meat.

Add the bean sprouts, shallots, chiles, cilantro, basil, and a lime wedge to each bowl. Pass the fish sauce and chili paste to season the soup to taste.

to freeze Cool the broth to room temperature. Divide it between 2 resealable 1-quart plastic freezer bags and refrigerate to chill. Freeze the chilled broth flat on a baking sheet lined with wax paper.

to defrost and serve Defrost the broth on a plate in the refrigerator for 6 to 12 hours, depending on the amount. Or thaw in a large bowl of cold water, changing the water every 15 minutes and breaking the broth into chunks as it defrosts.

side dish
Most supermarkets carry rice sticks in the ethnic section. Asian markets sell pungent, purple-leaved Thai or holy basil and fiercely hot Thai chiles.

cook smart
Trimming all the visible fat from around the beef shanks helps keep the broth lean.

Skimming the broth and simmering it gently are keys to keeping it as clear as possible.

If desired, shred the cooked beef, discarding the bones and gristle, and reserve to add to another soup or mix with pasta sauce.

Slice the meat, prepare the rice noodles as directed in For Serving Now on page 65, and divide them among 4 bowls.

To assemble the pho, bring the broth to a boil and ladle the boiling broth into the bowls. Garnish with the bean sprouts, shallots, chiles, cilantro, basil, and lime and serve. Pass the fish sauce and chili paste to season the soup to taste.

italian wedding soup

▶ freeze for up to
   8 weeks

▶ can be doubled

The wedding referred to is the marriage of meat and vegetables. Ground pork is often used, but I prefer it combined with turkey or mixed together with ground turkey and beef. The meatballs thaw quickly because of their small size, so I sometimes double that part of the recipe and serve the extra meatballs with spaghetti.

Makes 4 servings

meatballs

½ pound ground pork or turkey (93 percent lean)

½ pound ground beef (90–93 percent lean)

1 large egg

⅓ cup plain dried bread crumbs

⅓ cup grated pecorino cheese plus additional for passing

1 garlic clove, minced

Salt and freshly ground pepper

8 cups Quick Rich Chicken Broth (page 69) or canned chicken broth

1 medium carrot, thinly sliced

1 celery rib, thinly sliced

1 small onion, finely chopped

3 cups escarole, cut crosswise into thin strips, lightly packed

to serve

½ lemon, cut in 4 wedges

Preheat the oven to 350°F. Line a baking sheet with baking parchment paper and set aside.

In a mixing bowl, combine the ground meat, egg, bread crumbs, cheese, garlic, ½ teaspoon salt and ⅛ teaspoon pepper with a fork. Shape the mixture into 24 small meatballs and place them on the prepared baking sheet, 1 inch apart. Cover the pan loosely with foil.

for serving now Bake the meatballs until white in the center, about 15 minutes, then set aside, covered.

In a large saucepan, combine the broth, carrot, celery, and onion and set over medium-high heat. When the liquid boils, reduce the heat and simmer, covered, for 5 minutes. Add the escarole and simmer for 10 minutes, until it is almost tender. Add the meatballs and simmer until heated through. Season to taste with salt and pepper.

Divide the soup among 4 wide, shallow soup bowls, including 6 meatballs in each serving. Pass the lemon wedges and additional grated cheese in separately.

to freeze Bake the meatballs for 10 minutes, leaving them slightly pink in the center. Uncover and allow them to cool on the baking sheet.

In a large saucepan, simmer the broth with the carrot, celery, and onion for 5 minutes. Add the escarole and simmer for 5 minutes longer, leaving the vegetables slightly undercooked. Cool the soup, add the cooled meatballs, and ladle together into resealable 1-quart plastic freezer bags in 1- or 2-serving amounts. Refrigerate on a plate to chill. Freeze the bags of chilled soup flat on a baking sheet lined with wax paper.

to defrost and serve Defrost the soup in the refrigerator for 12 hours.

Place the defrosted soup in a large saucepan and heat, uncovered, over medium heat, taking care not to let it boil. Simmer, stirring occasionally, until the meatballs are heated through, about 10 minutes. Adjust the seasoning and pass the lemon wedges and cheese separately.

cook smart
Boiling these meatballs makes them tough and dry.

chinese lion's head soup

Rarely served in restaurants, this fragrant soup combines meatballs and mushroom-flavored broth with crisp vegetables. The secret is to freeze and store the meatballs and broth separately, then heat them together while stir-frying the vegetables.

▶ freeze for up to 6 weeks

▶ can be doubled

Makes 6 servings

meatballs

1 pound ground pork

2 tablespoons reduced-sodium soy sauce

1 tablespoon dry sherry

1 scallion, green and white parts, finely chopped

2 teaspoons grated ginger

1 teaspoon sugar

2 tablespoons rice flour

2 teaspoons roasted sesame oil

½ teaspoon salt

⅛ teaspoon freshly ground pepper

1 large egg, beaten

Preheat the oven to 350°F. Coat a baking sheet with nonstick spray.

In a bowl, use a fork to combine the pork, soy sauce, sherry, scallion, ginger, and sugar. Mix in the rice flour, sesame oil, salt, pepper, and egg. Form the mixture into 36 walnut-size meatballs, spacing them 1 inch apart on the prepared baking sheet. Cover the baking sheet loosely with foil.

Bake the meatballs until they are white in the center, 20 minutes, turning them once. Set them aside while you make the soup.

mushroom broth	to serve
2 large or 3 medium dried black mushrooms	1 tablespoon peanut oil
4 cups chicken broth	3 cups napa cabbage, cut crosswise into ½-inch slices
1 piece (2 inches) fresh ginger, cut into 8 slices	½ large onion, cut into thin crescents
Salt and freshly ground pepper	1½ cups mung bean sprouts
	⅓ cup scallions, green and white parts, chopped

In a small bowl, soak the mushrooms in ¼ cup of hot tap water until soft, 30 to 60 minutes. Remove the stems and squeeze the mushrooms over the bowl of soaking liquid. Strain and reserve the liquid. Finely chop the mushrooms.

In a large saucepan, combine the broth, reserved mushroom liquid, ginger, and 2 cups of water. Bring to a gentle boil over medium-high heat, cover, reduce the heat, and simmer for 10 minutes. Season to taste with salt and pepper.

for serving now Heat the oil in a wok or medium skillet over high heat. Add the cabbage and onion and stir-fry until crisp-tender. Divide among 6 large soup bowls. Add 6 meatballs to each bowl. Ladle hot soup into each bowl. Garnish servings with ¼ cup of the bean sprouts and equal portions of the scallions and chopped mushrooms.

to freeze Open-freeze the meatballs on a baking sheet. Transfer the frozen meatballs to a resealable 1-gallon plastic freezer bag. Or vacuum seal the meatballs in groups of 6.

Add the chopped mushrooms to the cooled broth, ladle it into resealable 1-quart plastic freezer bags in 1- or 2-serving amounts, and refrigerate on a plate to chill. Freeze the chilled broth flat on a baking sheet lined with wax paper.

to defrost and serve Defrost the meatballs in the refrigerator for 8 to 12 hours. Thaw the broth on a plate in the refrigerator or in a large bowl of cold water, changing the water every 15 minutes and breaking the broth into chunks as it defrosts.

Heat the defrosted broth and meatballs in a saucepan, uncovered, over medium heat until the soup simmers; take care not to let it boil. Adjust the seasoning to taste.

While the soup heats, heat the oil in a wok or medium skillet over high heat. Add the cabbage and onion and stir-fry until crisp-tender. Divide among large soup bowls. Ladle in the hot soup and meatballs, garnish with the bean sprouts and scallions, and serve.

freezer note Meatballs and other individual foods without a sauce store best vacuum sealed. They also freeze well in self-sticking freezer wrap.

quick rich chicken broth

Making chicken broth is economical if you collect chicken carcasses and vegetable parings in the freezer and use them to fill your stockpot. It is also time-consuming. Instead, use this trick for giving commercial broth almost homemade flavor.

▶ **freeze for up to 3 months**

▶ **can be doubled**

Makes 6 cups

2 containers (32 ounces each) chicken broth	1 piece (3 inches) parsnip, cut into ½-inch slices
1 small onion, quartered	5 flat-leaf parsley sprigs
½ small carrot, cut into ½-inch slices	½ celery rib, cut into ½-inch slices

In a large saucepan, combine the broth, onion, carrot, parsnip, parsley, and celery. Bring to a boil over medium-high heat, reduce the heat, cover, and simmer very gently for 30 minutes.

Uncover and allow to cool for 30 minutes. Strain the broth through a sieve set over a large bowl.

for serving now This broth keeps, tightly covered in the refrigerator, for 3 days.

to freeze Pour the cooled broth into resealable 1-quart plastic freezer bags in 1-cup to 4-cup amounts and refrigerate to chill. Freeze the bags of chilled broth flat on baking sheets lined with wax paper.

to defrost Defrost the broth on a plate in the refrigerator for 4 to 24 hours, depending on the amount. Or thaw in a large bowl of cold water, changing the water every 15 minutes and breaking the broth into chunks as it defrosts.

cook smart

Cool the broth in the pot for 30 minutes before straining, and its flavor will get even richer.

Freezing a few cups of broth in ice cube trays to use for cooking vegetables and pan sauces truly is worth doing. Store the frozen cubes in resealable 1-quart plastic freezer bags.

garden vegetable broth

▶ freeze for up
  to 3 months

▶ can be doubled

Carrots dominate the flavor and color of most commercial vegetable broths. As a result, they give dishes an orange or muddy color and carroty taste. These broths may also be high in sodium, and some contain MSG. To avoid all this, I created this clear, bright-tasting broth. Its sodium comes solely from the vegetables themselves, and it makes meatless soups, stews, and other dishes taste and look their best.

Makes 2 1/2 quarts

4 medium carrots, sliced

4 white mushrooms, quartered

2 cups chopped green cabbage

1 medium leek, white part only, chopped

1 medium onion, chopped

Peel of 1 white or yellow-fleshed potato, preferably organic

1 medium zucchini, chopped

1/4 pound green beans, cut into 1-inch pieces

1/2 small celery root, chopped (1 cup)

15 flat-leaf parsley sprigs

1 teaspoon black peppercorns

1 can (14 1/2 ounces) whole tomatoes

1 small bay leaf

1/2 teaspoon dried thyme

In a large pot, place the carrots, mushrooms, cabbage, leek, onion, potato peel, zucchini, beans, celery root, parsley, and peppercorns and add 3 quarts of cold water. Bring to a boil over medium-high heat, reduce the heat, and simmer, uncovered, for 30 minutes.

Add the tomatoes with their liquid, bay leaf, and thyme. Return to a simmer, then cook for 30 minutes. Let the broth cool for 15 minutes, then strain into a large bowl, pressing the vegetables with the back of a wooden spoon to extract as much liquid as possible.

for using now Refrigerate the cooled broth for up to 3 days in tightly sealed containers.

to freeze Pour the cooled broth into resealable 1-quart plastic freezer bags in 1-cup to 4-cup amounts and refrigerate to chill. Freeze the bags of chilled broth flat on baking sheets lined with wax paper. Alternatively, freeze the broth in ice cube trays, then store the cubes in resealable 1-quart plastic freezer bags.

to defrost Defrost the broth on a plate in the refrigerator for 4 to 24 hours, depending on the amount. Or thaw in a large bowl of cold water, changing the water every 15 minutes and breaking the broth into chunks as it defrosts.

grilling and skillet suppers

Why keep fajitas in the freezer when making them is so simple? Because when the supermarket has a special on flank steaks, you can save serious money—enough to serve Salsa Fajitas for a crowd at a backyard cookout weeks later without denting your budget. You can take advantage of the prices at warehouse clubs, too. For example, a 4-pound pack of ground turkey will make a double batch each of taco filling (page 81) and California Meatloaf Burgers (page 119). Preparing both recipes at the same time takes around 90 minutes and produces dinner for four for four nights.

Your freezer may even help your love life. For a date night dinner, serve Pork Chops with Honey-Sizzled Prunes, a seductively creamy and elegant dish you can make in 30 minutes and that no one would imagine came from the freezer.

- salsa fajitas
- cantonese flank steak
- turkish ground beef kebabs
- pecan chicken paillards with honey mustard cream
- chipotle turkey tacos
- sizzling sichuan sloppy joes
- shredded orange pork in lettuce cups
- smoked fish cakes with lemon mayonnaise
- my mother's gourmet chicken curry
- pork chops with honey-sizzled prunes

salsa fajitas

▶ freeze for up
  to 3 weeks

▶ can be doubled

▶ freeze now,
  cook later

▶ quick fix

Jarred salsa used as a marinade adds great flavor and tenderizes flank steak. Grilled, the marinated steak makes fabulous fajitas. If you are cooking for one, divide up a whole flank steak to freeze in several individual portions. For a crowd, simply multiply the recipe. A thin, smooth salsa will work best.

Makes 6 servings

1 ¼–1 ½ pounds flank steak

1 ½ cups red salsa

to serve

6 whole-wheat or flour tortillas (7- or 8-inch diameter)

2 tablespoons canola oil

1 large Spanish onion, cut into 6 (½ inch) slices

2 green bell peppers, seeded and cut into thin strips

¾ cup prepared or fresh salsa

⅓ cup lightly packed cilantro leaves

1 large lime, cut into 6 wedges

1 cup chopped ripe tomato (optional)

side dish

The steak can also be cooked in the salsa marinade in a skillet. When it is no longer pink in the center, remove the meat with a slotted spoon and boil the salsa briefly, adding more, if needed, to make ¼ cup sauce per serving. Serve the steak over cooked rice, spooning on additional salsa. Garnish with chopped cilantro.

cook smart

The meat must be dry to grill nicely.

Cut the flank steak across the grain into ½-inch slices. Place the sliced meat in a resealable 1-quart plastic freezer bag, add the salsa, and massage to distribute the salsa evenly. Press out the air and seal the bag.

for serving now Marinate the meat on a plate in the refrigerator for 12 to 24 hours.

Preheat the oven to 350°F.

Brush a grill rack for a gas or charcoal grill with oil and heat the grill to medium-hot, or heat a grill pan until water drops flicked into the pan ball up and dance.

Wrap the tortillas in foil and warm in the oven, 10 to 15 minutes.

To grill the vegetables, place the oil in a small bowl. Push 2 or 3 toothpicks horizontally into each onion slice to hold it together while cooking. Brush the slices lightly with oil and grill until well marked on each side. Using tongs, transfer the onion to a serving platter and remove the toothpicks. Cover the platter loosely with foil to keep the onion warm.

In a mixing bowl, add the remaining oil to the peppers and toss to coat them, then grill until the peppers are lightly charred and crisp-tender, 2 to 3 minutes, turning them several times. Add the peppers to the onion slices.

Line a baking sheet with a double layer of paper toweling. Drain the meat in a colander, then, 1 slice at a time, shake and place the meat on the lined baking sheet. Blot the sliced steak with the towels to dry the surface, wiping off any remaining chunks of salsa.

Lay the meat on the hot grill. When lightly marked, 1 minute, turn and grill until the slices are just pink in the center, 2 to 3 minutes in total. The meat will continue to cook, so remove it from the grill promptly and arrange the cooked steak on a second serving plate.

Serve the steak wrapped in the warmed tortillas, accompanied by the grilled vegetables and with bowls containing the ¾ cup salsa, the cilantro, lime wedges, and chopped tomato, if using.

to freeze Chill the meat in the salsa for 2 to 3 hours. Lay the bag with the chilled meat flat on a baking sheet and freeze.

to defrost and serve Defrost the frozen meat in the refrigerator for 4 to 24 hours, depending on the amount.

To serve, preheat the oven to 350°F. Place the tortillas in 1 stack, wrap them in foil, and warm them in the oven.

Grill the vegetables following the same steps as For Serving Now on the opposite page.

Line a baking sheet with a double layer of paper toweling. Drain the meat in a colander, then, 1 slice at a time, shake and place the meat on the lined baking sheet. Blot the sliced steak with the towels to dry the surface, wiping off any remaining chunks of salsa.

Grill the defrosted marinated steak as For Serving Now.

Serve the steak wrapped in the warmed tortillas, accompanied by the grilled vegetables and with bowls containing the ¾ cup salsa, the cilantro, lime wedges, and chopped tomato, if using.

cantonese flank steak

▶ freeze for up
  to 2 weeks

▶ can be doubled

▶ freeze now,
  cook later

▶ quick fix

Marinating flank steak in a combination of hoisin and black bean sauces gives it a delicious, dark crust when you grill it. This recipe is ideal if you enjoy meat cooked juicy and pink. The meat comes out equally well cooked outdoors or on the stove top in a grill pan. Serve with Garlic Smashed Potatoes (page 182) and steamed broccoli or as fajitas (see Side Dish).

Makes 4 to 6 servings

¼ cup hoisin sauce

2 tablespoons soy sauce

1 tablespoon Asian black bean sauce

1 tablespoon hot chile sauce, such as
  sriricha or oelek sambal

¼ cup dry sherry

1 tablespoon sugar

¼ cup chopped scallions, green and
  white parts

2 garlic cloves, thinly sliced lengthwise

¼ teaspoon freshly ground pepper

1 ¼–1 ½ pounds flank steak

side dish

For Asian-style fajitas, serve sliced Cantonese Flank Steak in warmed tortillas, topping the meat with chopped scallions and shredded lettuce, plus sliced red onion and strips of orange bell pepper tossed on the grill.

cook smart

An instant-read thermometer should read 145°F for meat cooked medium-rare, 160°F for medium.

In a bowl, whisk together the hoisin, soy sauce, black bean sauce, hot chile sauce, sherry, sugar, scallions, garlic, and pepper. Pour the marinade into a resealable 1-gallon plastic freezer bag and add the flank steak. Seal the bag, pushing as much air as possible out and folding the bag over.

for serving now Marinate the meat on a plate in the refrigerator for 2 to 8 hours.

Remove the steak from the refrigerator 30 minutes before cooking.

Brush the grill rack with oil and heat a gas or charcoal grill to high heat. Or heat a grill pan over high heat until a drop of water flicked onto the surface balls up and dances.

Pat the meat dry with a paper towel, brushing off the bits of garlic and scallion. Discard the marinade.

Grill the steak for 5 minutes on each side for medium-rare, 6 minutes for medium. In a grill pan, cook the steak for 3 minutes, then rotate 90 degrees and cook for 2 minutes. Turn and repeat on the second side. Let the steak rest on a plate for 5 minutes before slicing. Cut the steak across the grain at an angle into ½-inch slices. Serve hot or at room temperature.

to freeze Refrigerate the steak in the marinade until it is chilled, 2 to 3 hours.

Freeze the steak in the folded bag, laying it flat on a baking sheet lined with wax paper.

to defrost and serve Thaw the steak in the marinade on a plate in the refrigerator for 8 to 12 hours.

Let the meat stand at room temperature for 30 minutes. Remove from the marinade, and blot the steak with a paper towel, brushing off the bits of garlic and scallion.

Grill and slice the steak, following the directions as For Serving Now on page 75.

freezer note The flavor gets very intense and the meat becomes soft when it is frozen for longer than 2 weeks.

turkish ground beef kebabs

Turkish restaurants list these hot and spicy ground meat skewers on the menu as Adana kebabs. Making these sausage-shaped kebabs at home—to serve tucked into a warm pita, along with chopped vegetables and a drizzle of thick yogurt—is simple. Traditionally, they are grilled or cooked under the broiler, but I like cooking them in a toaster oven, which keeps the lean meat more moist and juicy.

▶ freeze for up
   to 8 weeks

▶ can be doubled

▶ freeze now, cook
   late

▶ quick fix

Makes 8 kebabs, 4 servings

1 pound ground beef (93 percent lean)

½ teaspoon ground cumin

½ teaspoon smoked or sweet ground paprika

¼ teaspoon ground cinnamon

¼ teaspoon garlic powder

1 teaspoon salt

¼ teaspoon freshly ground pepper

1 small onion, very finely chopped

to serve

8 pocketless pitas, warmed

¾ cup plain Greek yogurt

Chopped tomato, white onion, and parsley (garnish)

In a mixing bowl, combine the beef with the cumin, paprika, cinnamon, garlic powder, salt, pepper, and onion, mixing with a fork until very well blended. Divide the mixture into 8 portions. Place a portion in the palm of 1 hand and press it into a 3-inch x 2-inch patty. Lay a skewer lengthwise down the center of the patty and gently press the meat around it to form a 6-inch "hot dog" about 1-inch thick. Repeat with the remaining meat mixture. For maximum flavor, refrigerate the kebabs on a plate, covered, for 1 to 12 hours.

for serving now Preheat the broiler or set a toaster oven on broil. Arrange the kebabs on a broiler pan and broil for 8 to 10 minutes, turning them after 5 minutes. In a toaster oven, cook the kebabs for 15 minutes, turning them after 8 minutes.

To serve, slide the meat off the skewers and place a kebab in the center of each warmed pita. Stir the yogurt, season it to taste with salt and pepper, and drizzle about 2 tablespoons over each kebab. Spoon on some chopped tomato, white onion, and parsley.

to freeze Chill the kebabs on a plate, covered, for 1 hour. Wrap each kebab in plastic freezer wrap, then wrap them in pairs in foil. Label and freeze. Or open-freeze the chilled kebabs, then vacuum seal in pairs and return them to the freezer.

to defrost and serve Thaw the kebabs in the refrigerator for 4 to 8 hours.

Broil the defrosted kebabs under the broiler or in a toaster oven; see For Serving Now above.

Serve in warm pitas, garnished with the seasoned yogurt, chopped tomato, onion, and parsley.

freezer note When the kebabs are defrosted, the cumin disappears and garlic is the main seasoning you will taste. To refresh the cumin, mix ¼ teaspoon into the yogurt, along with the salt and pepper.

side dish
Reduced-fat or low-fat yogurt can be used for the seasoned Greek yogurt.

cook smart
Metal skewers conduct heat, helping kebabs to cook through more quickly. Bamboo skewers should be soaked in water for 30 minutes before using, but you can skip this step if freezing the kebabs.

pecan chicken paillards with honey mustard cream

▶ freeze for up
  to 6 weeks

▶ can be doubled

▶ quick fix

This is one of my favorite dishes. The nut crust keeps the chicken so moist that the paillards come out of the freezer even more succulent than when first coated. Pounding the cutlets to an even thickness helps them cook more quickly and evenly. I make zesty Honey Mustard Cream (page 80) while the paillards cook or reheat, if frozen.

Makes 4 servings

¾ cup pecans

2 tablespoons rice flour

½ teaspoon salt

¼ teaspoon freshly ground pepper

1 large egg white

4 boneless, skinless chicken cutlets (5–6 ounces each), pounded to ½-inch thick

2 tablespoons canola oil

to serve

Honey Mustard Cream (page 80)

Chopped dill or chives (optional, for garnish)

side dish

You can skip the creamy sauce and serve these cutlets with Red Cabbage and Cranberry Slaw (page 180) and steamed green beans.

cook smart

Rice flour in the coating helps the paillards hold the coating better when thawed when the coating contains rice flour.

Pulse the pecans in a food processor until finely ground. Transfer the ground nuts to a wide, shallow bowl and add the rice flour, salt, and pepper. Stir to combine. In another shallow bowl, whisk the egg white with 1 tablespoon of water until frothy. Dip the cutlets first in the egg white mixture, allowing the excess to drip back into the bowl, then coat them with the pecan mixture, pressing with your fingers to help it stick. Arrange the coated cutlets on a plate in 1 layer.

In a large skillet, heat the oil over medium-high heat. Add the chicken cutlets and cook until they are golden brown on the outside and white in the center, about 6 minutes, turning them once, after 3 minutes.

for serving now Divide the cooked paillards among 4 dinner plates. Spoon on Honey Mustard Cream and garnish with dill or chives, if using.

to freeze Cool the cooked paillards to room temperature. Wrap individually in plastic freezer wrap, arrange the chicken in 1 layer on a plate, and refrigerate to chill. Transfer the wrapped chicken to the freezer on a baking sheet lined with wax paper and, when solid, store the paillards in a resealable 1-quart plastic freezer bag. Or open-freeze the paillards, then vacuum seal and return the packaged chicken to the freezer.

to defrost and serve Defrost the wrapped chicken on a plate in the refrigerator for 6 to 8 hours.

To reheat for serving, preheat the oven to 350°F.

Arrange the thawed chicken on a baking sheet and bake for 15 to 20 minutes, until the paillards are well browned on the outside and heated through. Meanwhile, make the Honey Mustard Cream. Serve the cream sauce drizzled over the paillards and garnish with dill or chives, if using.

honey mustard cream

This handy little sauce dresses up simple grilled pork chops, salmon, or chicken cutlets, too. Making it takes about the same amount of time as they require to cook. It keeps in the refrigerator and reheats nicely.

Makes ⅔ cup

1 cup heavy cream
2 tablespoons honey mustard

In a small saucepan, boil the cream gently until reduced by one-third, about 10 minutes. Whisk in the mustard. Serve immediately, or refrigerate the cooled sauce for up to 3 days. Reheat the sauce in a small bowl in the microwave.

chipotle turkey tacos

When making the filling for these tacos, give it the degree of heat you prefer, from mildly spicy to three-alarm. This is one of the few dishes I like to thaw in the microwave, which lets you get this taco dinner from freezer to table speedily.

Makes 4 servings

2 tablespoons canola oil

1 medium onion, chopped

½ poblano chile, finely chopped

2 garlic cloves, finely chopped

1 package (1 ⅓ pounds) ground turkey (93 percent lean)

1 tablespoon chili powder

2 teaspoons dried oregano

1 teaspoon ground cumin

¼–1 teaspoon ground chipotle chile

1 cup tomato sauce or canned crushed tomatoes

Salt and freshly ground pepper

to serve

12 taco shells, warmed according to package directions

Shredded iceberg lettuce

Chopped tomatoes

Shredded Monterey Jack or Cheddar cheese

Sour cream

Prepared salsa, fresh or jarred

▶ **freeze for up to 6 weeks**

▶ **can be doubled**

▶ **quick fix**

In a medium skillet, heat the oil over medium-high heat. Add the onion and cook until it is translucent, 4 minutes, stirring frequently. Add the poblano and garlic and cook until the vegetables are soft, 5 minutes.

Add the turkey and cook, breaking up the meat with a wooden spoon. Stir frequently until the turkey loses its pink color, 8 to 10 minutes. Mix in the chili powder, oregano, cumin, and ground chipotle and cook, stirring, until the spices are fragrant, 1 minute. Add the tomato sauce and simmer for 3 minutes. Season to taste with salt and pepper.

for serving now Arrange the warm taco shells on a serving platter. Spoon about ⅓ cup of the filling into each shell. Place the lettuce, tomatoes, cheese, sour cream, and salsa in individual bowls and serve along with the tacos.

to freeze Cool the taco filling to room temperature. Divide the filling among 2 or more resealable 1-quart plastic freezer bags and refrigerate to chill. Freeze the chilled meat flat on a baking sheet. Or open-freeze the taco meat in 1 or more wide, shallow bowls, then vacuum seal and return to the freezer.

to defrost and serve Defrost the frozen taco meat on a plate in the refrigerator for 12 to 24 hours, depending on the amount. Or place the frozen filling in a microwaveable bowl, cover, and microwave in 1- to 2-minute bursts, stirring between each burst, until fully defrosted and hot. Adjust the seasonings to taste.

Spoon the hot filling into the taco shells and serve with the lettuce, tomatoes, cheese, sour cream, and salsa in bowls.

sizzling sichuan sloppy joes

▶ **freeze for up to 8 weeks**

▶ **quick fix**

A perfect fusion dish, these sloppy joes are prepared like the mild-mannered American classic but deliver the kick of bold, hot Asian flavor. Serve them with steamed broccoli, followed by either Spiced Tea Granita (page 238) or a slice of Akasha's Carrot Cake (page 216) for dessert for an unexpected and memorable meal.

Makes 4 servings

1 tablespoon sherry

1 tablespoon reduced-sodium soy sauce

2 teaspoons sugar

3 tablespoons peanut oil

1 pound ground pork

2 garlic cloves, finely chopped

1 piece (1 inch) fresh ginger, finely chopped

1 teaspoon black bean sauce with chili

1 cup tomato sauce

1 teaspoon salt

¼ teaspoon freshly ground pepper

to serve

½–1 teaspoon roasted sesame oil

4 hamburger buns or soft rolls

¼ cup chopped scallions, green and white parts

side dish
You can add a can of drained black beans to the sloppy joe mixture while it heats, then serve it over cooked rice.

In a small bowl, combine the sherry, soy sauce, and sugar and set aside.

Swirl 2 tablespoons of the peanut oil in a wok over the highest heat. Add the pork and stir-fry, breaking up the meat until no pink shows. Scoop the pork into a bowl.

Return the wok to the heat and add the remaining 1 tablespoon oil. Add the garlic and ginger and stir-fry until fragrant, 1 minute. Add the black bean sauce and stir-fry for 10 seconds. Return the pork to the wok. Add the tomato sauce, salt, and pepper, then restir the sherry mixture and add it to the wok.

for serving now Stir-fry until the meat is cooked through and the sauce has the consistency of tomato sauce, 3 to 4 minutes. Scoop the contents of the wok into a bowl. Add sesame oil to your taste.

Split the buns and place the bottoms each on a dinner plate. Spoon on one-fourth of the meat, garnish with 1 tablespoon of the scallions, and serve.

to freeze Transfer the sloppy joe mixture to a bowl and cool to room temperature. Spoon the mixture into 1 or 2 resealable 1-quart plastic freezer bags, and refrigerate to chill. Freeze the chilled meat flat on a baking sheet lined with wax paper. Or open-freeze the mixture in wide, shallow bowls, then unmold and vacuum seal. Return the packaged meat to the freezer

to defrost and serve Defrost the sloppy joe mixture on a plate in the refrigerator for 8 to 15 hours, depending on the amount.

In a saucepan, simmer the mixture over medium heat, uncovered, until the sauce thickens to the consistency of thick tomato sauce, 10 to 12 minutes. Mix in the sesame oil.

Spoon the meat over the split burger buns, garnish with the scallions, and serve.

cook smart
Do not cool sloppy joe mixture in the wok. It will pick up a metallic taste due to the acid in the tomatoes.

shredded orange pork in lettuce cups

▶ freeze for up
to 8 weeks

Chinese orange-flavor beef inspired this stir-fry. However, I make it with pork tenderloin, which is nearly fat-free, and stays more juicy and tender than beef when frozen. Combining the stir-fried pork with chopped vegetables after the meat is defrosted adds crispness and color as well as creating a balanced dish.

Makes 4 servings

1 pound pork tenderloin

3 tablespoons teriyaki sauce

¼ cup orange juice

1 tablespoon rice vinegar

¼ cup chicken broth

Grated zest of 1 orange

1 tablespoon cornstarch

3 tablespoons peanut oil

2 garlic cloves, chopped

1 teaspoon finely chopped fresh
ginger

Salt and freshly ground pepper

to serve

1 small head iceberg lettuce,
quartered

¼ cup finely chopped peeled
cucumber

¼ cup finely chopped red bell pepper

¼ cup chopped scallions, green and
white parts

2 tablespoons chopped peanuts

side dish

Serve over cooked rice instead of in lettuce cups, if you wish.

cook smart

Trim your tenderloin of the silverskin, a thin membrane that may cover 1 side, or get the butcher to remove it. This membrane can prevent the meat from fully absorbing the sauce.

Wrap the tenderloin in plastic wrap and freeze for 20 minutes. With a sharp knife, cut the meat into 2-inch slices. Lay each flat on your work surface and cut it into (¼-inch) slices. Stack 2 or 3 slices and cut them into the thinnest possible strips.

In a small bowl, combine the teriyaki sauce, orange juice concentrate, vinegar, broth, zest, and cornstarch and set aside.

Set a wok over high heat. Add in 2 tablespoons of the oil. When it is very hot, stir-fry the pork until it just loses its pink color, 2 minutes. With a slotted spoon, transfer the pork to a plate. Add the remaining 1 tablespoon oil, the garlic and ginger, and stir-fry until fragrant, 30 seconds. Stir the teriyaki mixture and add it into the wok. When the sauce bubbles, return the pork and accumulated juices to the wok and stir-fry until the meat is cooked through, 2 to 3 minutes. Season to taste with salt and pepper.

for serving now Lift 2 or 3 outer layers from each lettuce wedge, and set 1 of these lettuce cups on each of 4 dinner plates to use as a little bowl. Store the remaining lettuce for another use. Spoon the stir-fried pork into the lettuce cups.

Top with the cucumber, pepper, scallions, and peanuts and serve immediately.

to freeze Transfer the contents of the wok to a large bowl and cool to room temperature. Spoon the cooled stir-fry and its sauce into 1 or 2 resealable 1-quart plastic freezer bags and refrigerate to chill. Freeze the chilled stir-fry flat on a baking sheet lined with wax paper.

to defrost and serve Defrost the stir-fry on a plate in the refrigerator for 8 to 12 hours, depending on the amount. Reheat it in a saucepan over medium heat, uncovered; take care not to let it boil. Spoon the hot stir-fry into the cups of layered lettuce separated from the wedges, garnish with the chopped vegetables and peanuts, and serve immediately.

freezer note If the orange flavor has faded when the stir-fried pork is defrosted, grate on some orange zest after spooning the reheated meat into the lettuce.

smoked fish cakes with lemon mayonnaise

If you like mashed potatoes, you will love these lemon-accented, peppery fish cakes. Eating fish rich in omega-3s is important for good health, and mackerel is an excellent source of these essential fatty acids, as well as a fish many people underappreciate. It becomes a treat when smoked and blended into these light patties. Trust me, one bite and the fussiest eater will be happy.

▶ **freeze for up to 6 weeks**

▶ **can be doubled**

Makes 12 fish cakes, 4 servings

1 pound yellow-fleshed potatoes, halved crosswise

1 large egg, beaten

½ cup finely chopped scallions, green and white parts

½ teaspoon freshly ground pepper

⅛ teaspoon salt

8 ounces smoked mackerel, coarsely flaked

Grated zest of ½ lemon (see Cook Smart on page 89)

⅓ cup rice flour

¼ cup canola oil

to serve

Lemon Mayonnaise (page 89)

Place the potatoes in a large pot and cover with cold water to a depth of 2 inches. Bring to a boil over medium-high heat, reduce the heat, and simmer, covered, until the potatoes are tender in the center when pierced with a knife, 15 to 20 minutes. Drain, and when cool enough to handle, peel the potatoes and place in a mixing bowl.

Roughly mash the warm potatoes, using a fork. Mix in the egg, scallions, pepper, and salt until well combined with the potatoes. Gently mix in the fish and lemon zest.

Moisten your hands lightly with cold water and form the potato-and-fish mixture into twelve 3-inch x ½-inch patties, placing them on a plate in a single layer. Cover the fish cakes with foil and refrigerate for 2 hours to firm them.

Place the rice flour in a wide, shallow bowl. Heat the oil in a large skillet over medium-high heat. Coat the fish cakes thoroughly in the rice flour, then pan-fry until they are golden brown and crisp on the bottom, 2 minutes. Turn and crisp the second side, 2 minutes.

for serving now Serve the hot fish cakes immediately, topped with a dollop of Lemon Mayonnaise.

to freeze Cool the cooked fish cakes on a plate in 1 layer. Wrap each fish cake individually in plastic freezer wrap and refrigerate until chilled, 3 to 4 hours. Wrap 3 chilled fish cakes together in heavy-duty foil and freeze. Or open-freeze the chilled fish cakes, vacuum seal, and return the frozen fish cakes to the freezer.

to defrost and serve To defrost, remove the foil and thaw the fish cakes on a plate in the refrigerator for 8 to 12 hours.

To reheat, coat a skillet with nonstick spray. Add the thawed fish cakes and cook until they are crisp on both sides, 6 minutes, turning once. You can also heat the fish cakes on a baking sheet in a 350°F oven for 20 minutes, but they will not be crisp. Using a wide spatula, transfer 3 fish cakes to each of 4 plates, top with a dollop of Lemon Mayonnaise, and serve immediately.

Lemon Mayonnaise

Feel free to use a low-fat mayonnaise, if you wish. Use any leftover mayonnaise on sandwiches or serve with cold shrimp.

½ cup mayonnaise

Grated zest of ½ lemon (see Cook Smart)

1 tablespoon lemon juice

Salt and freshly ground pepper

In a small bowl, combine the mayonnaise with the lemon zest and juice and 1 tablespoon lemon juice. Season to taste with salt and pepper. Lemon Mayonnaise keeps, tightly covered in the refrigerator, for 1 day. Do not freeze.

freezer note Freezing reduces the lemon flavor in these fish cakes, but serving them with Lemon Mayonnaise keeps the zing in this dish.

side dish
Serve with Green Beans and Pine Nuts (page 183).

cook smart
Select potatoes of about the same size so that they all cook through at the same time.

When serving the fish cakes freshly made and accompanied by Lemon Mayonnaise, I zest a whole lemon, using half the zest in the fish cakes and the rest in the mayonnaise, and squeeze 1 tablespoon juice, then save the rest of the lemon for another use.

my mother's gourmet chicken curry

▶ freeze for up
to 4 weeks

Back when making ethnic dishes was considered adventurous, my mother was known for this Indian-style skillet supper. My version includes applesauce, which gives the sauce body and makes it gluten-free, too. The natural sweetness of the apples also balances nicely with the mild spices in this retro comfort food dish.

4 servings

2 tablespoons canola oil

2 pounds skinless split chicken breasts

1 cup chopped red onion

3 garlic cloves, chopped

2 tablespoons mild or hot curry powder

1 teaspoon ground cumin

1 teaspoon grated fresh ginger

2½ cups chicken broth

1 cup unsweetened applesauce

½ cup unsweetened coconut milk

1 cup frozen green peas (optional)

Salt and freshly ground pepper

to serve

3 cups cooked brown basmati rice

Chopped cilantro (optional, for garnish)

side dish
Dice a leftover baked potato, and add when reheating the curry instead of serving it over rice.

cook smart
Chicken breasts with ribs stay moister than boneless cutlets, and they cost less.

In a large skillet, heat 1 tablespoon of the oil over medium-high heat. Add the chicken, ribs facing up, and cook until browned, 8 minutes. Transfer the chicken to a plate.

Add the remaining 1 tablespoon oil to the skillet. Add the onion and cook for 3 minutes, stirring occasionally. Mix in the garlic and cook until the onion starts to brown, 3 minutes. Stir in the curry powder, cumin, and ginger and cook until fragrant, 30 seconds. Add the broth and applesauce, using a wooden spoon to scrape up the browned bits clinging to the bottom of the pan.

Return the chicken to the pan, ribs facing up, along with any accumulated juices. Reduce the heat, cover, and simmer until the chicken is cooked through, about 15 minutes. Remove the chicken to a plate.

When cool enough to handle, about 6 minutes, pull the chicken from the bones, tear the meat into bite-size pieces, and return them to the curry. Stir in the coconut milk and the peas, if using. Season the curry to taste with salt and pepper.

for serving now Continue cooking the curry over medium heat until the chicken is heated through. Mound ¾ cup of rice on each of 4 dinner plates, top with curry, and garnish with cilantro, if using.

to freeze Cool the curry to room temperature. Ladle it into resealable 1-quart plastic freezer bags in 1- or 2-cup amounts, and refrigerate on a plate to chill. Freeze the bags of chilled curry on a baking sheet lined with wax paper.

to defrost and serve Defrost bags of curry on a plate in the refrigerator for 8 to 16 hours, depending on the amount. Or thaw them in a large bowl of cold water, changing the water every 15 minutes and breaking the curry into chunks as it thaws.

Reheat the thawed curry in a saucepan over medium heat, covered, just until heated through, 8 to 10 minutes; do not let it boil. Adjust the seasoning to taste and serve over the cooked rice, garnished with cilantro, if desired.

pork chops with honey-sizzled prunes

This dish, including its lavish, sherry-accented sauce and caramelized prunes, is all made in 1 pan. It requires just 30 minutes of hands-on time, but when you serve these chops in their rich cream sauce, guests will think you cooked for hours. They certainly will never guess if you choose to serve it from the freezer.

▶ **freeze for up to 6 weeks**

▶ **elegant for entertaining**

Makes 4 servings

12 pitted prunes	2 tablespoons sherry vinegar
¼ cup cream sherry	1 cup chicken broth
1 tablespoon unsalted butter	8 thin boneless center-cut pork chops, about 1½ pounds
2 tablespoons canola oil	1 cup heavy cream
1 large shallot, thinly sliced	Salt and freshly ground pepper
2 tablespoons honey	

side dish
If you cook without alcohol, use brewed coffee or orange juice in place of the sherry.

In a small bowl, soak the prunes in the sherry until soft, 30 to 60 minutes. Drain, reserving the sherry. Cut each prune into 4 pieces and set aside.

In a large skillet over medium-high heat, melt the butter with 1 tablespoon of the oil. Add the shallot and cook, stirring constantly, until golden, 2 minutes. Add the prunes and stir until they are coated with butter. Add the honey and cook until it is bubbly, 1 minute. Pour in the vinegar and reserved sherry and cook until the mixture resembles liquid caramel, 2 to 3 minutes. Add the broth and boil until the liquid in the pan is reduced by half, 5 minutes. Pour the contents of the pan into a bowl and set aside.

cook smart
To stretch your budget for a big dinner party, prepare this dish when pork chops are on special and store it in your freezer. You will also save considerably buying the cream at Costco or other warehouse clubs.

Add the remaining 1 tablespoon oil to the pan. Brown the chops on both sides, 6 minutes. Remove them to a plate and pour in the cream. Return the sauce base reserved in the bowl to the pan, and use a wooden spoon to scrape up all of the browned bits clinging to the pan. Simmer over medium heat until the sauce is bubbling.

for serving now Return the chops to the skillet and cook until they are heated through in the sauce, 4 minutes. Divide the chops among 4 dinner plates. Spoon the sauce over them and serve immediately.

to freeze Place 2 or more pork chops in resealable 1-quart plastic freezer bags. Add a few tablespoons of the sauce and refrigerate to chill. Cool the remaining sauce to room temperature, pour into a resealable 1-quart plastic freezer bag, and chill alongside the cooked chops. Freeze the bags with the chilled pork and sauce flat on a baking sheet lined with wax paper.

to defrost and serve Defrost the bags of pork chops and sauce in the refrigerator for 12 to 18 hours. Combine them in a skillet, cover, and cook over medium heat until the pork is heated through and the sauce is hot; do not let it boil. Serve the chops with the creamy, prune-studded sauce spooned over them.

chapter 5

casseroles and other oven favorites

As a main dish, casseroles are hard to beat. I cannot think of a more satisfying or comforting meal than tuna noodle casserole or my personal favorite, Southern Pork Chop Casserole—layers of mashed sweet potato, juicy chops, and sliced oranges, finished with a buttery brown sugar topping.

Grilling chops or tossing a pasta meal together takes less time than producing a casserole. However, assembling casseroles two at a time requires about the same work as making one, so all of the recipes in this chapter can be doubled. Serving one immediately will have everyone looking forward to enjoying it again from the freezer, although you could certainly freeze both.

Because I prefer not to use the sodium- and additive-laden canned soup essential to many casseroles, I have created creamy sauces to use in their place, if you wish. They include Creamy Mushroom Sauce that is essential for Everybody's Favorite Tuna Noodle Casserole, and a version including cheese for Anytime Turkey Tetrazzini. When you make them, you know your family is getting the most wholesome comfort food. Plus, they taste even better than the originals. Since rice flour helps cream sauces freeze better than those made with wheat flour, these sauces are also gluten-free.

- southern pork chop casserole
- pizza noodle casserole
- anytime turkey tetrazzini
- everybody's favorite tuna noodle casserole
- lemon chicken and rice casserole
- mole chicken enchiladas
- baked four-cheese ziti
- spinach and pesto lasagna
- baked red peppers with quinoa and feta
- pomegranate-glazed chicken with wild rice
- prosciutto-stuffed chicken with creamy parmesan sauce
- california meatloaf burgers
- always good meatloaf

I include meatloaves in this chapter because making one is like putting together a casserole. Plus, you can bake meatloaf alongside a casserole to be ready to serve the next day or to freeze. While making California Meatloaf Burgers (page 119) and Turkish Ground Beef Kebabs (page 76), I also discovered how useful the toaster oven can be when cooking for one or two.

casserole tips A doubled recipe is designed to make two casseroles. If you want a single larger one made in a larger baking dish, such as lasagna in a 13-inch x 9-inch pan, the cooking time will need to be adjusted.

The benefit to making two casseroles when doubling recipes is that they defrost and reheat more quickly and without drying out.

A foil pan can replace baking dishes in all of these recipes. This is handy both for transporting dishes and if you prefer freezing in a baking dish to unmolding frozen casseroles for storage.

Cheese or crumb toppings have a better texture when added after defrosting frozen casseroles than when frozen along with the casserole. Either prepare the topping fresh, just before reheating the casserole, or make it when you prepare the casserole, and store it wrapped tightly and packaged together with the casserole.

southern pork chop casserole

Pork and sweet potatoes make a great combination. So do sweet potatoes and oranges. Putting all three together makes this lean and luscious casserole a trifecta of flavor, color, and goodness. The next time you bake sweet potatoes, add a few extra to use in making this delicious casserole.

Makes 4 servings

1 pound orange-fleshed sweet potatoes	Salt and freshly ground pepper
2 tablespoons unsalted butter	2 navel oranges, peeled and thinly sliced
1 teaspoon ground cinnamon	4 thin boneless center-cut pork chops
¼ teaspoon ground ginger	1 sweet onion, sliced
½ cup plus 2 tablespoons orange juice	1 tablespoon packed brown sugar

Bake the sweet potatoes in a 400°F oven until they are soft, 40 to 60 minutes.

Reduce the oven temperature to 350°F.

Peel, then mash the potatoes with a fork until smooth and creamy. Mix in 1 tablespoon of the butter, the cinnamon, ginger, and 2 tablespoons of the orange juice and season to taste with salt and pepper.

Coat a 1 ½-quart shallow baking dish with nonstick spray and spread the sweet potatoes in an even layer over the bottom of the dish. Arrange the orange slices to cover the sweet potato puree, overlapping them slightly. Place the chops in 1 layer over the oranges. Arrange the onion slices over the meat, overlapping them. Sprinkle on the sugar and dot with the remaining 1 tablespoon butter. Add the remaining ½ cup orange juice by dribbling it down the sides of the baking dish. Cover the casserole with foil, sealing it tightly.

for serving now Bake the casserole for 1 hour, until the pork chops are white in the center.

Uncover the casserole and let stand for 10 minutes before serving.

to freeze Bake the casserole for 45 minutes, leaving the chops slightly pink in the center.

▶ **freeze for up to 6 weeks**

▶ **can be doubled**

cook smart
When assembling this casserole, leave some space between the chops. After the casserole is frozen, you can then use a serrated knife to cut it into individual portions that will defrost and reheat more quickly.

Uncover and cool the casserole to room temperature. Immediately re-cover with foil and refrigerate to chill.

Transfer the chilled casserole to the freezer and open-freeze. Unmold the frozen casserole and wrap in plastic freezer wrap, then heavy-duty foil. Or vacuum seal the frozen casserole and return it to the freezer.

to defrost and serve To defrost, unwrap the frozen casserole and drop it back into the original baking dish. Cover with foil and thaw in the refrigerator for 18 to 24 hours. Bake the thawed, foil-covered casserole at 350°F until it is heated through, 45 minutes.

freezer **note** The ginger stays strong but the orange flavor may fade in the defrosted casserole. To refresh it, grate some orange zest over the casserole before reheating.

pizza noodle casserole

▌ freeze for up
   to 8 weeks

▌ can be doubled

▌ freeze now,
   cook later

Instead of making pizza, sometimes I combine the tomato sauce and creamy cheese I would use with ground beef and noodles, then spoon this mixture into a baking dish. The resulting casserole, marrying the pleasures of pizza and pasta, bakes up beautifully, whether freshly made or from the freezer. Including broccoli florets turns this into a well-rounded dinner.

Makes 4 servings

4 ounces medium egg noodles

1 tablespoon olive oil

1 pound ground beef (85–90 percent lean)

1 small onion, chopped

2 garlic cloves, finely chopped

Pinch of red-pepper flakes

3 cups Chunky Fresh Tomato Sauce (page 173) or 20-Minute Tomato Sauce (page 192)

2 cups steamed broccoli florets (optional) (see Cook Smart)

1 teaspoon dried basil

1 teaspoon dried oregano

2 tablespoons chopped flat-leaf parsley (optional)

1 cup (4 ounces) shredded mozzarella cheese (see Freezer Note)

1 cup (4 ounces) shredded Parmesan cheese (see Freezer Note)

Salt and freshly ground pepper

cook smart
Defrosted frozen spinach (well drained) or leftover cooked eggplant can be mixed into the casserole before freezing.

Cook the noodles in a large pot of salted boiling water, leaving them slightly al dente, 6 to 7 minutes. Drain the noodles in a colander, rinse under cold water, drain well, and set aside.

In a medium skillet, heat the oil over medium-high heat. Add the meat and cook until no pink shows, breaking up the meat with a wooden spoon, 10 minutes. Add the onion, garlic, and pepper flakes and cook until the onion is soft, 5 minutes, stirring often. Using a slotted spoon, transfer the meat mixture to a mixing bowl.

Add the tomato sauce to the mixing bowl, then the noodles, broccoli (if using), basil, oregano, and parsley (if using) and mix to combine. Mix in ½ cup of each of the cheeses. Season to taste with salt and pepper.

Coat an 8-inch x 8-inch x 2-inch baking dish with nonstick spray and pour the noodle casserole into the dish.

for serving now Preheat the oven to 350°F.

Sprinkle the remaining ½ cup mozzarella over the casserole, then the remaining ½ cup Parmesan. Cover the casserole with foil and bake for 20 minutes. Remove the foil and bake for 20 minutes longer, or until a knife inserted in the center of the casserole feels hot to the touch. Let the casserole sit for 5 minutes before serving.

to freeze Cover the top of the casserole with plastic wrap and refrigerate to chill for 2 hours. Open-freeze the casserole for 12 to 18 hours. Unmold the frozen casserole and seal in plastic freezer wrap, then center the casserole on a 24-inch length of heavy-duty foil. If desired, wrap the remaining mozzarella and Parmesan in plastic freezer wrap, place the package of cheese on top of the casserole, and seal the foil. Return the casserole to the freezer. Or vacuum seal the casserole, tape the cheese packet on top, and store them together. (See Freezer Note below.)

to defrost and serve Unwrap the casserole and drop it back into the original pan. Cover the top of the casserole with plastic wrap. Thaw the casserole and cheese in the refrigerator for 18 to 24 hours. Let stand at room temperature while the oven heats. Top the thawed casserole with the remaining mozzarella and Parmesan, cover, and bake for 20 minutes, then uncover and bake for 20 minutes longer, or until the casserole is heated through. Let stand for 5 minutes before serving.

freezer note The frozen casserole tastes better when the final topping of cheeses is added after it has thawed. To be efficient, some cooks pack this shredded cheese with the casserole and store them together in the freezer. Since freezing makes the mozzarella stick together, I prefer taking the couple of minutes needed to shred the cheeses right before the defrosted casserole goes into the oven.

what's your beef?
The leaner the meat, the higher the price. Beef that is 85 to 93 percent lean works in the recipes in this book, so decide which to use based on either cost or fat and cholesterol content.

anytime turkey tetrazzini

▶ freeze for up
to 4 weeks

▶ can be doubled

▶ freeze now,
cook later

This creamy casserole, created for a famous opera diva, has become the classic day-after-Thanksgiving way to use up turkey leftovers. Now, however, when you can buy and roast half a turkey breast anytime or quickly sauté turkey cutlets, think about making 2 Tetrazzinis to serve whenever or to hold in the freezer.

Makes 4 servings

6 ounces linguine

3 tablespoons unsalted butter

8 ounces white mushrooms, stemmed
and thickly sliced

¼ cup rice flour

1½ cups milk, at room temperature

1 cup chicken broth

2 tablespoons dry sherry

1 cup shredded Parmesan cheese

Salt and freshly ground pepper

1½ cups diced cooked turkey breast

½ cup diced boiled ham (optional)

½ teaspoon dried thyme

side dish

Lightly steamed spinach, broccoli, or green beans will go well with your Tetrazzini.

cook smart

Use only diced turkey from a roasted turkey or cutlets, never turkey roll or thinly sliced deli turkey breast.

Coat an 8-inch x 8-inch baking dish with nonstick spray and set aside.

Cook the pasta in a large pot of salted boiling water 1 to 2 minutes less than called for on the package, to keep the pasta very al dente. Drain the pasta, rinse under cool water, and drain very well. Place the pasta in a large mixing bowl and set aside.

In a large saucepan, melt 1 tablespoon of the butter over medium heat. Add the mushrooms and cook until they release their liquid, dry out, and brown, 8 to 10 minutes. Add the mushrooms to the pasta. Wipe out the pan.

In the same pan, melt the remaining 2 tablespoons butter. Whisk in the flour and cook for 1 minute, stirring often. Gradually pour in the milk while whisking, then add the broth and sherry. Bring the sauce to a boil over medium heat, reduce the heat, and simmer until the sauce is thick enough to coat a spoon, 5 minutes. Mix in ½ cup of the Parmesan and season to taste with salt and pepper.

Add the sauce to the pasta, along with the turkey, ham (if using), and thyme, stirring with a fork to combine. Turn the Tetrazzini into the prepared baking dish, spreading it in an even layer and smoothing the top.

for serving now Preheat the oven to 400°F.

Sprinkle the remaining ½ cup Parmesan over the top of the casserole.

Bake, uncovered, for 30 minutes, or until the cheese is melted and the sauce is bubbling. Let the Tetrazzini rest for 15 minutes before serving.

to freeze Press a piece of plastic wrap onto the top of the casserole and refrigerate to chill. Transfer the chilled casserole to the freezer and open-freeze for 8 to 12 hours. Remove the plastic wrap and unmold the frozen casserole onto plastic freezer wrap. Center the casserole on a 24-inch length of heavy-duty foil. Wrap the remaining Parmesan in plastic freezer wrap, place the package of cheese on top of the casserole, and seal the foil. Label and return the casserole to the freezer. Or place the packet of Parmesan on top of the casserole and vacuum seal them together.

to defrost and serve Unwrap the frozen casserole, drop it back into the original pan, and wrap in foil. Thaw the casserole and Parmesan in the refrigerator for 18 to 24 hours. Let both sit at room temperature while preheating the oven to 350°F.

Sprinkle on the remaining ½ cup Parmesan.

Bake the casserole, covered with foil, until heated through, 45 to 60 minutes. Let it rest for 15 minutes before serving.

everybody's favorite tuna noodle casserole

The Campbell Soup Company did not invent tuna noodle casserole, but their promotion of condensed cream of mushroom soup, starting in the 1940s, turned it into a constant favorite. My version can be made using either Creamy Mushroom Sauce (page 103) or canned condensed soup. Crushed potato chips make the best topping, in my opinion, but you can use an equal amount of crushed soda crackers in their place.

▶ freeze for up to 8 weeks

▶ can be doubled

Makes 6–8 servings

8 ounces wide egg noodles

2 cans (6 ounces each) chunk light or albacore tuna, drained

1 recipe Creamy Mushroom Sauce (page 103) or 2 cans (10.75 ounces each) cream of mushroom soup (if using canned soup, add ⅓ cup milk)

1 cup frozen green peas

½ cup finely chopped onion

1 cup (4 ounces) shredded sharp Cheddar cheese

Salt and freshly ground pepper

to serve

1 cup crushed potato chips

Preheat the oven to 375°F. Coat a deep 9-inch x 9-inch baking dish with nonstick spray and set aside.

Cook the noodles in a large pot of salted boiling water until al dente. Drain in a colander, then rinse the noodles under running water until cool. Drain very well and place the noodles in a large mixing bowl.

Add the tuna, mushroom sauce or canned soup plus milk, frozen peas, onion, and cheese to the noodles and use a fork to combine well. Season to taste with salt and pepper. Spoon the tuna-noodle mixture into the prepared baking dish, spreading it evenly.

for serving now Sprinkle the potato chips over the top of the casserole. Bake, uncovered, for 35 to 40 minutes, until the casserole is bubbling and the chips are very crisp. Let rest for 10 minutes before serving.

to freeze Cover the casserole with foil and bake for 30 minutes. Uncover and cool to room temperature.

Re-cover the cooled casserole with foil and refrigerate to chill. Press plastic wrap onto the surface of the chilled casserole and open-freeze. Unmold the frozen casserole and wrap in plastic freezer wrap. Set the casserole in the center of a 24-inch length of heavy-duty foil, seal, and return to the freezer. Or vacuum seal the unmolded frozen casserole and return to the freezer.

to defrost and serve To defrost, unwrap the casserole and drop it back into the original baking dish. Cover the top with foil and thaw the casserole in the refrigerator for 18 to 24 hours.

Preheat the oven to 350°F.

Sprinkle on the potato chips and bake the casserole, uncovered, for 45 minutes, or until a knife inserted into the center feels hot and the chip topping is very crisp. Let the casserole rest for 10 minutes before serving.

creamy mushroom sauce

An essential component of many cook-to-freeze casseroles, this sauce is a rare exception to the "do not refreeze" rule.

▶ freeze for up to 8 weeks

Makes 2 ½ cups

1 ½ cups milk

⅓ cup heavy cream

¼ cup chicken broth

1 tablespoon olive oil

1 package (10 ounces) white mushrooms, finely chopped

¼ cup finely chopped shallots or onion

3 tablespoons unsalted butter

3 tablespoons rice flour

Salt and freshly ground pepper

In a medium saucepan, combine the milk, cream, and broth and set over medium heat until hot, or warm the mixture in a microwaveable container. Set aside.

In a medium skillet, heat the oil over medium-high heat. Add the mushrooms and shallots or onion. Cook until the mushrooms release their liquid, the liquid boils off, and the mushrooms brown, 10 minutes, stirring often. Set aside.

In a medium, heavy saucepan, melt the butter over medium heat. Stir in the rice flour and cook for 2 minutes as it foams, whisking frequently. Slowly add the hot milk mixture, starting with ¼ cup, whisking during and after each addition until the sauce is smooth. Cook until the sauce is steaming and coats a spoon thickly, 6 minutes. Off the heat, mix in the mushrooms. Season to taste with salt and pepper.

to serve now Use the sauce immediately or transfer to a container, press plastic wrap onto the surface, and cool to room temperature. Cover tightly and refrigerate the sauce for up to 5 days.

to freeze Spoon the sauce into a resealable 1-quart plastic freezer bag. Cool the sauce to room temperature. Cover tightly and refrigerate the sauce to chill. Freeze the bagged sauce on a baking sheet.

to defrost and serve Defrost the sauce in the refrigerator for up to 12 hours. Or thaw in a bowl of cool water, changing it every 15 minutes.

side dish
Besides using this sauce in casseroles and pot pies, spoon it over sliced turkey for a hot turkey sandwich.

lemon chicken and rice casserole

▶ freeze for up
  to 6 weeks

▶ can be doubled

If you think lemon makes everything taste better, this combination of chicken and rice in a creamy sauce will be irresistible. Adding spinach rounds out the nutrition in this casserole. When serving this dish from the freezer, adding the crumb topping right before reheating assures just-made flavor.

Makes 6 servings

4 cups cooked rice

1 tablespoon unsalted butter

1 tablespoon canola oil

¾ cup finely chopped onion

1 garlic clove, minced

3 cups cooked chicken torn into
   1-inch pieces

1 package (10 ounces) defrosted
   frozen chopped spinach,
   squeezed dry

2 cups Cream of Chicken Sauce (page
   105) or 1 can (10 ounces) condensed
   cream of chicken soup

¾ cup sour cream

½ cup fresh lemon juice

1 cup chicken broth

Salt and freshly ground pepper

to serve

¼ cup Italian-style bread crumbs

side dish

Make this dish meatless by replacing the chicken with 1 cup crumbled feta cheese.

cook smart

Canned soups contain enough sodium that additional salt may not be needed.

Preheat the oven to 350°F. Coat an 8-inch x 8-inch baking dish with nonstick spray.

In a medium skillet over medium-high heat, melt the butter with the oil. Add the onion and garlic and cook until the onion is soft, 6 minutes. Add the contents of the pan to a large bowl and stir in the rice.

In another bowl, combine the cream of chicken sauce or canned soup, sour cream, lemon juice, and broth. Combine the sauce mixture with the chicken and rice, and season to taste with salt and pepper. Spoon the casserole mixture into the prepared baking dish, spreading it evenly.

Cover the baking dish with foil and bake the casserole for 30 minutes.

for serving now Sprinkle the bread crumbs over the top of the casserole and bake, uncovered, for 5 minutes, or until the crumbs are browned and the sauce is bubbling. Let the casserole sit for 10 minutes before serving.

to freeze Cool the baked casserole to room temperature. Cover with plastic wrap and refrigerate to chill. Transfer the chilled casserole to the freezer. When frozen, 6 to 8 hours, unmold and wrap the casserole in plastic freezer wrap, then center on a 24-inch length of heavy-duty foil, seal, and return to the freezer. Or vacuum seal the unmolded frozen casserole and return to the freezer.

to defrost and serve Unwrap and drop the frozen casserole back into its original baking dish. Cover with plastic wrap and thaw in the refrigerator for 12 to 18 hours.

While the oven preheats to 350°F, let the casserole sit at room temperature.

Remove the plastic wrap, cover the casserole with foil, and bake for 30 minutes. Sprinkle on the bread crumbs and bake, uncovered, for 15 minutes, or until the topping is browned and a knife inserted into the center comes out hot.

freezer note To speed freezing and defrosting, cut the cooled casserole into individual portions before freezing. Their smaller size also reheats more quickly.

creamy chicken sauce

Use in recipes calling for a can of condensed cream of chicken soup.

Makes 2 cups

1 cup milk	2 tablespoons rice flour
1 cup chicken broth	1/4 cup grated Parmesan cheese
2 tablespoons unsalted butter	Salt and freshly ground pepper

Warm the milk and broth together in a microwaveable container or combine them in a saucepan and warm over medium heat. Set aside.

In a medium, heavy saucepan, melt the butter over medium heat. Stir in the rice flour and cook for 2 minutes, whisking frequently. Slowly pour in the warm broth and milk, starting with 1/2 cup, while whisking constantly, until all the liquid is added and the sauce is smooth. Cook until the mixture coats a spoon enough for your finger to make a clear track along the back, 4 to 5 minutes. Season to taste with salt and pepper.

for serving now Use the sauce immediately, or transfer to a container, and cool to room temperature. Cover tightly and refrigerate for up to 5 days.

to freeze Spoon the sauce into a resealable 1-quart plastic freezer bag or a plastic container. If using a container, press plastic wrap on the surface, and cool to room temperature. Cover tightly and refrigerate the sauce to chill. Freeze the sauce, on a baking sheet if in a bag, or directly in the freezer if in a container.

to defrost and serve Defrost the sauce in the refrigerator for up to 12 hours, depending on the container. Or thaw in a bowl of cool water, changing it every 15 minutes.

mole chicken enchiladas

▶ freeze for up
  to 8 weeks

▶ can be doubled

Layers of intense flavor make a good Mexican mole sauce unforgettable, but preparing one can take hours. Here, I have simplified the process while keeping the result dark and delicious. Since mole keeps well, this recipe makes extra to freeze and use another time. For the chicken, you can use Three Dinner Chicken (page 154), poached breasts, leftovers already on hand, or store-bought barbecued chicken.

Makes 4 servings

mole sauce

½ cup raisins

1 tablespoon canola oil

1 medium onion, chopped

2 garlic cloves, chopped

3 vine tomatoes, seeded and chopped

½ cup raw almonds

1 tablespoon sesame seeds

1 teaspoon ground cinnamon

1 teaspoon ground coriander

1 teaspoon ground cumin

6 black peppercorns

2 tablespoons ground ancho chile

2 tablespoons chili powder

1 ½ cups chicken broth

2 tablespoons unsalted butter

1 ounce unsweetened chocolate, finely chopped

Salt and freshly ground pepper

2 cups shredded cooked chicken

8 soft corn tortillas (6- or 7-inch diameter)

to serve

½ cup (2 ounces) shredded queso blanco or Monterey Jack cheese

Thinly sliced red onion rings (garnish)

side dish

The extra mole sauce, defrosted in the refrigerator, can be used to turn pan-seared pork chops, turkey cutlets, or sautéed shrimp into a flavorful skillet supper.

Soak the raisins in ½ cup of warm water until plump, 20 minutes. Drain the raisins and set aside.

In a medium skillet, heat the oil over medium-high heat. Add the onion and garlic and cook until soft, 5 minutes, stirring often. Scrape the contents of the pan into a blender and wipe out the pan. Add the tomatoes, almonds, sesame seeds, cinnamon, coriander, cumin, peppercorns, ancho chile, chili powder, and soaked raisins to the blender. Pour in ½ cup of the broth and whirl until the mixture is pulpy. Add ½ cup more broth and puree until the sauce is as smooth as possible.

Melt the butter in the skillet over medium heat. Pour in the contents of the blender and add the chocolate and remaining ½ cup broth. Cook until the sauce simmers and darkens, stirring occasionally, 5 minutes. Season to taste with salt and pepper. There will be 3½ cups of sauce.

Preheat the oven to 350°F. Coat an 11-inch x 7-inch baking dish with nonstick spray.

To assemble the enchiladas, in a bowl, mix 1 cup of the sauce with the chicken. Spread another ½ cup of the sauce in the bottom of the prepared baking dish. Two at a time, coat the tortillas lightly with nonstick spray, lay them on a baking sheet, and heat in the oven until supple, 2 to 3 minutes. Spoon ¼ cup of the chicken mixture horizontally across each tortilla near the edge towards you and roll up tightly. Place the filled tortillas seam side down in the baking dish. Repeat, packing the tortillas together tightly. Spoon 1 cup of mole sauce over them.

for serving now Cover the baking dish loosely with foil. Bake the enchiladas for 30 minutes, or until heated through. Divide the enchiladas among 4 dinner plates, sprinkle 2 tablespoons of the cheese over each serving, and serve immediately, garnished with the red onion.

to freeze Open-freeze the enchiladas in the baking dish. Unmold in a block onto plastic freezer wrap and seal, then wrap in heavy-duty foil, and return the enchiladas to the freezer. Or vacuum seal the unmolded enchiladas and return to the freezer.

Freeze the extra 1 cup of mole sauce in a tightly sealed container, pressing plastic freezer wrap onto the surface.

to defrost and serve To defrost, unwrap the frozen enchiladas and drop them back into the original baking dish. Cover with plastic wrap and thaw in the refrigerator for 12 hours.

Preheat the oven to 350°F. Cover the baking dish with foil and bake for 35 to 40 minutes, until the enchiladas are heated through. Just before serving, sprinkle the cheese and the onions over the enchiladas.

four-cheese baked ziti

▶ freeze for up to
   8 weeks

▶ can be doubled

Bring this abundant pasta casserole to a potluck and you will take home a very empty baking dish. Make sure to buy smooth penne for the pasta, not thicker penne rigate, which has ridges. Substituting most brands of commercially made tomato sauce for the Chunky Fresh Tomato Sauce still makes a delicious dish, but for the cheeses, always use a good-quality brand with full fat or the result can be a bland or even watery casserole.

Makes 4 servings

8 ounces (½ package) penne pasta

2½ cups Chunky Fresh Tomato Sauce
   (page 173)

1 container (15 ounces) ricotta cheese

1½ cups (6 ounces) shredded
   mozzarella cheese

2 tablespoons pecorino cheese

1 teaspoon dried oregano

1 teaspoon salt

⅛ teaspoon freshly ground pepper

¼ cup (1 ounce) shredded
   Parmesan cheese

cook smart
Freezing softens pasta, so undercook it quite a bit (just shy of al dente) if you plan to freeze this casserole.

Cook the pasta in a large pot of salted boiling water until al dente. Drain well in a colander and set aside.

Coat a 9-inch x 9-inch baking dish with nonstick spray. Spread ¾ cup of the sauce over the bottom of the pan; there will be gaps.

In a large mixing bowl, combine the ricotta with ¾ cup of the tomato sauce. Add 1 cup of the mozzarella, the pecorino, oregano, salt, and pepper and mix until the cheese is fluffy. Add the pasta and mix thoroughly. Turn the pasta and cheese into the prepared baking dish, spreading it in an even layer. Spoon the remaining 1 cup tomato sauce over the top, sprinkle on the remaining ½ cup mozzarella, then top with the Parmesan.

for serving now Preheat the oven to 400°F.

Bake the casserole, uncovered, for 30 minutes, or until the sauce is bubbling around the edges and the cheese topping is colored. Let the baked ziti stand for 10 minutes before serving.

to freeze Lay plastic wrap over the filled baking dish, pressing it lightly onto the surface of the casserole. Open-freeze until the casserole is solid, 6 to 8 hours. Unmold the frozen casserole and wrap tightly in plastic freezer wrap, then heavy-duty foil, and return to the freezer. Or vacuum seal the frozen casserole.

to defrost and serve To defrost, unwrap the frozen casserole and drop it back into the original baking dish. Cover with plastic wrap and defrost in the refrigerator for 12 to 18 hours.

Preheat the oven to 350°F. While the oven heats, let the casserole stand at room temperature.

Cover with foil and bake the casserole for 25 minutes. Uncover and bake for 15 minutes longer, or until the sauce is bubbling and the cheese on top is colored. Let the dish rest for 10 minutes before serving.

spinach and pesto lasagna

▶ **freeze for 8 weeks**

▶ **can be doubled**

side dish

Keep 3 cups (a half recipe) of Tomato and Roasted Red Pepper Sauce in the freezer and you can quickly assemble this lasagna to serve anytime.

A prepared pasta sauce of good quality will change the flavor but also makes a delicious lasagna.

cook smart

If your ricotta cheese is loose and wet, drain it in a fine strainer set over a bowl in the refrigerator for 3 to 4 hours.

For a meatless meal, lasagna is hard to beat. It is also easy to assemble when you use no-cook lasagna noodles and prepared pesto. Then you can invest the time saved to prepare Tomato and Roasted Red Pepper Sauce (page 176). Its bright, intense flavor, along with the basil-perfumed pesto and creamy cheeses, puts this lush yet light lasagna over the top.

Makes 4 servings

3 cups (½ recipe) Tomato and Roasted Red Pepper Tomato Sauce (page 176)

9 sheets no-cook lasagna noodles

1 container (15 ounces) ricotta cheese

½ package (5 ounces) defrosted chopped spinach, squeezed dry

⅓ cup prepared pesto

1 large egg

1 teaspoon salt

¼ teaspoon freshly ground pepper

2 cups shredded mozzarella cheese (see Freezer Note)

1 cup shredded Parmesan cheese (see Freezer Note)

Coat an 8-inch x 8-inch baking dish with nonstick spray and set aside. If serving now, preheat the oven to 375°F.

Spread ½ cup of the Tomato sauce over the bottom of the prepared pan. Arrange 3 sheets of the pasta over the sauce. In a large mixing bowl, combine the ricotta, spinach, pesto, egg, salt, and pepper. Spread half of this cheese mixture over the pasta and sprinkle on ½ cup of the mozzarella and ¼ cup of the Parmesan. Spoon on another ½ cup of the tomato sauce. Repeat, making another layer of pasta, ricotta mixture, cheeses, and tomato sauce and finishing with the remaining 3 lasagna sheets and 1 ½ cups tomato sauce.

for serving now Sprinkle the lasagna with the remaining 1 cup mozzarella and ½ cup Parmesan. Cover the pan loosely with nonstick foil or foil coated with nonstick spray. Bake for 30 minutes. Uncover and bake for 15 minutes longer, or until the cheese on top is lightly browned and the sauce is bubbling. Let the lasagna rest for 15 minutes before serving

to freeze Press a sheet of plastic wrap onto the surface of the lasagna and refrigerate to chill. Open-freeze the chilled lasagna. Unmold, wrap tightly in plastic freezer wrap, then heavy-duty foil, and return the lasagna to the freezer.

If desired, combine the remaining 1 cup mozzarella and ½ cup Parmesan in a 1-cup freezer container, press plastic wrap over the cheeses, cover, and freeze. However, I recommend waiting until the lasagna is thawed and ready to bake before shredding these cheeses for the topping.

to defrost and serve Unwrap the frozen lasagna and drop it back into the original baking dish. Cover with foil and thaw in the refrigerator for 12 hours. If you have frozen them, defrost the cheeses for the topping in the refrigerator for 6 hours.

Sprinkle the final 1 cup mozzarella and ½ cup Parmesan frozen or freshly grated, over the top of the lasagna. Bake the lasagna, covered with foil, in a 375°F oven for 35 to 40 minutes, or until warm in the center. Uncover and continue baking until the cheese and sauce are bubbling. Let the lasagna rest for 15 minutes before serving.

freezer note Topping the frozen lasagna with the final layer of cheeses after it has thawed produces a better-tasting baked lasagna. To be efficient, some cooks pack these cheeses, already shredded, together with the lasagna in the freezer. Since freezing makes the mozzarella stick together and shredding it takes only a couple of minutes, I prefer doing this right before the lasagna goes into the oven. Plus, freshly shredded cheese melts more nicely than defrosted cheese.

baked red peppers with quinoa and feta

Pairing roasted red peppers and protein-rich quinoa with corn and tangy feta makes these colorful peppers an excellent meatless dish. Baking them in a hot oven brings out the natural sweetness of the peppers and cooks them in about half the time usually required. It also keeps them delightfully succulent. Use the fleshy hothouse-grown peppers with thick walls (usually from Europe or Israel), not the field-grown domestic ones, which have thinner walls. Also, pick through the bin to select smaller peppers that will hold about 1 cup of the filling.

Makes 4 servings

4 thick-walled red bell peppers

Quinoa Pilaf with Garden Vegetables (page 189)

½ cup (2 ounces) crumbled feta cheese

to serve

¼ cup fresh lemon juice

2 tablespoons extra virgin olive oil

½ teaspoon dried thyme

½ teaspoon salt

Freshly ground pepper

▶ freeze for up to 4 weeks

▶ can be doubled

▶ freeze now, cook later

Cut the tops off the bell peppers just below the curved shoulder. Discard the tops and scoop out the seeds and ribs, then coat the inside of the peppers with nonstick spray.

In a mixing bowl, combine the Quinoa Pilaf with Garden Vegetables and the feta. Pack this filling into the peppers, mounding it lightly.

for serving now Preheat the oven to 450°F. Line a baking dish just large enough to hold the filled peppers with foil.

Stand the filled peppers in the prepared pan; they should be almost touching. Pour in ¾ cup of water. Set a 4-inch square of foil over each pepper, like a little hat.

Bake for 30 minutes, or until a knife easily penetrates the peppers but they are not overly soft. Set the pan on a cooling rack, uncover the peppers, and let them stand for 10 minutes.

In a small bowl, combine the lemon juice and oil. Season with the thyme, salt, and pepper to taste and spoon one-fourth of the mixture over the filling in each pepper. Serve hot or at room temperature.

side dish
Make the pilaf using long-grain brown rice in place of the quinoa, if you wish.

to freeze Set the filled peppers on a plate, cover with plastic wrap, and refrigerate to chill.

Wrap the chilled peppers individually in plastic freezer wrap and then in heavy-duty foil. Set the wrapped peppers on a baking sheet and freeze.

to defrost and serve Remove the foil and defrost the plastic-wrapped peppers in the refrigerator for 12 to 15 hours.

Preheat the oven to 450°F.

Unwrap and set the peppers in a foil-covered baking dish just large enough to hold them and let stand at room temperature until the oven is heated. Top each pepper with a 4-inch square of foil and bake for 30 minutes, or until the peppers are tender and a knife inserted into the center of the filling comes out hot to the touch. Combine the lemon juice, olive oil, thyme, salt, and pepper to taste. Spoon the mixture over the peppers and serve, hot or warm.

pomegranate-glazed chicken with wild rice

Perhaps you will recognize this as my version of a popular Martha Stewart dish. Brushing the chicken repeatedly with a garnet-colored glaze makes it high-maintenance, but every mouthful says this casually elegant dish is worth the effort. Serve it once and I predict you will be doubling the recipe so you can enjoy it again and again.

Makes 4 servings

2 cups pure pomegranate juice (see Side Dish)

1 garlic clove, minced

1 tablespoon finely chopped flat-leaf parsley

1 tablespoon Dijon mustard

1 ½ teaspoons ground cumin

1 tablespoon extra virgin olive oil

1 teaspoon salt

¼ teaspoon freshly ground pepper

4 skinless split chicken breast halves with ribs, 8 ounces each

1 can (8 ounces) jellied cranberry sauce, chopped into small pieces

to serve

4 cups cooked wild rice

Chopped flat-leaf parsley (optional, for garnish)

In a glass or stainless steel deep, medium saucepan, combine the pomegranate juice, garlic, parsley, mustard, and 1 teaspoon of the cumin. Bring to a boil over medium-high heat, reduce the heat, and boil gently until the marinade is reduced to 1 cup, about 20 minutes. Add the oil and ½ teaspoon of the salt, plus the pepper. As the marinade cools to room temperature, it will thicken.

Pour half of the marinade into a resealable 1-gallon plastic freezer bag, leaving the rest in the saucepan. Add the chicken and squeeze out as much air as possible from the bag. Marinate the chicken on a plate in the refrigerator for 1 hour.

Preheat the oven to 400°F. Line a 9-inch x 9-inch baking pan with heavy-duty foil. Set a wire rack over the pan. Coat the foil and rack with nonstick spray and set aside.

Add the cranberry sauce and remaining ½ teaspoon cumin to the marinade in the saucepan. Over medium heat, simmer until the cranberry sauce dissolves, increase the heat, and boil gently until there is 1 cup of glaze. Season with the remaining ½ teaspoon salt and pepper to taste.

Remove the chicken from the marinade. Discard the marinade and, using paper towels, dry the chicken. Arrange the breasts rib side down on the rack and brush them liberally with the warm glaze.

▶ **freeze for up to 4 weeks**

▶ **elegant for entertaining**

side dish

PomWonderful is the pomegranate juice I like best for its intense, tart-sweet flavor and almost syrupy thickness.

cook smart

Lining the pan with foil and spraying the wire rack speeds cleanup.

Reduce the oven to 375°F and bake the chicken for 10 minutes. Brush with the glaze and bake 10 minutes longer. After repeating these steps 2 more times, pour the remaining glaze into the baking pan.

for serving now Continue baking until an instant-read thermometer inserted in a breast at the thickest point reads 170° F, or until the meat is white when slit with a knife.

Make a bed of wild rice on 4 dinner plates. Set a chicken breast on top of the rice and spoon over one-fourth of the sauce from the baking pan. Garnish with parsley, if desired.

to freeze When an instant-read thermometer reads 165°F, or the chicken still looks slightly pink inside, remove it from the oven. When it's cool enough to handle, separate the meat from the ribs and tear the chicken into bite-size pieces. Place the chicken into 2 or more resealable 1-quart plastic freezer bags, add the glaze from the pan, and cool to room temperature, then refrigerate the chicken to chill. Squeeze out as much air as possible and freeze the chilled chicken flat on a baking sheet lined with wax paper.

to defrost and serve Defrost the chicken on a plate in the refrigerator for 10 to 24 hours, depending on the amount. Place the chicken and glaze in a glass or stainless steel medium saucepan, cover, and simmer gently over medium heat until heated through.

To serve, spoon the chicken and sauce over the wild rice and garnish with parsley, if using.

prosciutto-stuffed chicken with creamy parmesan sauce

These ham-and-cheese stuffed chicken rolls coated with flavorful bread crumbs are perfect for a dinner party. They take time to defrost, so remove them from the freezer the night before. You can prepare the creamy Parmesan sauce while the chicken bakes, or hold it in the freezer to defrost and reheat at the same time as the chicken.

▸ freeze for up to 6 weeks

▸ can be doubled

▸ elegant for entertaining

Makes 4 servings

1 cup milk	4 slices prosciutto
1 tablespoon unsalted butter	4 tablespoons shredded mozzarella cheese
1 tablespoon rice flour	
¼ cup shredded Parmigiano-Reggiano cheese	1 teaspoon dried basil
	1 large egg
Salt and freshly ground pepper	¼ cup milk
4 boneless, skinless chicken breast halves, 6–7 ounces each	½ cup Italian-style bread crumbs

Heat the milk in a microwaveable measuring cup or small saucepan until steaming. Set aside.

In a small saucepan, melt the butter over medium heat. Whisk in the rice flour and cook for 2 minutes, whisking constantly.

While whisking, slowly add ¼ cup of the hot milk. When the mixture is smooth, continue adding the milk ¼ cup at a time while whisking. Cook until the sauce is steaming and coats a spoon thickly, 4 to 5 minutes, stirring occasionally. Off the heat, add the Parmigiano-Reggiano and whisk until it has melted and the sauce is smooth. Season to taste with salt and pepper. Set the sauce aside. There will be 1 cup of sauce, which keeps, covered in the refrigerator, for 5 days.

Place each chicken breast smooth side up between 2 sheets of wax paper and pound to an even ¼-inch thickness. The pounded breasts should be about 6 inches across and 6 inches long at their widest point.

Place each breast on a work surface with the widest part away from you. Cover each breast with a slice of prosciutto. Sprinkle 1 tablespoon of the mozzarella and ¼ teaspoon of the basil on each breast. Fold up the bottom, then fold in the sides to enclose the filling, and roll the breast away from you while pulling it tight with your fingers. Wrap the rolled breasts in plastic wrap and refrigerate on a plate for 1

side dish

If you have only plain bread crumbs, mixing in some grated Parmesan or pecorino cheese, dried oregano, and salt and pepper will approximate the Italian kind.

hour. Unwrap and insert toothpicks at the seam to hold the rolls closed.

Preheat the oven to 350°F. Coat a baking dish just large enough to hold the chicken with nonstick spray.

In a wide dish, whisk the egg with the milk. Spread the bread crumbs in a second dish. One at a time, dip each roll first in egg mixture, then bread crumbs, patting to help them adhere. Place the coated rolled chicken seam side down in the prepared baking dish.

Bake the chicken, uncovered, for 30 to 35 minutes, or until the rolls feel firm and an instant-read thermometer inserted into the center registers 170°F, or the chicken looks white when a roll is cut open.

for serving now If necessary, reheat the sauce over medium heat, whisking constantly until it is warmed through.

Place a baked chicken roll on each of 4 dinner plates. Spoon on about 3 tablespoons of the creamy Parmesan sauce and serve.

to freeze Cool the baked chicken rolls to room temperature. Wrap individually in plastic freezer wrap and refrigerate to chill. Enclose the wrapped chicken individually in heavy-duty foil and freeze on a baking sheet. Or freeze the chicken in plastic wrap, remove the wrap, vacuum seal, and return to the freezer. Transfer the sauce to a 1-cup freezer container, press plastic freezer wrap onto the surface, and cool to room temperature. Cover the sauce tightly, refrigerate to chill, and then freeze.

to defrost and serve Defrost the chicken in the refrigerator on a rack set on a plate for 12 to 16 hours. Defrost the sauce in the refrigerator for 8 to 12 hours.

Preheat the oven to 350°F. Coat a baking dish just large enough to hold the chicken with nonstick spray.

Arrange the thawed chicken in the baking dish, cover with nonstick foil or foil coated with nonstick spray, and bake for 30 minutes.

Spoon on the thawed sauce and bake, uncovered, until the chicken is heated through and the sauce is hot, 10 minutes.

california meatloaf burgers

The recipe for this meatloaf served as a burger is the bestseller at Restaurant Akasha in Los Angeles, where I have dined next to A-list movie stars. Shredded Cheddar blended into the patty keeps it extra juicy, while jalapeño chile pepper and green olives add bold flavor. Instead of grilling, though, I bake these plump, burger-shaped patties because this avoids the unhealthy compounds that form when meat chars during grilling and broiling. Then I serve them on a bun with all the trimmings, just like at Akasha'a. As the individual patties cook, expect the cheese to release liquid.

▶ freeze for up to 4 weeks

▶ can be doubled

▶ freeze now, cook later

Makes 6 servings

- 1 pound ground turkey (93 percent lean)
- 1 cup (3 ounces) shredded sharp Cheddar cheese
- ½ cup finely chopped red onion
- ¼ cup finely chopped pitted green olives
- 2 tablespoons tomato paste
- 1 small jalapeño chile pepper, seeded and finely chopped
- 1 teaspoon salt
- ⅛ teaspoon freshly ground pepper

to serve

- 6 whole-grain hamburger buns, toasted
- Tomato and red onion slices
- Ketchup and mustard
- 6 pickle spears

In a large mixing bowl, mix the turkey, cheese, onion, olives, tomato paste, jalapeno, salt, and pepper with a fork until well combined. Shape the mixture into six 3-inch patties.

for serving now

using oven Preheat the oven to 425°F.

Line a shallow baking pan with foil, set a wire rack on the pan, and arrange up to 6 burgers on the rack so the pan can catch liquid released during cooking.

Bake for 8 minutes, turn, and bake until an instant-read thermometer inserted in the center reaches 170°F, about 8 minutes longer.

using toaster oven Preheat the toaster oven to 450°F.

Bake the burgers, 1 or 2 at a time, for 20 minutes, or until an instant-read thermometer registers 170°F, turning them after 10 minutes.

side dish
Replace the jalapeno with chopped sweet red bell pepper if you do not like heat.

cook smart
Shaped like burgers, these mini meatloaves cook in one-fourth the time required to bake one big meatloaf.

Serve the burgers on the toasted buns, topped with tomato and onion slices, ketchup, and mustard and accompanied by a pickle.

to freeze Individually wrap the uncooked burgers in plastic freezer wrap, then wrap 2 burgers together in heavy-duty foil. Refrigerate, then transfer the chilled burgers to the freezer. Or open-freeze individual burgers, then vacuum seal them, up to 4 in a package, and return to the freezer.

to defrost and serve Remove the foil and defrost the burgers on a plate in the refrigerator for 3 to 4 hours.

Bake the defrosted meatloaf burgers on a wire rack set over a foil-lined baking pan in a 425°F oven for 16 minutes, turning them midway, or in a 450°F toaster oven.

Serve the burgers on toasted buns, with the tomato and onion slices, ketchup, mustard, and pickles.

always good meatloaf

These days, meatloaf recipes abound for versions that are rustic, upscale, ethnic, even fanciful. Still, nothing beats Mom's classic when it is made with good-quality beef (85 percent lean, please), soaked bread, and an egg flavored with ketchup and spicy mustard; then baked under smoky bacon strips. Ground beef is usually the best budget choice, but turkey or the combination of veal, pork, and beef traditionally used is also good in this recipe. Since cold meatloaf makes great sandwiches, planned leftovers are always a good idea.

▶ **freeze** for up to 8 weeks

▶ **can be doubled**

▶ **feeds a crowd**

Makes 8 servings

2 slices white bread, crusts removed

¼ cup milk

1 large egg

1 medium carrot, cut in 1-inch pieces

1 small celery rib, cut in 1-inch pieces

½ medium onion, diced

1 garlic clove

½ poblano or green bell pepper, diced

1 tablespoon extra virgin olive oil

1½ pounds ground beef (85–90 percent lean)

⅓ cup ketchup

2 tablespoons spicy brown mustard

1 teaspoon salt

¼ teaspoon freshly ground pepper

4 strips preservative-free bacon

side dish
Cover the meatloaf with plum tomato slices in place of the bacon if you wish.

Preheat the oven to 350°F. Coat a 9-inch x 5-inch x 3-inch loaf pan with nonstick spray.

Tear the bread into 1-inch pieces. In a large mixing bowl, soak the bread in the milk until soft. Add the egg and beat with a fork to combine.

Whirl the carrot, celery, onion, garlic, and poblano or bell pepper in a food processor until finely chopped. Heat the oil in a medium skillet over medium-high heat. Add the vegetables and cook until soft, 5 minutes, stirring often. Set the vegetables aside for 10 minutes.

Add the cooled vegetables, beef, ketchup, mustard, salt, and pepper to the soaked bread mixture and mix until well combined. Pack the mixture into the prepared pan and rap sharply on the counter to eliminate air pockets. Cover the top of the meatloaf with the bacon strips. Wrap the pan in foil, sealing it well.

Bake the meatloaf for 60 to 75 minutes, or until an instant-read thermometer inserted into the center registers 170°F.

to serve now Let the meatloaf sit for 10 minutes. Remove and discard the bacon. Slice the meatloaf in the pan and serve. Or cool in the pan, then unmold the meatloaf and discard the bacon. Refrigerate the meatloaf, covered, for up to 4 days, slicing and reheating it in foil in a 350°F oven, or making sandwiches with cold meatloaf.

to freeze Cool the baked meatloaf in the pan. Cover with foil and refrigerate to chill. Unmold the cold meatloaf and cut into 8 slices. Wrap the slices individually in plastic freezer wrap, then heavy-duty foil. Freeze on a baking sheet, then store in resealable 1-quart plastic freezer bags. Or open-freeze unwrapped slices, vacuum seal, and store.

to defrost and serve Defrost wrapped meatloaf slices on a plate in the refrigerator for 8 hours. Discard the plastic wrap and seal the slices in foil. Bake in a 350°F oven until heated through, 25 to 30 minutes.

chapter 6

stews and slow simmers

Stews and other slowly braised dishes, as well as chili, truly do taste better the day after they are made. In addition, these succulent dishes hold up well in the freezer, making them ideal to prepare and store away.

Many of the dishes here have ethnic flavors, from Greek-style Beef Stew with Red Wine and Cinnamon to Catfish Jambalaya, which successfully meets the challenge of freezing fish. The chilis—zesty Chicken Chili Verde and meatless Best Ever Lentil Chili—offer lighter choices with big flavor.

The fillings for pot pies are actually stews that freeze nicely, too. So does Sunday Red Sauce, an old-world Italian one-pot meal including meatballs and sausages that will have people looking in your kitchen for an Italian *nonna*, and a coq au vin as good as Julia's.

Boiling toughens meat and poultry and also makes them dry. So when reheating stews and braises like Coffee Pot Roast and Sake-Soy Short Ribs, for best results always use gentle heat and keep an eye on them.

- chicken chili verde
- catfish jambalaya
- spanish chicken and chickpea stew
- beef stew with red wine and cinnamon
- sunday red sauce with sausage, meat, and meatballs
- frankie's meatballs
- best ever lentil chili
- vegetarian mushroom goulash
- coffee pot roast
- pulled jerk pork with carolina barbecue sauce
- coq au vin blanc
- sake-soy short ribs
- lamb shanks with white beans and lemon
- chicken pot pies
- salmon and mushroom pot pies
- three dinner chicken

chicken chili verde

▶ freeze for up
to 6 weeks

▶ can be doubled

I call this mild chili a "slap-hands" dish because everyone wants to dip a spoon into the pot while it cooks. I use chicken cutlets for convenience, but less expensive split breasts or boneless and skinless thighs cut into pieces are fine—just allow for longer cooking after adding the sauce.

Makes 4 servings

1 ½ cups chicken broth

1 can (11 ounces) tomatillos

1 vine tomato, seeded and chopped

1 large onion, chopped

2 garlic cloves, chopped

¼ cup packed cilantro leaves

2 tablespoons chopped flat-leaf parsley

1 teaspoon ground cumin

2 tablespoons canola oil

2 teaspoons dried oregano, preferably Mexican

1 pound chicken cutlets, cut into 1-inch pieces

Salt and freshly ground pepper

to serve

4 cups cooked brown rice

Cilantro leaves (optional, for garnish)

Hot-pepper sauce (optional)

side dish

An alternative method is to make the sauce and freeze it before adding the chicken. That way, you can simmer thin pork chops or tilapia in the sauce as alternatives to chicken.

cook smart

Using canned tomatillos saves time spent peeling and scrubbing away the sticky coating on fresh ones.

In a blender, whirl 1 cup of the broth with the tomatillos, tomato, ¼ cup of the onion, and half the garlic until the mixture is pulpy. Pour it into a medium bowl, then add the remaining ½ cup broth to the blender, along with the cilantro, parsley, and cumin, and whirl until pulpy. Add the mixture to the tomatillos, completing the sauce.

In a large skillet, heat 1 tablespoon of the oil over medium-high heat and add all of the sauce. When it starts to bubble, reduce the heat and simmer until the sauce darkens and thickens slightly, about 15 minutes. Return the sauce to the bowl and set aside. Wipe out the pan.

Add the remaining 1 tablespoon oil and the remaining onion. When the onion is translucent, 4 minutes, add the oregano and remaining garlic and cook until the onion is soft, 2 minutes, stirring frequently. Add the chicken and cook, using tongs to turn the chicken until the pieces no longer look pink, about 2 minutes. Add the sauce and simmer the chili, covered, until the chicken is white in the center, 5 to 6 minutes. Season to taste with salt and pepper.

for serving now Divide the rice among 4 wide, shallow bowls. Ladle the chili over the rice, garnish with cilantro (if using), and serve. Pass a bottle of hot-pepper sauce separately for those who want more heat.

to freeze Cool the chili to room temperature. Ladle it into resealable 1-quart plastic freezer bags and refrigerate to chill. Freeze the bags of chilled chili flat on a baking sheet lined with wax paper.

to defrost and serve Thaw the chili in the refrigerator on a plate for 12 to 18 hours, depending on the amount. Or defrost in a bowl of cool water, changing the water every 15 minutes and breaking the chili into chunks as it defrosts. Reheat the thawed chili in a saucepan, covered, just until the chicken is heated through and the sauce is hot. Adjust the seasoning with salt and pepper, plus cumin and oregano, if desired. Serve the chili over the cooked rice, garnished with cilantro, if desired.

catfish jambalaya

▶ freeze for up to 4 weeks

▶ can be doubled

Catfish goes well with the herbs and tomatoes used in Creole cooking. It is also a fish that freezes particularly well. Making a roux can be tricky, but not when you do it my way. Using rice flour, which does not lump up, in my simplified version for this Louisiana-style stew makes it almost foolproof. The chorizo, which adds smoky flavor, can be either hot or mild.

Makes 4 servings

3 tablespoons canola oil

3 ounces hard chorizo, finely chopped

1 cup chopped onion

2 tablespoons rice flour

1 cup hot water

1 large celery rib, chopped

1 small green bell pepper, seeded and chopped

1 can (14½ ounces) diced tomatoes, or 2 cups

1 can (8 ounces) tomato sauce

2 garlic cloves, chopped

1 bay leaf

1 teaspoon dried oregano

1 teaspoon dried thyme

½ teaspoon dried basil

¼ teaspoon cayenne pepper

1 pound catfish fillets, cut into 1-inch pieces

2 scallions, green and white parts, chopped

1 tablespoon fresh lemon juice

Salt and freshly ground pepper

to serve

4 cups cooked long-grain white or brown rice

Salt and freshly ground pepper

side dish

When serving now, jambalaya can be made using small or medium shrimp in place of the catfish. It cannot be frozen because most shrimp is previously frozen, so freezing it a second time turns it mushy.

In a small Dutch oven, heat the oil over medium-high heat. Add the chorizo and cook until it has colored the oil, 2 minutes. Remove the chorizo with a slotted spoon, drain on paper towels, and set aside.

Add the onion and cook until golden, 8 minutes, stirring occasionally. Mix in the rice flour. When it bubbles, whisk constantly until the roux turns deep gold, 8 to 10 minutes. Off the heat, add the hot water, standing back, as it will splatter. Return the pot to medium heat and boil gently, whisking constantly, until the roux thickens, 3 minutes.

Add the celery and bell pepper and cook for 5 minutes, stirring occasionally. Add the tomatoes (with juice), tomato sauce, garlic, bay leaf, oregano, thyme, basil, and cayenne and simmer until the vegetables are just tender, 10 minutes.

Add the catfish, scallions, lemon juice, and reserved chorizo. Simmer until the catfish is white in the center, 5 minutes.

for serving now Mix in the rice. Season the jambalaya to taste with salt and pepper. When the rice is heated through, divide the jambalaya among 4 wide bowls.

to freeze Cool the jambalaya to room temperature, and then divide it between 2 resealable 1-quart plastic freezer bags. Chill the jambalaya on a plate in the refrigerator. Freeze the chilled jambalaya flat on a baking sheet lined with wax paper.

to defrost and serve Thaw the jambalaya on a plate in the refrigerator for 8 to 16 hours, depending on the amount. Place the jambalaya in a heavy pot. Add the rice and simmer over medium heat, covered, about 8 minutes, stirring occasionally. Do not let the jambalaya boil. Adjust the seasoning to taste with salt, pepper, and lemon juice and cook until heated through, about 8 minutes longer.

spanish chicken and chickpea stew

▶ freeze for up
to 8 weeks

▶ can be doubled

In Spain, *cocidos* are substantial one-pot dishes that fall between a soup and a stew. This one, made with chicken, rice, and chickpeas, makes a hefty and easy meal in a bowl. Whenever chicken thighs are on special, I dig out this recipe and my jar of smoky Spanish paprika and stock the freezer.

Makes 4 servings

¾ pound boneless, skinless chicken thighs (see Cook Smart, page 154)

3 cups chicken broth

1 medium carrot, diced

1 celery rib, cut into ½-inch pieces

1 leek, white part only, halved lengthwise and thinly sliced crosswise

1 medium onion, chopped

2 large garlic cloves, minced

1 can (15 ounces) chickpeas, drained, or 2 cups cooked dried chickpeas

1 cup canned whole plum tomatoes, coarsely chopped

1 teaspoon Spanish smoked sweet paprika

1 dried red chile pepper or ⅛ teaspoon red-pepper flakes

1 ounce finely chopped serrano ham or prosciutto

to serve

2 cups cooked long-grain brown rice or frozen brown rice

Salt and freshly ground pepper

Chopped flat-leaf parsley (optional, for garnish)

side dish

Crusty bread, grilled or toasted, then rubbed with a cut garlic clove and drizzled with extra virgin olive oil, completes this meal.

cook smart

Frozen cooked brown rice is becoming widely available. It saves enough time to warrant the cost.

In a small Dutch oven, combine the chicken, broth, and 1 cup of water. Bring to a boil over medium-high heat, reduce the heat, and simmer until the chicken is cooked through, about 35 minutes. Remove the thighs to a plate. Strain the liquid into a large bowl and let sit for 30 minutes, then skim off the fat. When the chicken is cool enough to handle, tear the meat into bite-size pieces, cover, and set aside.

Return the broth to the pot. Add the carrot, celery, leek, onion, garlic, chickpeas, tomatoes, paprika, and chile pepper or pepper flakes. Bring the stew just to a simmer and cook until the vegetables are crisp-tender, 15 minutes.

for serving now Add the chicken, ham, and rice and simmer until they are heated through and the vegetables are tender, about 10 minutes. Season to taste with salt and pepper. Divide the stew among deep soup bowls. Garnish with parsley, if using.

to freeze Transfer the stew to a large bowl and cool to room temperature. Mix in the cooked chicken and the ham. Ladle the stew into resealable 1-quart plastic freezer bags in 2-cup portions. Refrigerate the stew on a plate to chill. Freeze the chilled stew flat on a baking sheet lined with wax paper.

to defrost and serve Thaw the stew on a plate in the refrigerator for 6 to 8 hours. In a saucepan, heat the stew with the cooked rice, covered, over medium heat, taking care not to let it boil. Adjust the seasoning to taste with salt and pepper. Serve garnished with parsley, if desired.

freezer note After freezing, smoky paprika will be even more noticeable than when this stew is freshly made. Serving it with the garlic-rubbed bread balances this.

beef stew with red wine and cinnamon

Cinnamon, bay leaf, and red wine, frequently used together in Greek cooking, warm the flavor of this lean stew. When served from the freezer, adding the vegetables during reheating keeps their colors bright and helps their flavors stand out.

Makes 4 servings

1 tablespoon canola oil

2 pounds chuck, well trimmed, cut into 1-inch cubes

1 teaspoon salt

¾ cup dry red wine

1 can (15 ounces) beef broth

2 tablespoons red wine vinegar

¼ cup tomato paste

3 whole garlic cloves, smashed and peeled

1 piece (2 inches) cinnamon stick

1 large bay leaf

1 teaspoon whole peppercorns

to serve

1 tablespoon unsalted butter

2 cups peeled fresh or frozen pearl onions (½ of a 10-ounce bag)

1 cup baby carrots, cut into ¾-inch pieces

½ tablespoon packed brown sugar

▶ **freeze for up to 8 weeks**

▶ **can be doubled**

side dish
Orzo pasta or rice makes a good side dish with some of the stew's liquid spooned over.

cook smart
Using ground in place of stick cinnamon will make the stew's juices cloudy.

In a large Dutch oven or deep skillet, heat the oil over medium-high heat. Sprinkle the meat with the salt and add half of the beef to the pan, leaving space between the pieces. Brown the meat well on all sides, 12 to 15 minutes, turning it with tongs.

Remove the meat to a plate and brown the remaining pieces, 8 to 10 minutes, and add to the first batch. Pour out any fat and return the pan to the heat.

Pour in the wine and use a wooden spatula to scrape up any browned bits clinging to the pan. Add the broth, vinegar, tomato paste, garlic, cinnamon, bay leaf, and peppercorns, stirring to dissolve the tomato paste. Return the browned meat and its accumulated juices to the pan. When the liquid starts to bubble, reduce the heat, cover, and simmer until the meat is fork-tender, 1 hour 15 minutes. Remove and discard the bay leaf and cinnamon stick.

for serving now Melt the butter in a medium skillet over medium heat. Add the pearl onions, carrots, and brown sugar and cook, stirring often, until they are shiny and lightly colored, 5 minutes. Add the glazed vegetables to the stew and simmer until they are tender, 10 minutes. Divide the stew among wide, shallow bowls.

to freeze Cool the stew to room temperature. Divide the meat and liquid among 3 resealable 1-quart plastic freezer bags and refrigerate. Freeze the bags of chilled stew flat on a baking sheet lined with wax paper.

to defrost and serve Thaw the stew on a plate in the refrigerator for 18 to 24 hours.

Place the defrosted stew in a heavy pot. Glaze the onions and carrots in the melted butter and brown sugar and add them to the stew. Simmer over medium heat, covered, until the vegetables are tender and the meat is heated through, 20 to 25 minutes, depending on the amount. (Boiling will toughen the meat.) Adjust the seasoning as needed, including the vinegar (see Freezer Note).

freezer note The cinnamon flavor in this stew holds up in freezing, but the flavors of the vinegar and bay leaf fade. To resharpen the stew's flavor, add ¼ teaspoon of vinegar per serving when reheating.

sunday red sauce with sausage, meat, and meatballs

When you make this dish, everyone will believe an Italian *nonna* taught you her secret recipe. Traditionally served on Sundays, this is called *ragù* in southern Italy and gravy by Americans of Italian heritage. They serve the intensely flavorful tomato sauce in a bowl, along with the meat and sausages simmered in it, plus meatballs, then use the remaining sauce to make baked pasta or spoon over Baked Polenta (page 190). For freezing, I pack some of the sauce alone, some mixed with meat and sausage, and some with only meatballs.

▶ freeze for up to 10 weeks

▶ feeds a crowd

Makes 6 cups sauce, 2 cups meat, and 8 meatballs

2 tablespoons extra virgin olive oil

1 large onion, finely chopped

2 garlic cloves, chopped

3 cans (28 ounces) whole plum tomatoes in tomato sauce

½ pound Italian sausages, sweet or hot

½ pound lean boneless beef chuck steak

2 teaspoons dried oregano

1 large bay leaf

1 teaspoon sugar (optional)

1 recipe Frankie's Meatballs, uncooked (on page 134); (optional)

Salt and freshly ground pepper

to serve

¾ pound spaghetti (optional)

In a large Dutch oven, heat the oil over medium-high heat. Add the onion and cook for 3 minutes, stirring. Add the garlic and cook until the onion is translucent, 3 minutes, stirring occasionally.

Add the tomatoes, one at a time, holding each over the pot and crushing it through your fingers. Add the tomato sauce remaining in the cans. Simmer the sauce, uncovered, for 20 minutes.

Meanwhile, rinse a medium skillet in cold water, shake out the excess water, and add the sausages. Set the pan over medium-high heat and cook the sausages, turning them until browned on all sides, 8 to 10 minutes. Add the browned, whole sausages to the simmering sauce. Return the skillet to the heat.

Brown the chuck steak in the skillet until it is crusty in places, 4 to 5 minutes per side, and add it to the sauce, along with the oregano, bay leaf, and, if the tomatoes taste too acidic, the sugar. Add the uncooked meatballs, if using. Cover, reduce the heat to medium low, and simmer the sauce until the chuck steak falls apart when pulled with a fork, 2 hours.

side dish

Use this meat sauce to make lasagna, in baked pasta, or cooked rice. Or add steamed broccoli or cauliflower to the sauce just before serving.

cook smart

Investing in a good brand of canned plum tomatoes gives the sauce better flavor and body. Bella Terra Organic from Racconto is one of my favorites.

Remove the meat to a plate and pull it apart, using 2 forks. Place the shredded meat in a mixing bowl. Remove the sausages from the sauce and slice and add them to the meat. With a slotted spoon, transfer the meatballs to a second bowl and cover loosely with foil. Adjust the seasoning of the sauce to taste with salt and pepper.

for serving now In wide, shallow bowls, for each serving, either combine ½ cup of sauce with ½ cup of the meat and sausages, or spoon the sauce over 2 meatballs.

Alternatively, cook the spaghetti according to the package directions and divide the pasta among 4 individual pasta bowls. Add ½ cup of the shredded meat and sliced sausages or a couple of the meatballs, and spoon on ½ cup of the sauce.

to freeze Place the cooled meatballs in plastic freezer containers just large enough to hold them and fill the containers with enough sauce to cover.

Return the sliced sausage and shredded meat to the pot with the remaining sauce and cool to room temperature. Divide the meat sauce among resealable 1-quart plastic freezer bags and refrigerate to chill. Freeze the chilled sauce flat on a baking sheet lined with wax paper.

to defrost and serve Thaw on a plate in the refrigerator for 8 to 16 hours, depending on the amount. Or thaw the bags of sauce in a bowl of cold water, changing the water every 15 minutes and breaking the sauce into chunks as it defrosts, 20 to 30 minutes.

Simmer the thawed meat sauce or meatballs with their sauce in a saucepan, uncovered, adding ¼ cup of water if the sauce is too thick.

frankie's meatballs

▶ freeze for up
   to 8 weeks

▶ can be doubled

Italian cooks know that simmering meatballs in tomato sauce is the best way to keep them juicy and tender. This is why I like to make these meatballs at the same time as Sunday Red Sauce (page 131) and add them to the big pot of sauce. Using the packaged blend of beef, veal, and pork labeled meatloaf mixture at your market also makes these meatballs moist and flavorful.

Makes 8 meatballs, 4 servings

1 pound meatloaf mixture (one-third each ground beef, pork, and veal)

¼ cup dry bread crumbs

¼ cup chopped flat-leaf parsley

¼ cup grated pecorino cheese

1 large egg, at room temperature, lightly beaten

⅛ teaspoon freshly ground pepper

Sunday Red Sauce (page 131) or 3 cups prepared marinara sauce

side dish

For a meatball hero, halve a crusty 8-inch Italian roll lengthwise. Spoon some sauce over the bottom, add 2 halved meatballs, more sauce, and shredded mozzarella cheese. Bake in a 350°F oven or a toaster oven until the cheese melts.

cook smart

Cooking meatballs in tomato sauce is neat and efficient, with no spattering fat or standing over a pan to turn them.

If not cooking the meatballs as part of a batch of Sunday Red Sauce, you can simmer them in 3 cups of a good-quality commercially made marinara sauce.

In a large bowl, use a fork to mix the meat, bread crumbs, parsley, cheese, egg, and pepper until well combined. Using your hands, divide the meat into 8 loosely formed 2-inch meatballs.

Drop the uncooked meatballs into the pot along with the sausages and beef when making Sunday Red Sauce and simmer until done. Or, in a saucepan, bring the prepared tomato sauce to a gentle boil. Add the meatballs and simmer until firm in the center, 30 to 40 minutes.

for serving now Serve the meatballs in a bowl with just Sunday Red Sauce, over spaghetti, or halved in a meatball sandwich.

to freeze Cool the cooked meatballs to room temperature on a plate, loosely covered with foil. Cool the sauce separately. Divide the sauce between 2 plastic containers and add the meatballs, leaving ½-inch headspace, seal, and refrigerate to chill. Transfer the containers to the freezer.

to defrost and serve Thaw containers of meatballs and sauce in the refrigerator for 12 to 18 hours, depending on the amount.

Place the defrosted sauce and meatballs in a saucepan, cover, and cook over medium heat until the sauce is gently bubbling and the meatballs are heated through, about 15 minutes.

best ever lentil chili

Lentils make a satisfying meatless chili, particularly when you use the small, rounded, red-brown lentils that are orange inside when split. Their firm texture and earthy taste make this vegan dish as fortifying as a bowl of Texas Red. Chipotle chile adds medium heat and big, smoky flavor.

▶ freeze for up to 6 weeks

Makes 6 servings

1 pound brown lentils

3 cups vegetable broth

2 tablespoons canola oil

1 cup finely chopped onion

¾ cup finely chopped green bell pepper

2 garlic cloves, chopped

1 tablespoon chili powder

1 tablespoon ground cumin

1 teaspoon chipotle chile powder

1 cup ground or crushed tomatoes

1 tablespoon dried oregano

Salt and freshly ground pepper

to serve

1 cup lightly packed chopped cilantro leaves (garnish)

1 cup finely chopped sweet onion (garnish)

Cooked brown rice (optional)

In a large, deep saucepan, combine the lentils, broth, and 2 cups of water. Bring to a boil over medium-high heat, cover, reduce the heat, and simmer for 20 minutes.

Meanwhile, in a medium Dutch oven, heat the oil over medium-high heat. Add the onion and bell pepper and cook until the onion is translucent, 3 minutes. Add the garlic and cook until the onion is soft, 2 minutes. Mix in the chili powder, cumin, and chipotle powder. Cook, stirring, until the spices are fragrant, 1 minute.

Add the lentils, including their cooking liquid, the tomatoes, and oregano to the vegetables. When the chili starts to bubble, cover partially, reduce the heat, and simmer until the lentils are tender, 20 minutes. Season to taste with salt and pepper.

for serving now Divide the chili among 6 deep bowls. Pass the cilantro and sweet onion in bowls for garnish. Or, if desired, serve the chili over cooked brown rice.

to freeze Cool the chili to room temperature. Divide it among resealable 1-quart plastic freezer bags in single (1 ½ cups) or double (3 cups) servings. Refrigerate on a plate to chill. Freeze the chilled chili flat on a baking sheet lined with wax paper.

side dish
To add color and boost the protein, sprinkle shredded Cheddar cheese over the chili when serving.

cook smart
Almost deep terra-cotta in color, these petite lentils make a denser chili than the large and flat, greenish brown kind.

to defrost and serve Thaw the chili on a plate in the refrigerator for 8 to 16 hours, depending on the amount. Or thaw in a large bowl of cold water, changing the water every 15 minutes and breaking the chili into chunks as it defrosts.

Reheat the chili in a saucepan, covered, over medium heat, about 15 minutes. Serve in deep bowls, passing the cilantro and sweet onion in smaller bowls, for garnish. Or serve the chili over cooked brown rice.

vegetarian mushroom goulash

▶ freeze for up
  to 8 weeks

Hungarians love mushrooms and use them in many dishes, including this meatless stew. Growing up around Hungarian cooks, I learned some of their secrets, including how to use paprika to thicken a dish. To keep the mushrooms firm, be sure to cook them until dry, especially if you plan to freeze this vegan goulash.

Makes 4 servings

1 can (14½ ounces) diced tomatoes

3 large portobello mushroom caps

8 ounces white mushrooms, stemmed

3 tablespoons extra virgin olive oil

1 medium onion, chopped

1 large Cubanelle or Italian frying pepper, seeded and chopped

1 small red bell pepper, seeded and chopped

2 garlic cloves, chopped

4 teaspoons sweet Hungarian paprika

Salt and freshly ground pepper

to serve

4 cups cooked medium egg noodles or 3 cups cooked rice

4 tablespoons sour cream

2 tablespoons chopped fresh dill

cook smart
The gills of portobello mushrooms can turn dishes dark in color. To remove them, slice horizontally across the inverted mushroom cap just below its curved rim.

Set a strainer over a bowl and drain the tomatoes very well. Reserve ½ cup of the tomato liquid and set the drained tomatoes aside. Save the remaining liquid for another use or discard.

Trim the gills from the portobello mushrooms, using a small knife. Cut the portobellos and white mushrooms into 1-inch pieces and set aside.

Heat the oil in a large skillet over medium-high heat. Add the onion and peppers and cook, stirring often, until they are soft, 5 minutes. Add the garlic and cook until the vegetables are browned, 4 minutes.

Add all of the mushrooms and cook, stirring occasionally, until they release their liquid, 8 minutes. Continue cooking until the mushrooms are dry and a spoon leaves a track when dragged across the pan, 15 minutes longer. Add the drained tomatoes and mix in the paprika. Simmer for 10 minutes, until the mushrooms have absorbed most of the liquid.

for serving now Add the reserved tomato liquid and continue cooking until the goulash is a rich red and the mushrooms are meaty, 3 to 5 minutes. Season to taste with salt and pepper. Divide the noodles or rice among 4 wide, shallow bowls, spoon over one-fourth of the goulash, and top with a dollop of sour cream and a sprinkling of dill.

to freeze After it has cooked for 10 minutes, cool the goulash. Divide it among resealable 1-quart plastic freezer bags in 1- or 2-cup portions. Refrigerate on a plate to chill. Freeze the bags of chilled goulash flat on a baking sheet lined with wax paper. Freeze the reserved tomato liquid in a ½-cup freezer container; this helps to keep the mushrooms meaty when the frozen goulash is defrosted.

to defrost and serve Thaw the goulash on a plate and the tomato liquid in its container in the refrigerator for 8 to 12 hours, depending on the amount.

Combine the goulash and tomato liquid in a saucepan and simmer, uncovered, over medium heat, stirring occasionally, until the mushrooms are tender and the goulash thickens. It should be moist but not soupy, about 15 minutes. Adjust the seasoning with salt and pepper.

Serve over noodles or rice, topped with the sour cream and dill.

coffee pot roast

▶ freeze for up
   to 6 weeks

▶ feeds a crowd

So what if pot roast is a quintessential cold-weather meal. Anytime the weather is raw and damp, having this meltingly tender, deeply flavorful dish in the freezer cheers the day. Better yet, you can heat up just 1 or 2 portions whenever you like. Brisket is not the least expensive cut for pot roast, but it is one of the leanest, plus it holds together and slices nicely.

Makes 8 servings

1 tablespoon finely ground coffee

1 teaspoon sweet paprika

1 teaspoon dried thyme

1 teaspoon salt

½ teaspoon freshly ground pepper

1 (4-pound) first-cut beef brisket, well trimmed

1 tablespoon canola oil

2 pounds onions, about 4 large, halved lengthwise and cut crosswise into thin slices

2 garlic cloves, halved

2 cups beef broth

¾ cup freshly brewed coffee

½ cup pomegranate juice

1 teaspoon dried thyme

1 bay leaf

2–4 teaspoons balsamic vinegar

side dish

Combine leftover sauce with beef broth to enhance the flavor of onion, cabbage, or barley soups.

cook smart

The coffee in the dry rub seasoning and cooking liquid adds more than just flavoring. It also helps tenderize the meat.

Removing all visible fat from the meat before cooking it produces a considerably leaner sauce.

In a small bowl, combine the ground coffee, paprika, thyme, salt, and pepper. Trim any remaining visible fat from the brisket. Wipe the meat with a paper towel, then coat it completely with the dry rub. Set the meat on a plate, cover with plastic wrap, and refrigerate for 1 to 4 hours.

Place a rack in the lower third of the oven. Preheat the oven to 300°F.

In a large ovenproof Dutch oven or soup pot with a tight-fitting lid, heat the oil over medium-high heat. Swirl to coat the bottom and lower sides of the pot. Brown the brisket well on all sides, 10 minutes, using tongs to turn it. Transfer the meat to a plate. Pour all but 2 tablespoons of fat from the pot. Add the onions and cook until they are limp, 5 minutes. Add the garlic and cook until the onions are pale gold, 5 minutes. Spread the onions to cover the bottom of the pot.

Add 1 cup of the broth, the brewed coffee, pomegranate juice, thyme, and bay leaf. When the liquid simmers, return the meat to the pot; the liquid should come one-third to one-half of the way up the sides of the meat. Cover and place the pot in the oven.

Check after 20 minutes to be sure the liquid is simmering gently and lower the oven temperature 10 to 15 degrees, if necessary. After 30 minutes, turn the brisket. Turn it again after 90 minutes and add the remaining broth as needed, ½ cup at a time, to keep the liquid at the right level. Bake until the meat is fork-tender, a total of 3½ to 4 hours.

Transfer the brisket to a cutting board, tent loosely with foil, and let the meat rest for 15 minutes. Cut the meat across the grain into ½-inch slices. Pour the remaining contents of the pot into 1 or 2 containers, removing and discarding the bay leaf. Chill until the fat has risen to the top, then skim it off. Season the sauce to taste with salt, pepper, and vinegar, starting with ½ teaspoon per cup of sauce. To thicken the sauce, if desired, puree 1 cup and mix it back into the remaining sauce.

for serving now Arrange the sliced pot roast on a deep serving platter. Heat the sauce in a saucepan over medium heat and spoon over the meat, covering it generously. Pour the remaining sauce into a bowl to pass separately.

to freeze Divide the sliced pot roast and sauce among 2 or more resealable 1-quart plastic freezer bags. Pour any remaining sauce into another container and cover tightly. Refrigerate the meat and sauce to chill. Freeze the bags of chilled pot roast flat on a baking sheet lined with wax paper, and the sauce in its container. Or arrange the sliced meat in shallow bowls and cover with some of the sauce. Cover the surface of the liquid with a piece of plastic wrap and open-freeze, then unmold and vacuum seal the meat with the sauce.

to defrost and serve Thaw the pot roast and sauce in the refrigerator for 12 to 24 hours, depending on the amount. Reheat the sliced pot roast and sauce in a shallow baking dish, covered with foil, at 350°F until heated through, 30 to 40 minutes. Adjust the seasoning of the sauce with salt, pepper, and vinegar before serving.

pulled jerk pork with carolina barbecue sauce

▶ freeze for up to 8 weeks

▶ feeds a crowd

A slow cooker makes this juicy barbecue a matter of set it and forget it. Slathering the pork with Jamaican jerk paste is an unexpected choice that keeps the meat beautifully moist. It also creates a feisty-tasting pot likker that reducing turns into a mouth-tingling barbecue sauce.

Makes 10 servings

jerk paste

1 small onion, diced

3 scallions, green and white parts, coarsely chopped

2 teaspoons salt

2 teaspoons freshly ground pepper

1 teaspoon ground allspice

1 teaspoon dried thyme

½ teaspoon ground cinnamon

½ teaspoon freshly grated nutmeg

1 Scotch bonnet or habanero chile pepper, seeded and quartered, or ½ teaspoon cayenne pepper

½ teaspoon liquid smoke (optional)

1 (4–4½-pound) Boston butt, with the bone and skin on 1 side (see Cook Smart)

1 can (14½ ounces) beef broth

for the sauce

2 cups cider vinegar

3–4 tablespoons sugar

Red-pepper flakes (optional)

Salt and freshly ground pepper

to serve

10 hamburger or other soft buns, split

cook smart

Boston butt is the meatier top half of a whole pork shoulder. If necessary, ask the butcher to remove the skin and fat from all but 1 side.

Shredding the pork while it's warm yields more meat and lets you remove more fat and gristle than when it is room temperature.

In a food processor, whirl all the jerk paste ingredients except the both to a pulpy puree.

Pat the jerk paste all over the meat, coating it liberally. Place the pork in a 4-quart slow cooker. Pour in the broth, cover, and cook on high for 4 to 5 hours, or on low for 7 to 8 hours, or until the meat shreds easily when pulled with a fork.

Transfer the meat to a plate and reserve the cooking liquid, about 3½ cups. When the meat is cool enough to handle, remove and discard the skin, then pull the meat away from the bone in chunks, discarding the bone and gristle. On a platter, use 2 forks to pull the chunks apart into fine shreds. There will be 7 to 8 cups of shredded meat.

For the sauce, pour the reserved cooking liquid into a medium saucepan and boil until reduced to 2½ cups. Reserve 1 cup of the reduced liquid, saving the rest to use for soup stock, or discard. Add the vinegar, sugar, and pepper flakes (if using), to the reduced liquid and boil over medium-high heat until the sugar dissolves, 2 minutes. Season the sauce to taste with salt and pepper. Makes 3 cups.

for serving now Combine the pulled pork in a saucepan with enough of the sauce to moisten it and heat over medium heat, stirring occasionally. For each serving, spoon ¾ cup of the meat over the bottom of a bun. Moisten with more of the sauce and serve, passing extra sauce separately.

to freeze Cool the sauce to room temperature. Combine 2 cups of the pulled pork with ½ cup of the sauce in resealable 1-quart plastic freezer bags and seal. Seal any remaining sauce in another bag. Refrigerate the pulled pork and extra sauce on plates until chilled. Lay the chilled meat and sauce on a baking sheet lined with wax paper and freeze.

to defrost and serve Defrost the pulled pork on a plate in the refrigerator, about 8 hours. Thaw the sauce on another plate for 4 hours. Or thaw in a large bowl of cold water, changing the water every 15 minutes. Heat the pork with as much of the sauce as needed, tasting to adjust the seasoning as needed. Serve the pulled meat on the buns, passing extra sauce.

freezer note Anytime the flavor in defrosted meat and sauces seems bland, adding an acid, such as vinegar or lemon juice, sharpens it up.

coq au vin blanc

French country cooking is a lesson in frugality and good sense. Here, marinating chicken legs helps turn this inexpensive part into a special occasion dish that is meltingly tender and intensely flavorful. Using a white wine keeps the chicken more attractive looking. I recommend a fruity Chardonnay for flavor that complements the shallots and mushrooms. Start marinating the chicken on a Friday and it will be ready to cook and serve on Saturday, or to freeze.

▶ **freeze for up to 6 weeks**

▶ **can be doubled**

▶ **elegant for entertaining**

Makes 4 servings

- 1 small onion, chopped
- 3 garlic cloves, 2 unpeeled and smashed, 1 finely chopped
- 12 fresh thyme sprigs
- 3 marjoram sprigs or 1 teaspoon dried marjoram
- 2 cups white wine, such as Woodbridge, a California Chardonnay
- 3 tablespoons extra virgin olive oil
- 4 whole chicken legs
- 2 ounces pancetta or nitrite-free bacon, chopped
- 3 tablespoons all-purpose flour

- 1 teaspoon salt
- ⅛ teaspoon freshly ground pepper
- 3 tablespoons unsalted butter
- 1 large shallot, finely chopped, and 8 small whole shallots, peeled
- 1 cup chicken broth
- 8 ounces medium cremini mushrooms, halved
- 5 flat-leaf parsley sprigs
- 1 bay leaf

to serve

Cooked long-grain white rice or noodles

For marinating, in a resealable 1-gallon plastic freezer bag, combine the onion with the smashed garlic cloves, half the thyme, the marjoram, 1 cup of the wine, and 1 tablespoon of the olive oil. Add the chicken and massage for 1 minute. Place the bag on a plate and marinate the chicken in the refrigerator for 4 to 24 hours.

Preheat the oven to 350°F.

Remove the chicken from the marinade and pat dry with paper towels. Discard the marinade.

In a deep, ovenproof skillet with a tight-fitting lid, heat 1 tablespoon of the remaining oil over medium-high heat. Add the pancetta or bacon and cook until browned and crisp, 6 minutes. With a slotted spoon, remove the pancetta or bacon and set it aside on a plate. Remove the pan from the heat.

side dish

Use the money you saved by using this inexpensive chicken part toward what you spend on the wine, and you will be amply rewarded.

cook smart

If you are in a time pinch, you can omit marinating the chicken, but I highly recommend including this step.

In a paper bag, shake together the flour, salt, and pepper. Add 2 chicken legs and shake to coat, then set the chicken on a plate. Repeat with the remaining chicken. Discard the remaining flour.

Melt 2 tablespoons of the butter in the skillet. Add the chicken and brown on all sides, 10 minutes, turning it with tongs. Add the chicken to the pancetta or bacon. Toss the chopped shallot into the pan, pour in the broth and remaining 1 cup wine and as the liquid boils, scrape the bottom of the pan with a wooden spatula to loosen all of the browned bits. Return the chicken and pancetta or bacon to the pan, cover tightly, and transfer it to the oven. Bake for 30 minutes.

In another skillet, melt the remaining 1 tablespoon butter with the remaining 1 tablespoon olive oil over medium-high heat. Add the mushrooms, chopped garlic, and whole shallots and cook, stirring often, until the mushrooms are golden brown, about 12 minutes. Add the parsley, bay leaf, and remaining thyme and cook until fragrant, about 1 minute. Add the mushroom mixture to the chicken, cover, and bake for 30 minutes longer, or until the chicken is very tender. Remove and discard the thyme sprigs, parsley, and bay leaf.

for serving now Make a bed of the cooked rice or noodles on each of 4 dinner plates. Set a chicken leg on top. Divide the mushrooms and shallots among the plates and spoon on a generous amount of sauce from the pan.

to freeze Transfer the cooked coq au vin, including the vegetables and sauce, to a bowl and cool to room temperature. Place 2 chicken legs each in resealable 1-quart plastic freezer bags. Add the vegetables and sauce and refrigerate to chill. Freeze the bags of chilled coq au vin flat on a baking sheet lined with wax paper.

to defrost and serve Thaw the coq au vin on a plate in the refrigerator for 18 to 24 hours. Or place the bags in a large bowl of cold water and change the water every 15 minutes.

Preheat the oven to 375°F.

Place the thawed coq au vin in a shallow, covered casserole just large enough to hold the number of servings. Add ¼ to ½ cup of water. Cut a piece of baking parchment paper to fit under the lid of the casserole, moisten the paper under running water, and set it over the chicken. Cover and bake for 30 minutes, until the liquid is bubbling and the chicken is heated through.

sake-soy short ribs

When cold weather or life's events call for serious comfort, I make these Asian-flavored short ribs. Serving their meltingly soft meat off the bone lets you remove much of its fat. Make sure to skim the intensely flavorful cooking liquid carefully to further reduce the fat in this rich dish.

▶ **freeze for up to 3 months**

▶ **feeds a crowd**

Makes 6 to 8 servings

- 1 tablespoon canola oil
- 4½–5 pounds meaty beef short ribs, cut into 3–4-inch pieces, well trimmed
- 4 shallots, sliced
- 5 large garlic cloves, chopped
- 5 whole star anise
- 4 dried red chile peppers
- 4 (3-inch) cinnamon sticks
- 1 piece (2 inches) fresh ginger, peeled and cut into ¼-inch slices
- 1½ cups sake
- ⅓ cup tamari or reduced-sodium soy sauce
- 2 tablespoons firmly packed brown sugar

In a very large Dutch oven or skillet, heat the oil over medium-high heat. Brown the short ribs on both wide, flat sides until crusty in places, 10 minutes, turning them once with tongs. If necessary, do this in batches, transferring the browned ribs to a plate, in 1 layer. Pour off most of the fat from the pan.

Add the shallots and cook, stirring, until they wilt, 2 minutes. Add the garlic, star anise, chiles, cinnamon, and ginger. Cook, stirring, until the shallots are golden and the spices are fragrant, 2 to 3 minutes. Pour in the sake, scraping with a wooden spoon to gather up browned bits clinging to the pan. Add the tamari or soy sauce and 4 cups of water. Mix in the sugar. When the liquid boils, add the short ribs, preferably in 1 layer so they are almost covered by the liquid, or with 2 or 3 pieces on top of immersed ribs. Reduce the heat until the liquid bubbles gently, cover, and cook until the meat is falling off the ribs and shreds easily with a fork, about 3 hours. Check every 30 to 45 minutes, and if the liquid level goes down, add water. If it bubbles too vigorously, reduce the heat.

Use a slotted spoon to transfer the cooked ribs to a platter. Pour the liquid from the pot through a strainer into a bowl to remove the solids. When the ribs are cool enough to handle, remove the meat from the bone in large chunks or shreds, then separate the meat from the fat and gristle.

side dish

Serve the warm short ribs over Baked Polenta (page 190) or accompanied by Garlic Smashed Potatoes (page 182) to soak up the sauce.

cook smart

I prefer using chunky English-cut short ribs over the longer cut called flanken. Avoid boneless short ribs, which have less flavor.

If there is time, refrigerating the liquid for 1 hour makes it easier to skim. If doing this, also tent the meat with foil to keep it from drying out.

for serving now Skim as much fat as possible from the cooking liquid (see Cook Smart on page 145). Place the meat in a skillet or saucepan and ladle the liquid over the top, allowing ¼ cup per serving. Simmer, covered, over medium heat until heated through. Serve with sauce spooned over the meat.

to freeze Place the cooled meat in a container, cover, and refrigerate to chill. Refrigerate the cooking liquid in a microwaveable container until the fat congeals. Skim off the fat, then heat the liquid in the microwave until it is no longer gelled. Divide the meat among 2 or more resealable 1-quart plastic freezer bags and add ⅓ to ½ cup of the liquid per serving. Refrigerate the bags on a plate to chill the meat and liquid. Place the bags on a baking sheet lined with wax paper and freeze. Or open-freeze the meat and sauce in wide, shallow bowls covered with plastic wrap, then unmold, vacuum seal the meat and sauce, and return to the freezer.

to defrost and serve Thaw the meat and sauce on a plate in the refrigerator for 6 to 24 hours, depending on the amount. Reheat in a saucepan over medium heat, covered, until heated through, 10 minutes.

lamb shanks with white beans and lemon

Lemon and lamb are great partners, while the beans help soak up the tangy sauce in this Mediterranean one-pot dinner. Gremolata, a colorful, aromatic garnish combining lemon zest, garlic, and parsley, finishes it off. I make at least 4 shanks because this dish can be enjoyed several ways after it is defrosted.

Makes 4 to 6 servings

▶ **freeze for up to 6 weeks**

2 lemons

1 tablespoon extra virgin olive oil

4–6 lamb shanks (1–1¼ pounds each)

1 pound plum tomatoes, seeded and chopped

1 medium onion, finely chopped

3 garlic cloves, finely chopped

1½ cups chicken broth

1 tablespoon chopped fresh rosemary

1½ teaspoons dried thyme

Salt and freshly ground pepper

to serve

2 cans (15 ounces) cannellini or great Northern beans

Gremolata (page 148), chopped dill, or flat-leaf parsley (garnish)

Peel 6 strips of zest from 1 lemon and squeeze the juice from both lemons, making ⅓ to ½ cup juice. Set the zest and juice aside.

Set a rack in the lower third of the oven. Preheat the oven to 350°F.

In a large Dutch oven, heat the oil over medium-high heat. Working in 2 batches, sear the chunks, turning them with tongs until browned on all sides, 10 minutes. Remove the shanks to a plate and pour off all but 1 tablespoon of fat from the pot.

Add tomatoes, onion, and garlic to the pot and cook, stirring often, until the onion is soft and the tomatoes start to break down, 5 minutes. Pour in the broth, and with a wooden spoon, scrape up the browned bits sticking to the pan.

Add thyme, rosemary, and reserved lemon zest and juice and bring the liquid to a gentle boil. Add the lamb shanks, arranging them snuggly head-to-toe in the pot, making 2 layers if necessary. Cover tightly and transfer the pot to the oven. Check after 15 minutes to make sure the liquid is bubbling gently, and reduce the heat if necessary.

Bake the shanks for 30 minutes. Turn the shanks over and, if in 2 layers, switch the shanks on the bottom to the top. Continue baking, turning the shanks every 30 minutes, until the meat is falling off the bone, about 2 hours total.

side dish

If you prefer, omit the beans and serve the shanks over North African or Israeli couscous. Any leftover juices are also good served with rice or other grains.

cook smart

A whole shank makes an impressive presentation, but it is too much meat for some appetites. Serving the shanks without the bone lets you discard fat and gristle as well as stretch the number of servings. The dish freezes better this way, too.

for serving now Transfer the lamb shanks to a platter. Pour the liquid and vegetables into a large bowl and cool until you can skim off the fat.

Return the skimmed liquid to the pot, add the beans and lamb, cover, and simmer over medium heat for 10 minutes, or until the beans are heated through. Season to taste with salt and pepper.

Divide the liquid and beans among wide, shallow bowls. Add a lamb shank or a generous ½ cup of meat off the bone. Garnish with the gremolata, chopped dill, or parsley.

to freeze When the shanks are cool enough to handle, pull the meat from the bones with your fingers, discarding the fat and gristle. Cover and set aside. Cool the liquid in a bowl to room temperature and skim off the fat. Divide the liquid among at least 2 resealable 1-quart plastic freezer bags. Add the lamb and refrigerate on a plate to chill. Freeze the bags of chilled shanks flat on a baking sheet lined with wax paper.

to defrost and serve Thaw the lamb shanks on a plate in the refrigerator for 8 to 12 hours, depending on the amount.

Place the lamb and liquid in a saucepan, add the beans, and simmer, uncovered, until heated through, stirring occasionally. Season to taste with salt and pepper. Place each shank in a wide, shallow bowl. Add some of the beans and a generous amount of the braising liquid. Garnish with the gremolata, chopped dill, or parsley.

freezer note The rosemary flavor fades quickly in freezing, letting the tangy taste of the lemon stand out. To refresh the taste of the rosemary, sprinkle 1 teaspoon of the fresh herb, finely chopped, into the pot when reheating the lamb with the beans.

gremolata

    2 tablespoons chopped flat-leaf parsley
    1 teaspoon minced garlic
    1 teaspoon lemon zest

In a small bowl, combine the parsley, garlic, and zest. Serve immediately or within 1 hour.

chicken pot pies

Assembling these pot pies is as simple as making a stew, then serving it with a crust topping. For the crust, I use either Flaky Pie Crust (page 236) or premade pie crust dough. Either way, everyone is delighted. Adding the crust just before serving saves freezer space and guarantees a savory pie with a perfect crust.

▶ freeze for up to 4 weeks

▶ can be doubled

Makes 4 servings

3 cups chicken broth

1 tablespoon canola oil

3 slim carrots, cut into ¼-inch slices

1 small onion, finely chopped

¾ cup frozen green peas

3 tablespoons unsalted butter

⅓ cup flour

1 cup milk, at room temperature
  ½ teaspoon dried thyme

Salt and freshly ground pepper

2 cups poached chicken, cut into bite-size pieces (see Three Dinner Chicken, on page 154, or Cook Smart, on page 151)

to serve

Flaky Pie Crust (page 236) or refrigerated prepared pie crust (see Side Dish)

1 egg yolk

1 tablespoon milk

In a saucepan, bring the broth to a boil over high heat and cook until reduced to 2 cups. Set aside.

In a medium skillet, heat the oil over medium-high heat. Add the carrots and onion and cook until crisp-tender, 5 minutes. Transfer the vegetables to a mixing bowl, add the frozen peas, and set aside.

In a medium saucepan, melt the butter over medium heat. Whisk in the flour and cook for 2 minutes, whisking often as it bubbles. Add the reduced broth, ½ cup at a time, whisking after each addition until the sauce is smooth. Mix in 1 cup milk and the thyme. Cook until the sauce is as thick as a cream soup, 4 to 5 minutes, whisking often. Season to taste with salt and pepper. Add the sauce to the vegetables and mix in the chicken.

Coat four 10-ounce ovenproof ramekins or 2-inch deep individual baking dishes with nonstick spray. Spoon the filling into the prepared dishes and cool to room temperature, 30 to 40 minutes.

side dish

If buying the pie crust dough, be aware that what supermarkets sell varies. Be sure to get enough to cut out lids that cover the 4 pies in the particular baking dishes you will use.

for serving now Let the pie crust dough sit at room temperature until it can be rolled out, 15 to 30 minutes. Measure the ramekins or baking dishes to the outside rim. On a lightly floured surface, roll out the crust until you can cut out 4 rounds, each 2 inches larger than the diameter of the baking dishes. Set the crusts on a baking sheet and refrigerate while the pie filling cools.

Place a rack in the lower third of the oven. Preheat the oven to 400°F.

Moisten the rim of the baking dishes with water. Set a pastry lid over each dish and press firmly around the top rim and sides to seal. Set the pies on a baking sheet. With sharp knife, cut 4 slits in the pastry. In a small dish, beat the egg yolk with 1 tablespoon milk, then brush the crusts with the egg mixture, avoiding the slits.

Bake the pies for 25 to 30 minutes, until the pastry is golden brown and the filling is hot. If the crust is coloring too quickly, cover it loosely with foil.

Let the pies stand for 5 minutes before serving.

to freeze Press plastic wrap onto the surface of the cooled filling in the baking dishes. Open freeze the pies on a baking sheet. Wrap the frozen pies in plastic freezer wrap, then foil. Return the frozen pies to the freezer.

to defrost and serve Unwrap the pies, leaving the plastic wrap covering the filling. Defrost the pies in the refrigerator for 12 hours.

Preheat the oven to 400°F.

Roll out the dough, cover the pies, and bake, following the directions in For Serving Now.

cook smart

If you plan to freeze these pot pies, do not use previously frozen raw or cooked chicken, as it is not safe to freeze it a second time.

To poach the chicken for this recipe, combine 1 1/4 pounds skinless split breasts on the rib in a large saucepan with 3 cups cold water, 2 cups chicken broth, a carrot and celery rib each cut into 1-inch pieces, a quartered onion, and a leek halved lengthwise. Add any spare chicken necks or other parts you have been saving in the freezer.

Cook over medium-high heat until the liquid starts to bubble, reduce the heat, and simmer gently for 25 minutes, or until the chicken is cooked through. Remove the chicken and, when cool enough to handle, shred the meat. Strain the broth through cheesecloth into a bowl. Makes 2 cups shredded meat, plus 4 cups broth.

salmon and mushroom pot pies

▶ freeze for up
to 4 weeks

▶ can be doubled

▶ elegant for
entertaining

At once sophisticated and comforting, these refined pot pies are perfect for a dinner party or candlelight supper for 2. To accompany the meal, choose either a light white wine that is somewhat but not bone dry, such as a Riesling or Chablis, or serve a Beaujolais, lightly chilled.

Makes 4 servings

1 tablespoon unsalted butter

1 medium leek, thinly sliced

1 shallot, thinly sliced

8 ounces cremini mushrooms, stemmed and halved or quartered

2 cups Creamy Mushroom Sauce (page 103) or 1 can (10½ ounces) condensed cream of mushroom soup plus ¼ cup heavy cream

½ cup dry white wine

Pinch of cayenne pepper

Salt and freshly ground pepper

1 pound skinless salmon fillet, cut into 1-inch pieces

to serve

4 sheets (2 packages) frozen puff pastry

1 egg white (optional)

side dish

Halibut fillet can be used in place of salmon.

cook smart

Pepperidge Farms is the only brand of puff pastry available nationwide, but in some areas you may find a local brand made with butter. If so, your pot pies will be noticeably better. Some specialty stores also offer their own home-made frozen pastry.

Coat the inside of four 10-ounce round baking dishes with nonstick spray and set aside.

In a medium skillet, melt the butter over medium heat. Add the leek and shallot and cook until the shallot is soft, 5 minutes. Add the mushrooms and cook, stirring occasionally, until their liquid has released and evaporated, 8 to 10 minutes. Add the mushroom sauce or soup and cream, wine, and cayenne. Season the filling to taste with salt and pepper. Add the salmon and stir to coat it with the sauce.

Divide the filling among the prepared baking dishes.

for serving now Defrost the puff pastry according to the package directions.

From each sheet of pastry, cut a square large enough to overhang the baking dish by 1 inch on all sides. With your fingers, wet the rim and outside the top of each baking dish with cold water. Drape the pastry over the dish and press it gently but firmly to seal it around the top and sides of the dish, leaving long points at each corner of the pastry. Using a sharp knife, cut a 1-inch hole in the center of the top. If desired, beat the egg white in a small bowl with 1 tablespoon of water until frothy. Brush the crust of each pie with the egg wash. Refrigerate the filled pies for 30 minutes and up to 4 hours before baking.

Preheat the oven to 375°F while the pies chill.

Set the pies on a baking sheet and bake for 25 minutes, or until the crusts are puffed and golden brown. Cool the pies for 10 minutes before serving.

to freeze Cool the filled pies to room temperature, press plastic wrap against the surface of the filling, and open-freeze the pies on a baking sheet. Wrap the pies individually in plastic freezer wrap, then heavy-duty foil, and return to the freezer.

to defrost and serve Remove the foil and thaw the frozen pies in the refrigerator.

Defrost the puff pastry according to the package directions.

From each sheet of pastry, cut a square large enough to overhang the baking dish by 1 inch on all sides. With your fingers, wet the rim and outside the top of each baking dish with cold water. Drape the pastry over the dish and press it gently but firmly to seal it around the top and sides of the dish, leaving long points at each corner of the pastry. Using a sharp knife, cut a 1-inch hole in the center of the top. If desired, beat the egg white in a small bowl with 1 tablespoon of water until frothy. Brush the crust of each pie with the egg wash. Refrigerate the filled pies for 30 minutes and up to 4 hours before baking.

Preheat the oven to 375°F while the pies chill.

Set the pies on a baking sheet and bake for 25 minutes, or until the crusts are puffed and golden brown. Cool the pot pies for 10 minutes before serving.

three dinner chicken

▶ freeze for up
to 8 weeks

You cannot beat this for economy and efficiency. A whole chicken yields enough meat for at least 3 dishes, plus broth. Buying a whole bird is most cost-effective and the poached meat is beautifully moist. What is frozen can be used only in dishes to serve immediately, so decide thoughtfully how much to freeze and what to use freshly cooked.

Makes 6 cups chicken and 8 to 12 cups broth

4½–5 pound roasting chicken

1 pound chicken wings, necks, or backs

1 large carrot, cut into 1-inch pieces

1 large celery rib, with leaves, cut into 1-inch pieces

1 large leek, the white part plus 1–2 inches of the pale green, cut into 1-inch pieces

1 large onion, quartered

1 small parsnip, cut into 1-inch pieces (optional)

cook smart

Experts advise that cooking chicken fully kills any bacteria, while washing raw poultry spreads bacteria around the sink and kitchen, so do not rinse it before cooking.

Place the roasting chicken in a large, deep pot. Add the chicken parts, carrot, celery, leek, onion, and parsnip (if using). Pour in 5 quarts of cold water, covering chicken by about 2 inches. Set the pot over medium-high heat until it bubbles, 15 to 20 minutes. Reduce the heat so occasionally bubbles are breaking the surface steadily but gently, skim off any scum that rises. Cook for 1 hour.

Carefully remove the whole chicken to a platter, leaving the extra parts in the pot. Adjust the heat so the liquid continues to bubble gently and cook until the broth is well flavored, 1 to 2 hours.

When the chicken is cool enough to handle, remove the skin and pull the meat from the bones; there should be 6 cups of bite-size pieces. Pack the chicken into 1 or more containers, cover, and refrigerate. Use the cooked chicken within 3 days.

Strain the broth into a large bowl; there should be 8 to 12 cups. Discard the solids. Cool the broth to room temperature, cover with plastic wrap, and refrigerate until very cold, or overnight. Skim off the fat from the surface and divide the broth among containers. Cover tightly and refrigerate up to 3 days, or freeze.

to freeze Pack cooled cooked chicken in 1-quart resealable freezer bags. Place bags on a baking sheet lined with wax paper and freeze. Freeze chilled broth similarly.

to defrost and serve Thaw chicken on a plate in the refrigerator for 6 to 24 hours, depending on the amount. Use according to your recipe. *Never refreeze defrosted chicken.* Thaw the broth in the refrigerator or using a cold water bath. Broth can be refrozen if cooked when making a soup, stew, or other hot dishes.

chapter 7

side dishes and sauces

How often have you planned to make a special side dish but ended up serving steamed broccoli or boiled brown rice to accompany the main course? Since life's too short to tolerate boring meals, your freezer is perfect for helping you keep all of a meal interesting, even when you do not have time to do it all from scratch.

When you stock the freezer with side dishes, you can serve Frozen Coleslaw and Maple Baked Beans with grilled pork chops on a Tuesday night. Or pick up a rotisserie chicken and present it accompanied by Creamy Twice-Baked Potatoes with Parmesan or Cranberry Cornbread Dressing anytime you feel like it. For vegetarians, Creamy Corn Pudding with Cheese and Broccoli, or Decadent Potato and Leek Gratin, can even be the main course. And because serving steamed broccoli is inevitable, there is also Golden Cheese Sauce, which defrosts quickly and makes any cooked green vegetable enticing.

- green beans in greek tomato sauce
- shaker tomato pudding
- maple baked beans
- frozen coleslaw
- creamy corn pudding with cheese and broccoli
- acorn squash dressing
- cranberry cornbread dressing
- creamy twice-baked potatoes with parmesan
- upside-down pineapple sweet potatoes
- decadent potato and leek gratin
- chunky fresh tomato sauce
- golden cheese sauce
- tomato and roasted red pepper sauce

green beans in greek tomato sauce

▶ freeze for up
  to 4 weeks

▶ can be doubled

Greek cooks enhance the flavor of tomato sauce with oregano and red wine. Green beans simmered in this deep red sauce look most appealing, and their taste pleases even vegetable haters.

Makes 4 servings

1 tablespoon extra virgin olive oil

½ cup finely chopped onion

1 garlic clove, finely chopped

1 cup canned ground tomatoes

2 tablespoons dry red wine

1 teaspoon dried oregano, preferably wild

Salt and freshly ground pepper

1 pound fresh green beans, trimmed

to serve

Chopped dill (optional, for garnish)

cook smart

Ground tomatoes have more body than tomato sauce, plus they add just-picked flavor to a dish.

In a medium skillet, heat the oil over medium-high heat. Add the onion and cook until translucent, 4 minutes, stirring occasionally. Add the garlic and cook until the onion is golden, 4 minutes, stirring often. Mix in the tomatoes, wine, and oregano and simmer for 4 minutes, stirring occasionally. Season to taste with salt and pepper.

Meanwhile, cook the green beans in a pot of salted boiling water for 4 minutes. Drain the beans.

for serving now Add the blanched green beans to the tomato sauce, cover, and simmer until the green beans are tender, about 10 minutes. Season with salt and pepper and serve, garnished with dill, if using.

to freeze Immediately plunge the hot green beans into a bowl of ice water. When fully cool, drain the green beans well and set aside.

Transfer the tomato sauce to a large bowl and cool to room temperature,

Combine the green beans with the tomato sauce and spoon into 1 or 2 resealable 1-quart plastic freezer bags. Chill the green beans in the refrigerator on a plate. Freeze the chilled beans flat on a baking sheet lined with wax paper.

to defrost and serve Defrost the beans on a plate in the refrigerator for 8 to 12 hours, depending on the amount. Or thaw in a bowl of cold water, changing the water every 15 minutes.

Simmer the beans and sauce in a stainless steel or other nonreactive pot, covered, until they are tender, 10 minutes. Add 2 to 3 tablespoons of water if the sauce gets too thick. Adjust the seasoning to taste with salt and pepper and serve, garnished with dill, if using.

freezer note Freezing intensifies the garlic flavor in this dish, so use a small clove if you plan to freeze it.

shaker tomato pudding

▌ freeze for up
  to 4 weeks

▌ can be doubled

▌ freeze now,
  cook later

The Shakers, a 19th-century religious sect, lived austerely. Expert gardeners, they grew their own food and were also gourmet cooks. This side dish, which falls between a gratin and a bread pudding, is a luscious example. It requires fully ripe tomatoes. When served from the freezer, it prolongs the summer pleasure a while longer.

Makes 4 servings

3 slices firm white bread, crusts removed

4 tablespoons unsalted butter plus 1 teaspoon

1 tablespoon canola oil

1 medium onion, finely chopped

2 garlic cloves, finely chopped

3 pounds beefsteak tomatoes, peeled, seeded, and coarsely chopped

2 tablespoons chopped flat-leaf parsley

1 tablespoon packed brown sugar

Salt and freshly ground pepper

to serve

1 tablespoon unsalted butter

2 slices firm white bread, crusts removed

side dish

Serve with eggs for a light meal or as a side dish with broiled fish. You can make the buttered crumbs along with the pudding and freeze them with it in a plastic bag, if desired.

cook smart

Stirring the tomatoes frequently as they cook reduces spattering.

Cube the bread by cutting 3 stacked slices into ¼-inch strips, rotating the stack 90 degrees, and cutting it into ¼-inch cubes.

Coat an 8-inch x 8-inch shallow baking dish with 1 teaspoon of the butter and set aside. In a medium skillet, melt 2 tablespoons of the butter over medium heat. Add the cubed bread and toss to coat with the butter. Cover the bottom of the prepared baking dish with the buttered bread cubes and set aside. Do not wash out the skillet.

Add 2 more tablespoons of the butter and the oil to the skillet and set over medium-high heat. Add the onion and cook until translucent, 4 minutes. Add the garlic and cook until the onion is soft, 3 minutes. Add the tomatoes and simmer, stirring frequently, until the mixture is thick enough to plop from a spoon, 15 to 20 minutes. Stir in the parsley and sugar and season to taste with salt and pepper. Spoon the mixture over the bread in the baking dish, smoothing it with the back of the spoon. The dish can be covered with plastic wrap at this point and refrigerated for up to 2 days.

for serving now Preheat the oven to 350°F.

Spread 1 tablespoon butter over the 2 bread slices, cut into 1-inch pieces, and whirl the buttered bread in a food processor to make 1 ½ to 2 cups of buttered crumbs. Sprinkle the crumbs over the tomatoes. Cover the baking dish with foil and bake for 20 minutes. Uncover, turn the oven to broil, and set the dish under the broiler until the topping is golden and crisp, 1 to 2 minutes. Let the pudding sit for 5 minutes, cut into 4 pieces, and use a wide spatula to transfer the pieces to individual plates.

to freeze Cool the assembled, unbaked casserole, without the topping, to room temperature, cover with plastic wrap, and refrigerate to chill. Open-freeze, then unmold the pudding onto plastic freezer wrap, seal, and wrap in heavy-duty foil. Return the frozen pudding to the freezer. Or vacuum seal the frozen pudding and return to the freezer.

to defrost and serve Unwrap the frozen pudding, butter the original baking dish, and drop the pudding back into it. Cover with plastic wrap and thaw in the refrigerator for 10 to 12 hours.

Preheat the oven to 350°F.

Spread the 1 tablespoon butter over the 2 bread slices, cut them into 1-inch pieces, and whirl the buttered bread in a food processor to make 1 ½ to 2 cups of buttered crumbs. Sprinkle the crumbs over the defrosted pudding, cover with foil, and bake for 20 to 30 minutes. Turn the oven to broil and set the pudding under the broiler until golden on top, 1 to 2 minutes. Let the pudding sit for 5 minutes, cut into 4 pieces, and use a wide spatula to transfer the pieces to individual plates.

maple baked beans

▶ freeze for up
 to 8 weeks

▶ feeds a crowd

Dried beans cooked from scratch beat canned beans hands down. A slow cooker makes preparing them set-it-and-forget-it simple, as these vegetarian beans prove. They are so good you will be glad to have a generous amount.

Makes 6 to 8 servings

1 pound dried navy beans (see Side Dish)

½ cup tomato sauce

2 tablespoons dark maple syrup

2 tablespoons packed dark brown sugar

2 tablespoons unsulphured molasses

2 teaspoons dry mustard

½ teaspoon ground ginger

2 cups boiling water

2 whole cloves

1 medium onion, halved

Salt and freshly ground pepper

side dish

Navy beans are traditionally used for baked beans, but they can be hard to find. Great Northern beans, which are slightly larger and sweeter tasting, are a good substitute.

cook smart

To use the Quick-Soak method for dried beans: Place the beans in a large saucepan and add 8 cups of water. Cover the pot, bring to a boil, and then let the covered pot sit off the heat for 1 hour. Drain the beans.

In a large bowl, cover the beans with cold water by 2 inches and soak for 6 to 8 hours, or use the Quick-Soak method (see Cook Smart). Drain the beans.

Place the soaked beans in a 4-quart slow cooker. In a small saucepan over medium heat, bring the tomato sauce, maple syrup, sugar, molasses, mustard, and ginger to a boil, stirring until the sugar has dissolved. Pour the mixture over the beans and add the boiling water. Stick the cloves into the onion and add it to the pot.

Cook the beans in the slow cooker on medium-high for 1 hour. Reduce the heat to low and cook until the beans are soft, 7 to 8 hours. If needed, add water, 1 cup at a time, as the beans cook. Season to taste with salt and pepper.

for serving now If possible, refrigerate the cooked beans overnight to let their flavors meld. Reheat in a covered pot over medium heat, adding a splash of water, if needed, and stirring twice so the beans reheat evenly.

to freeze Divide the beans in 2-cup portions among resealable 1-quart plastic freezer bags and refrigerate on a plate to chill. Freeze the chilled beans flat on a baking sheet lined with wax paper. Or spoon the beans into vacuum bags, freeze unsealed, then vacuum seal and return to the freezer.

to defrost and serve Thaw the frozen beans at room temperature, about 2 hours, or in cold water for 45 minutes, changing the water every 15 minutes. Defrost larger amounts in the refrigerator for 6 to 18 hours, depending on the amount. Adjust the seasoning to taste.

freezer note Freezing makes the beans even more tender and creamy.

frozen coleslaw

Surprisingly, freezing works wonders, wilting the cabbage in this picnic favorite while turning it rosy pink and melding its flavors. Plus, freezing lets you do all of the chopping at a convenient time, then serve the result anytime.

Makes 8 servings

½ cup white vinegar

¼ cup sugar

1 teaspoon salt

¼ teaspoon mustard powder

¼ teaspoon celery seeds

1 wedge (½ pound) green cabbage

1 wedge (½ pound) red cabbage

1 large carrot

to serve

1 medium green bell pepper, halved and seeded

½ cup chopped scallions, green part only

¼ sweet onion, finely chopped, about ½ cup

Freshly ground pepper

▶ freeze for up to 4 weeks

▶ feeds a crowd

In a stainless steel or other nonreactive saucepan, combine the vinegar, sugar, salt, mustard powder, and celery seeds, plus ¼ cup of water. Bring to a boil, stir to dissolve the sugar, and set aside to cool.

Meanwhile, cut the cabbage lengthwise into thin wedges. Shred the cabbage and carrot in a food processor fitted with the medium shredding disk. Or slice the cabbage thinly and shred the carrot on a box grater. Transfer the shredded vegetables to a large bowl, add the cooled dressing, and toss to combine well.

for serving now Cut the bell pepper lengthwise into thin strips and halve the strips crosswise. Add to the slaw, along with the scallions and onion, and toss to combine. Season to taste with pepper. Refrigerate the slaw, covered, for 4 to 24 hours before serving.

to freeze Spoon the cabbage, carrot, and dressing into a resealable 1-quart plastic freezer bag. Massage the bag well to push out all of the air before sealing. Refrigerate on a plate to chill. Freeze the chilled slaw flat on a baking sheet lined with wax paper.

to defrost and serve Defrost the slaw on a plate in the refrigerator for about 12 hours. If the slaw is very wet, drain off most of the liquid.

Mix in the bell pepper, scallions, and onion and adjust the seasoning. Chill for 2 to 4 hours before serving. Use the defrosted slaw within 24 hours.

side dish

Adding the remaining vegetables to the slaw after thawing keeps their colors and flavors bright and distinct.

cook smart

Using packaged shredded cabbage is tempting, but it produces a bland slaw. Shredding the cabbage in the food processor takes just minutes, and the result is far superior.

creamy corn pudding
with cheese and broccoli

▶ freeze for up
  to 4 weeks

▶ can be doubled

▶ freeze now,
  cook later

Since it is equally good as a meatless main course or as a side dish served with pork chops or roast chicken, think of this colorful casserole when you have vegetarians and carnivores sharing a meal.

Makes 6 servings

½ cup stone-ground yellow cornmeal

½ cup all-purpose flour

1 teaspoon baking powder

2 tablespoons sugar

½ teaspoon salt

⅛ teaspoon freshly ground pepper

2 cups bite-size broccoli florets

1 can (15 ¼ ounces) corn, drained, or
   2 cups fresh kernels

1 can (14 ¾ ounces) creamed corn

1 large egg, beaten

4 tablespoons (½ stick) unsalted
   butter, melted

1 small onion, chopped

½ cup chopped scallions, green and
   white parts

½ cup shredded Cheddar cheese

1 can (4 ounces) green chiles, drained

to serve

½ cup shredded Cheddar cheese

side dish

Use the reduced-fat three-cheese blend sold in supermarkets in place of the Cheddar if you wish.

cook smart

Using cornbread mix is convenient, but the inexpensive ones include hydrogenated shortening, while the natural mixes cost as much as a gallon of milk. At the end of the day, it's just smarter to make this dish from scratch.

Coat an 8-inch x 8-inch baking dish with nonstick spray and set aside.

In a bowl, combine the cornmeal, flour, baking powder, sugar, salt, and pepper. Set aside.

In a large pot of boiling water, cook the broccoli for 2 minutes. Drain the broccoli in a colander, then cool it under cold running water to keep the florets crisp and bright. Drain very well and set aside.

In a large mixing bowl, combine the corn, creamed corn, egg, and butter. Add the dry ingredients and mix just to combine. Mix in the broccoli, onion, scallions, ½ cup cheese, and the chiles. Spread the pudding in the prepared baking dish.

for serving now Preheat the oven to 350°F.

Sprinkle ½ cup cheese over the top of the pudding and bake for 40 minutes, or until the pudding is puffed and golden on top and a knife inserted into the center comes out clean. Cool on a wire rack for 15 minutes and serve.

to freeze Open-freeze the uncooked pudding. Unmold it onto plastic freezer wrap, seal, and place in the center of a 2-foot length of heavy-duty foil. Seal and return the frozen pudding to the freezer. Or vacuum seal the frozen pudding and return it to the freezer.

to defrost and serve Unwrap the frozen pudding and drop it back into the original baking dish. Cover with plastic wrap and defrost in the refrigerator for 18 hours.

Preheat the oven to 350°F.

Let the pudding stand at room temperature while the oven heats. Sprinkle ½ cup cheese over the top of the pudding and bake, as previously described, for 45 to 50 minutes.

acorn squash dressing

A signature dish back in my catering days, this dressing combines a generous amount of squash with the bread so you can serve it as either a carb or a vegetable. Its golden color looks especially great on holidays if you bake it in small acorn squash halves or miniature pumpkins (see Side Dish on page 164).

▶ **freeze for up to 6 weeks**

▶ **can be doubled**

Serves 8

8 slices firm white bread, crusts removed, cut into ½-inch cubes

1 navel orange

1 acorn squash, about ¾ pound, peeled, seeded, and chopped in ½-inch pieces

1 leek, white only, chopped

1 medium onion, finely chopped

4 tablespoons (½ stick) unsalted butter, melted

2–3 tablespoons finely chopped fresh ginger

1 tablespoon poultry seasoning (see Side Dish)

2 teaspoons salt

⅛ teaspoon freshly ground pepper

1 cup chicken or vegetable broth, heated

Spread the bread cubes on a baking sheet and dry at room temperature for 24 hours, stirring the cubes 3 or 4 times. The cubes should be hard. (For faster drying, see Cook Smart on page 164.) The dried bread cubes can be stored in an airtight container for up to 3 days.

Preheat the oven to 400°F.

For special occasions, brush scooped-out small acorn squash halves with oil, fill with the dressing, and bake at 375°F until the squash is tender and the dressing is heated through 35 to 45 minutes.

cook smart

To dry the bread quickly, spread the cubes on a baking sheet in 1 layer and bake in a 350°F oven for 20 to 30 minutes, stirring every 10 minutes, or until the bread feels dry and almost hard. Do not let the cubes color. To prevent them from burning, transfer the bread cubes to another baking sheet to cool.

In place of poultry seasoning, use 1 teaspoon dried thyme, ½ teaspoon dried sage, and ½ teaspoon dried marjoram.

Place the orange on a cutting board. Cut off both ends and then work a knife down the sides of the orange, removing the peel and white part in strips. Holding the orange over a bowl, cut out the sections, releasing them into the bowl. Squeeze the juice from the membrane into the bowl. Set the orange aside.

In a large mixing bowl, toss the squash, leek, and onion with 3 tablespoons of the butter until well coated. Spread the vegetables on a baking sheet and roast until the squash is al dente, 20 minutes, stirring midway. Return the roasted vegetables to the mixing bowl. Reduce the oven temperature to 375°F.

Add the ginger, bread cubes, and orange with juice to the vegetables. Using a fork, break up the orange sections. With your hands, toss the mixture until well combined. Sprinkle in the poultry seasoning, salt and pepper. Pour in ½ cup of the hot broth, and mix with your hands until the liquid is absorbed. Continue adding broth, ¼ cup at a time, as needed, until no hard bits of bread remain. If freezing the dressing, leave it on the dry side.

Brush a 9-inch x 9-inch baking dish with the remaining 1 tablespoon butter and pack the dressing firmly into the dish. Bake until the top is golden brown and crusty, 40 to 45 minutes.

for serving now Let the dressing sit for 10 minutes, then serve from the dish or transfer to a serving bowl.

to freeze Cool the dressing to room temperature in the dish on a wire rack. Cover with plastic wrap and refrigerate to chill. Open-freeze the dressing in the dish, covered with plastic wrap. Unmold the dressing and wrap in plastic freezer wrap, seal in foil, and return to the freezer. Or, before freezing, cut the dressing into portions, wrap in plastic freezer wrap and then heavy-duty foil, and freeze on a baking sheet.

to defrost and serve To defrost the whole pan of dressing, coat the original baking dish with nonstick spray, drop the frozen dressing back into it, and thaw on a wire rack in the refrigerator for 12 to 15 hours.

Preheat the oven to 350°F. Let the dressing sit at room temperature while the oven heats.

Cover the dish with foil and bake for 40 minutes, or until heated through. For individual portions, wrap in foil and heat on a baking sheet for 30 minutes, or until heated through.

cranberry cornbread dressing

Cornbread gives dressings a slightly sweet, southern flavor, along with lovely golden color. This one, studded with cranberries and apples, elevates a casual supper of greens and beans to an occasion. It is also good served with poultry and pork dishes.

Makes 4 to 6 servings

- 4 cups cornbread cut into ¾-inch cubes (see Cook Smart)
- 3 tablespoons unsalted butter plus 1 teaspoon
- 1 cup chopped peeled Golden Delicious apple
- 1 large celery rib, chopped
- ½ cup chopped red onion

- 1 large egg, lightly beaten
- ¾ cup chicken broth, heated
- ¾ cup fresh or frozen cranberries, coarsely chopped
- ½ cup packed flat-leaf parsley
- 1 teaspoon salt
- ⅛ teaspoon freshly ground pepper

Spread the cubed cornbread on a baking sheet and dry at room temperature for 24 hours, stirring the cubes 3 or 4 times. The cornbread should be hard.

Preheat the oven to 350°F. Coat an 8-inch x 8-inch baking dish with 1 teaspoon of the butter and set aside.

Place the cornbread in a large mixing bowl. In a medium skillet, melt the remaining 3 tablespoons butter over medium heat. Add the apple, celery, and onion and cook until the onion is translucent, 5 minutes, stirring occasionally. Add the apple mixture to the cornbread, scraping the pan well. Add the egg to the cornbread and use a fork to mix until the ingredients are thoroughly combined. The cornbread cubes should be well coated and starting to crumble around the edges. Add ¼ cup of the hot broth and mix very well. Continue adding broth by the quarter cup, using just enough to make the dressing moist and the cornbread cubes tender. They should still hold their shape. Mix in the cranberries, parsley, salt, and pepper. Spoon the dressing into the prepared dish, smoothing it into an even layer. Cover the dish tightly with foil.

Bake the dressing for 30 minutes; it should be fluffy and golden but not mushy.

for serving now Let the dressing sit, uncovered, for 10 minutes. Cut it into 4 or 6 pieces and spoon the portions onto dinner plates as a side dish.

▶ **freeze for up to 6 weeks**

▶ **can be doubled**

cook smart

Many markets sell ready-made cornbread. You need about 1½ pounds, or an 8-inch x 8-inch x 2-inch pan, to make the cubes for this recipe. Since Jiffy and other inexpensive mixes are too sweet and most contain hydrogenated fat, I usually buy the cornbread.

For faster drying, spread the cubed cornbread on a baking sheet in 1 layer and bake in a 375°F oven for 30 minutes, stirring every 10 minutes, until the cubes feel dry and almost hard. Do not let them color. Transfer the cornbread cubes to another baking sheet to cool. When cooled completely, the cornbread cubes can be stored in an airtight container for up to 3 days.

to freeze Cool the baked dressing to room temperature in the dish on a wire rack. Cover with plastic wrap and refrigerate to chill. Wrap the dressing, either whole or cut into portions, in plastic freezer wrap, then heavy-duty foil and freeze on a baking sheet. Store portions of the frozen dressing together in a resealable plastic freezer bag, if desired.

to defrost and serve For individual portions, discard the plastic freezer wrap, then rewrap in foil and heat on a baking sheet in a 350°F oven for 25 to 30 minutes, or until heated through.

To defrost a whole pan of dressing, coat the original pan with nonstick spray and drop the frozen dressing into it. Thaw the dressing on a wire rack in the refrigerator for 6 to 12 hours.

Preheat the oven to 350°F. Let the dressing sit at room temperature while the oven heats. Cover the pan with foil and bake for 30 minutes, or until heated through.

creamy twice-baked potatoes
with parmesan

▶ freeze for up
   to 6 weeks

▶ can be doubled

The fluffy filling and crisp skin of these potatoes please both mashed and baked potato lovers. My special touch, brushing their tops with melted butter just before baking them the second time, gives them exceptional flavor. You can add chopped broccoli or spinach to the filling to make this an easy, all-in-one meal.

Makes 4 servings

2 large russet baking potatoes

3 tablespoons unsalted butter, diced

¼ cup grated Parmesan cheese

¼ cup sour cream

Salt and freshly ground pepper

to serve

2 tablespoons unsalted butter, diced

cook smart
Use powdery, finely grated Parmesan cheese.

Preheat the oven to 400°F.

Pierce the potatoes in 3 or 4 places. Bake for 45 to 55 minutes, or until the potatoes feel soft when squeezed. Immediately halve the potatoes lengthwise and scoop their flesh into a mixing bowl, leaving ½ inch of flesh on the skin.

Add the 3 tablespoons butter to the potatoes and mash with a fork until they are fluffy. Mix in the cheese, then the sour cream, and season to taste with salt and pepper. Spoon the filling back into the scooped-out skins, mounding it slightly and smoothing the tops with the back of the spoon.

for serving now Reduce the oven to 350°F. Place the stuffed potatoes on a baking sheet. In a small saucepan, melt the 2 tablespoons butter over medium heat until it is golden brown and smells nutty, 3 to 4 minutes. Brush the browned butter over the tops of the stuffed potatoes and bake for 40 minutes, or until the potatoes are puffed and golden brown on top.

to freeze Cool the stuffed potatoes to room temperature and wrap in plastic freezer wrap, then heavy-duty foil, and freeze. Or open-freeze the potatoes on a baking sheet lined with wax paper, then vacuum seal and return to the freezer.

to defrost and serve Remove the foil and defrost the stuffed potatoes on a plate in the refrigerator for 8 hours.

Preheat the oven to 350°F.

Melt the 2 tablespoons butter in a small saucepan until golden brown and brush it over the potato tops.

Bake the potatoes for 50 minutes, or until the tops are puffed and golden brown.

freezer note If you choose to add broccoli or spinach to the potatoes to make them an all-in-one meal, cook the broccoli or spinach, then press it in a colander until well drained. Press the vegetables in paper towels so they are thoroughly dry, then finely chop them.

upside-down pineapple sweet potatoes

▶ freeze for up
  to 6 weeks

▶ can be doubled

▶ feeds a crowd

▶ elegant for
  entertaining

My godmother gave me this recipe, which I consider a family jewel. We serve it at both Thanksgiving and Christmas because it is so good. One night I had a whole pan left over and discovered this dish freezes beautifully. Now I always double the recipe, serving one and freezing the other.

Makes 8 servings

4 tablespoons (½ stick) unsalted butter

½ cup lightly packed brown sugar

7 slices canned pineapple, drained and dried

21 dried cranberries or tart cherries

2½ pounds orange-fleshed sweet

potatoes, roasted, peeled, and mashed

2 large eggs, beaten

½ teaspoon ground cinnamon

½ teaspoon baking powder

Salt and freshly ground pepper

side dish
A friend adds another ¼ cup of brown sugar and serves this, slightly warm, as a dessert.

Preheat the oven to 350°F. Coat a 9-inch round cake pan with nonstick spray and set aside.

In a small saucepan over medium heat, melt the butter and sugar together. Pour the mixture into the prepared pan, tilting to coat the bottom evenly. Arrange 6 pineapple slices in the pan in a ring and place 1 slice in the center. Put 3 dried cranberries or cherries in the center of each pineapple ring.

In a mixing bowl, whisk the sweet potatoes, eggs, cinnamon, and baking powder together until well combined. Season to taste with salt and pepper. Spoon the potato mixture into the baking pan, spreading it evenly over the fruit and smoothing the top evenly. Rap the pan sharply on the countertop to knock out air bubbles.

Bake, uncovered, for 40 minutes, or until the top feels dry and springy to the touch. A knife inserted into the center should come out clean.

for serving now Cool in the pan on a wire rack for 10 minutes. Run a knife around the sides of the pan, invert a serving plate over the pan, and—holding it firmly in place—flip the two so the potatoes drop onto the plate. Serve warm.

to freeze Cool the potatoes completely in the pan on a wire rack. Open-freeze, then invert onto plastic freezer wrap, seal, wrap in heavy-duty foil, and return the potatoes to the freezer.

to defrost and serve Coat the original baking pan with nonstick spray. Drop the frozen potatoes back into the pan, cover with plastic wrap, and thaw on a wire rack in the refrigerator.

Preheat the oven to 350°F. Let the defrosted dish sit at room temperature while the oven heats.

Bake, uncovered, until the potatoes are heated through, about 45 minutes. Cool for 10 minutes, invert a serving plate over the pan, and—holding it firmly in place— flip the two so the potatoes drop onto the plate. Serve warm.

decadent potato and leek gratin

For an over-the-top dinner, serve this lavish casserole alongside fillet of beef or a rib roast. Thanks to its cheese-rich sauce, vegetarian friends request it as a main course, too.

Makes 6 to 9 servings

1 ½ pounds red-skinned potatoes

2 cups milk

4 tablespoons (½ stick) unsalted butter, plus 2 teaspoons

1 large leek, white part only, thinly sliced

3 tablespoons rice flour

3 cups (12 ounces) shredded Gruyère, Emmental, or Comté cheese

½ teaspoon mustard powder

Pinch of cayenne pepper

Salt and freshly ground pepper

to serve

4 teaspoons unsalted butter

1 cup panko

½ teaspoon ground sweet paprika

> ▶ **freeze for up to 6 weeks**
>
> ▶ **freeze now, cook late**
>
> ▶ **elegant or festive**

side dish
For a pretty presentation, bake or freeze the gratin in individual gratin dishes. This may require extra topping. Reduce the baking time, whether freshly made or frozen.

Place the potatoes in a large saucepan with cold water to cover by 2 inches. Boil the potatoes until a knife inserted into the center meets slight resistance, 15 to 18 minutes. Drain, cool to room temperature, then cover the potatoes on a plate and refrigerate until they are well chilled, 4 to 24 hours.

Peel the potatoes, then shred, using the coarsest side of a hand grater set on a sheet of wax paper. Gently slide the shredded potatoes into a large mixing bowl.

Heat the milk until steaming in the microwave or a saucepan over medium heat. Set aside.

cook smart
Do not shred the potatoes in a food processor. It makes them gluey.

In a heavy, medium saucepan, melt 1 tablespoon of the butter over medium heat. Add the leek and cook until soft, 4 minutes. Add 3 tablespoons of the remaining butter. When it is melted, add the rice flour and stir frequently for 2 minutes as the mixture bubbles. Add 1 cup of the hot milk, ¼ cup at a time, whisking vigorously after each addition until the mixture is smooth before making the next addition. Pour in the remaining milk while whisking constantly, and cook until the sauce has the consistency of cream soup, 5 minutes.

Off the heat, mix the cheese, mustard powder, and cayenne into the sauce base. Season to taste with salt and pepper. The sauce will be dense and stringy. Pour the hot sauce over the potatoes and use a silicon spatula to mix gently until combined.

Coat an 8-inch x 8-inch baking pan or ovenproof oval 2-quart baking dish, using the remaining 2 teaspoons butter. Spread the potato mixture evenly in the prepared pan.

for serving now Melt the 4 teaspoons butter in a small saucepan. Mix in the panko, paprika, ½ teaspoon salt, and a few grinds of pepper. Sprinkle the topping evenly over the gratin.

Preheat the oven to 350°F.

Bake the gratin, uncovered, for 30 to 35 minutes, until the edges are bubbling and the topping is crisp and golden brown. Let stand for 10 minutes before serving.

to freeze Cool the gratin to room temperature. Press a sheet of plastic wrap over the surface and refrigerate to chill the gratin. Open-freeze the chilled gratin, unmold and wrap in plastic freezer wrap, then heavy-duty foil, and return to the freezer. Or vacuum seal the frozen gratin and return to the freezer.

to defrost and serve Coat the original baking dish with nonstick spray. Unwrap the gratin and drop it back into the prepared baking dish. Cover with plastic wrap and thaw on a wire rack in the refrigerator for 18 to 24 hours.

Preheat the oven to 350°F. Let the gratin sit at room temperature while the oven heats up.

Meanwhile, melt the 4 teaspoons butter in a small saucepan. Mix in the panko, paprika, ½ teaspoon salt, and a few grinds of pepper. Sprinkle the topping evenly over the gratin.

Bake, uncovered, for 45 to 50 minutes, until the edges are bubbling, the topping is crisp and golden, and the gratin is heated through. Let the gratin stand for 10 minutes before serving.

chunky fresh tomato sauce

Plum tomatoes make a reliably good sauce any time of year. The secret is letting pale, out-of-season tomatoes sit on the counter until they turn deep red. This ripening can take up to 6 days but improves their flavor substantially, as well as the amount of lycopene, an important antioxidant abundant in tomatoes. I use this sauce on pasta and in any recipe calling for fresh tomato sauce.

▶ freeze for up to 8 weeks

Makes 4 cups

1 small celery rib, with leaves, finely chopped

1 small onion, finely chopped

1 large garlic clove

¼ cup loosely packed flat-leaf parsley

2 tablespoons extra virgin olive oil

5 pounds ripe plum tomatoes, peeled, seeded, and chopped, about 7 cups (see Cook Smart)

1 tablespoon chopped fresh oregano or 1 teaspoon dried

Salt and freshly ground pepper

In a food processor, whirl the celery and celery leaves, onion, garlic, and parsley until finely chopped and moist, stopping to scrape down the sides of the bowl once or twice.

In a large stainless steel or other nonreactive skillet, heat the oil over medium-high heat. Add the chopped vegetables and cook until they are golden, 4 to 5 minutes, stirring often. Add the tomatoes and oregano, reduce the heat, and simmer until the tomatoes are very soft but still chunky, 20 minutes. Season to taste with salt and pepper.

for serving now Use the freshly cooked sauce, or cool it in a large bowl, then refrigerate in a sealed container for up to 5 days.

to freeze Spoon the cooled sauce in 2-cup portions into resealable 1-quart plastic freezer bags. Refrigerate on a plate to chill. Freeze the chilled sauce flat on a baking sheet lined with wax paper.

to defrost and serve Thaw the sauce on a plate in the refrigerator for 8 to 12 hours. Or place the bag in a large bowl of cold water, changing the water every 15 minutes and breaking the sauce up into chunks when partially defrosted to speed the process.

Simmer the thawed sauce in a nonreactive saucepan, uncovered, until it thickens to its original consistency, 10 to 20 minutes, depending on the amount.

side dish

For variety, you can add 2 tablespoons of grated Parmesan cheese per cup of sauce, or mix in fresh basil or a couple of chopped anchovies.

cook smart

Using a swivel-blade peeler with a serrated edge speeds peeling tomatoes. Alternatively, plunge a few tomatoes at a time in boiling water until their skins crack, 30 to 60 seconds. Immediately transfer the tomatoes to a bowl of ice water and use your fingers to pull off the loosened skin.

golden cheese sauce

▶ freeze for up
  to 12 weeks

Imagine always having the perfect, cheese sauce handy to spoon over steamed vegetables or a baked potato; mix with pasta; or use in casseroles. Keep this creamy sauce in the freezer and do it anytime. Using rice flour makes this sauce gluten-free.

Makes 2½ cups

1½ cups milk

3 tablespoons unsalted butter

3 tablespoons rice flour

2 cups (8 ounces) shredded sharp
  Cheddar cheese

½ teaspoon dry mustard

Salt and freshly ground pepper

side dish

Combine Golden Cheese Sauce with cooked macaroni, shells, or bow ties for instant stove-top macaroni and cheese.

Heat the milk in a microwaveable measuring cup or small saucepan. Set aside.

In a heavy, medium saucepan, melt the butter over medium heat. Whisk in the rice flour and cook for 2 minutes as it foams, whisking constantly.

While whisking, slowly add ½ cup of the hot milk. When the mixture is smooth, slowly add the remaining milk, continuing to whisk. Cook until the sauce is steaming and coats a spoon thickly, 5 minutes, stirring occasionally. Off the heat, add the cheese and whisk until it has melted and the sauce is smooth. Whisk in the mustard and season to taste with salt and pepper.

for serving now Spoon the cheese sauce over steamed broccoli and other vegetables or cooked pasta. Golden Cheese Sauce keeps, tightly covered in the refrigerator, for 3 days. Reheat as for the defrosted sauce, below.

to freeze Spoon the hot sauce into a resealable 1-quart plastic freezer bag, seal, and cool on a plate until room temperature. Refrigerate to chill, then freeze on a baking sheet lined with wax paper. Or divide the sauce among several plastic freezer containers and press plastic freezer wrap onto the surface. Cool to room temperature, then refrigerate to chill. Cover tightly and freeze.

to defrost and serve Thaw the sauce in the refrigerator for up to 12 hours, depending on the amount. A bag of frozen sauce can be thawed in a large bowl of cold water, changing the water every 15 minute and breaking the sauce into chunks as it defrosts.

Heat the sauce in a small, heavy saucepan over medium heat, stirring constantly, for 8 to 15 minutes, depending on the amount.

tomato and roasted red pepper sauce

▶ freeze for up
to 4 weeks

Roasted peppers and garlic give unexpected depth of flavor to this meatless sauce. Glorious in Spinach and Pesto Lasagna (page 110), it is good to have on hand to spoon over grilled eggplant or to turn sautéed shrimp into a special yet quick dinner.

Makes 6 cups

2 tablespoons extra virgin olive oil

¾ cup finely chopped onion

3 roasted garlic cloves, peeled

2 cans (28 ounces) crushed tomatoes

2 roasted red peppers, peeled, seeded, and finely chopped (see Cook Smart)

1 teaspoon dried basil

Salt and freshly ground black pepper

side dish
Store-bought roasted peppers taste slightly bitter and less sweet than fresh ones you roast.

cook smart
To oven-roast sweet peppers, start with the fleshy, thick-walled kind, halved and seeded. Set the peppers cut side down on an oiled baking sheet. Bake at 450°F until their skins are blistered, 30 minutes. Transfer to a bowl, cover with a plate, and steam the peppers for 20 minutes, then use your fingers to lift off the skins.

Heat the oil in a large Dutch oven over medium-high heat. Add the onion and cook until soft, 6 minutes, stirring frequently. Mash the garlic into the onion. Add the tomatoes and roasted peppers. When the sauce starts to boil, reduce the heat, add the basil, and simmer, uncovered, until the peppers are so soft they blend in with the tomatoes, 20 minutes.

Cool the sauce for 10 minutes, then puree until almost smooth, using an immersion blender or in a blender, which may require 2 batches. Season to taste with salt and black pepper.

for serving now Use the freshly cooked sauce, or cool it in a large bowl, then refrigerate in a sealed container for up to 3 days.

to freeze Spoon the cooled sauce, in 2- to 4-cup portions, into resealable 1-quart plastic freezer bags. Refrigerate on a plate to chill. Freeze the chilled sauce flat on a baking sheet lined with wax paper.

to defrost and serve Thaw the sauce on a plate in the refrigerator for 8 to 24 hours, depending on the amount. Or place the bag in a large bowl of cold water, changing the water every 15 minutes and breaking the sauce up into chunks when partially defrosted to speed the process.

Simmer the thawed sauce in a nonreactive saucepan, uncovered, until it thickens to its original consistency, 10 to 20 minutes, depending on the amount.

chapter 8

add something special and fresh

A casserole is in the oven or a stew is heating up. Alongside them, I like to add something that completes the meal, particularly a colorful salad, fresh vegetables with a twist, or an appealing grain. Here are some of my favorites that I serve often because they are easy to prepare.

Honey Dijon Spinach Salad with Apples is the ideal partner for Lemon Chicken and Rice Casserole (page 104) or Spiced Butternut Squash and Carrot Soup (page 60). Texas Tabbouleh goes perfectly with Chicken Chili Verde (page 124), and Garlic Smashed Potatoes help soak up the delicious sauces of Beef Stew with Red Wine and Cinnamon (page 129) or Coffee Pot Roast (page 138). Baked Polenta and New England Cornbread are whole-grain dishes when made with stone-ground cornmeal. So is Quinoa Pilaf with Garden Vegetables, which adds vegetables to your dinner, too.

- honey dijon spinach salad with apples
- iceberg wedge with real russian dressing
- red cabbage and cranberry slaw
- moroccan carrot salad
- garlic smashed potatoes
- green beans with pine nuts
- texas tabbouleh
- indian rice pilaf
- cocoa-mashed sweet potatoes
- quinoa pilaf with garden vegetables
- baked polenta
- new england cornbread
- 20-minute tomato sauce

honey dijon spinach salad with apples

▶ can be doubled

Dried cranberries and pumpkin seeds, plus citrus in the dressing, add a tapestry of flavors to this side salad. Tender baby spinach or the darker, more substantial leaves of the darker crinkly kind work equally well. Serve this salad with Smoky Black Bean Soup (page 47) or Best Ever Lentil Chili (page 135).

Makes 4 servings

dressing

¼ cup orange juice

1 tablespoon fresh lemon juice

1 tablespoon honey

1 teaspoon Dijon mustard

1 teaspoon salt

⅛ teaspoon freshly ground pepper

2 tablespoons extra virgin olive oil

6 cups lightly packed spinach leaves, stemmed

¼ cup dried cranberries or tart cherries

2 tablespoons sunflower or pumpkin seeds

side dish

Add grilled chicken to make this a main-dish salad.

In a small bowl, whisk together the orange and lemon juices, honey, mustard, salt, and pepper until well combined. Whisk in the oil gradually until the dressing is combined and thick. Makes ⅓ cup dressing.

In a mixing bowl, toss the spinach with 3 to 4 tablespoons of dressing. Divide the glistening leaves among 4 wide, shallow salad bowls. Garnish with the dried fruit and seeds. Serve immediately.

iceberg wedge with real russian dressing

Who needs a steakhouse when you can make this lettuce and tomato salad liberally topped with the zingiest dressing and enjoy it at home? Chili sauce gives the dressing a punch that ketchup misses. Try it and see what a difference this makes. Serve with California Meatloaf Burgers (page 119) or Everybody's Favorite Tuna Noodle Casserole (page 101).

Makes 4 servings

dressing

½ teaspoon sugar

½ teaspoon white vinegar

¼ teaspoon Worcestershire sauce

3 tablespoons chili sauce

⅓ cup mayonnaise, regular or reduced-fat

1 small head iceberg lettuce, cut into 4 wedges

12 grape or cherry tomatoes, halved

2 thin slices red onion

In a small bowl, whisk together the sugar, vinegar, and Worcestershire sauce until the sugar dissolves. Mix in the chili sauce. Add the mayonnaise and whisk until combined.

Put a lettuce wedge on each of 4 salad plates. Spoon 2 tablespoons of the dressing over each wedge. Sprinkle the halved tomatoes around the lettuce. Separate the onion slices into rings and scatter one-fourth over each salad.

▶ **can be doubled**

side dish
Serve the dressing as a dip with celery and carrot sticks, and with boiled shrimp at parties.

red cabbage and cranberry slaw

▶ can be doubled

▶ feeds a crowd

Few salads are as versatile and rich in antioxidants as this colorful slaw. Since it keeps well, you can make it well ahead and savor its sharp-sweet flavor for several days. Serve with Pomegranate-Glazed Chicken with Wild Rice (page 115) or Southern Pork Chop Casserole (page 95).

Makes 8 servings

½ cup dried cranberries

⅓ cup pomegranate juice

1 pound red cabbage, cut into wedges and sliced crosswise into thin strips, about 6 cups

1 large carrot, coarsely shredded

1 small red onion, cut into thin crescents

½ cup lightly packed chopped flat-leaf parsley

½ cup chopped walnuts

dressing

1 tablespoon balsamic vinegar

1 ½ teaspoons salt

¼ teaspoon freshly ground pepper

1 tablespoon roasted walnut oil or canola oil

side dish
This salad is great with turkey burgers, rotisserie chicken, and other turkey, chicken, and pork dishes.

cook smart
If you do not have pomegranate juice, soak the cranberries in ⅓ cup of apple juice. For the dressing, use 2 tablespoons of the berry-flavored apple juice with 2 tablespoons of red wine vinegar and the balsamic vinegar.

In a small bowl, soak the cranberries in the pomegranate juice until plumped, 30 minutes. Drain, reserving the juice.

In a large mixing bowl, combine the cranberries, cabbage, carrot, and onion. Mix in the parsley and walnuts.

Add the vinegar, salt, and pepper to the reserved juice. Whisk in the oil, then pour the dressing over the cabbage mixture and toss with a fork until well combined. Let the slaw sit for 30 minutes, toss, and serve. This salad keeps, covered in the refrigerator, for 4 days.

moroccan carrot salad

The spice flavors in this colorful salad are so satisfying that you won't notice it is made without oil. Shredding the carrots coarsely is important. Serve with Turkish Ground Beef Kebabs (page 76).

Makes 4 servings

4 medium carrots, coarsely shredded, about 4 cups

½ cup golden raisins

Juice of 1 lemon

1 small garlic clove, finely minced

1 tablespoon honey

¼ teaspoon ground cinnamon

¼ teaspoon ground ginger

1 teaspoon kosher salt

In a mixing bowl, combine the carrots and raisins. In a small bowl, whisk together the lemon juice, garlic, honey, cinnamon, ginger, and salt. Pour the dressing over the carrots and toss with a fork to combine. Serve immediately or within 1 to 2 hours, before the flavors in the dressing start to dissipate.

side dish

Youngsters love the natural sweetness of this salad. To make it even more kid-friendly, omit the garlic.

garlic smashed potatoes

Rough and rustic, these are potatoes the way a chef would make them. Garlic mashed into the potatoes, still in their skins, adds flavor and makes them creamier. Serve with Always Good Meatloaf (page 121), Sake-Soy Short Ribs (page 145), or Coffee Pot Roast (page 138).

▶ **can be doubled**

Makes 4 servings

¾ pound small yellow-fleshed potatoes

2 large garlic cloves, unpeeled

1 tablespoon extra virgin olive oil

Salt and freshly ground pepper

Place the potatoes and garlic in a large saucepan and cover by 2 inches with cold water. Boil over medium-high heat, uncovered, until the potatoes are easily pierced with a knife, about 20 minutes. Drain and transfer the potatoes to a mixing bowl. Peel the garlic and add to the potatoes.

With a fork, break each hot potato into 3 or 4 chunks. Add the oil, ½ teaspoon of salt, and several grinds of pepper and mash the potatoes roughly with the garlic, leaving lots of potato chunks. Season to taste with salt and pepper and serve immediately.

side dish

Combined with eggs in a casual frittata, these potatoes are so good that you may want to double the recipe just for the leftovers.

cook smart

For this dish, use your best extra virgin olive oil, one with robust flavor, along with a nice sea salt.

green beans with pine nuts

Tossed with butter and toasted nuts, green beans become a special-occasion dish. Serve with My Mother's Gourmet Chicken Curry (page 90), Anytime Turkey Tetrazzini (page 100), or Prosciutto-Stuffed Chicken with Creamy Parmesan Sauce (page 117).

Makes 4 servings

¾ pound fresh green beans, trimmed

1 tablespoon unsalted butter

1 teaspoon olive oil

¼ cup pine nuts or slivered almonds

Salt and freshly ground pepper

½ teaspoon fresh lemon juice

Cook the beans in boiling water until crisp-tender, 4 minutes. Drain in a colander, then immediately transfer the beans to a bowl of ice water. When the beans are completely cooled, drain and pat dry on paper towels.

In a large skillet, melt the butter with the oil over medium-high heat. When the butter stops bubbling, stir in the nuts. Cook, stirring, until the nuts just start to color, 1 to 2 minutes. Watch carefully, as they burn quickly.

Add the beans to the skillet and spoon the nuts over them, tossing them together until the nuts are golden and the beans are heated through, about 3 minutes. Season to taste with salt and pepper. Add the lemon juice, toss, and serve immediately.

side dish

For a leaner version, use just the olive oil.

texas tabbouleh

▶ can be doubled

I call this tabbouleh because, like the Middle Eastern salad, it is made with lots of parsley and lemon juice. But in place of bulgur, I use black-eyed peas, making it higher in protein, lower in carbs, and gluten-free. Serve with Salsa Fajitas (page 72) or Baked Red Peppers with Quinoa and Feta (page 113).

Makes 4 servings

¾ cup dried black-eyed peas, or 1 can (15 ounces), rinsed and drained

1 cup packed chopped flat-leaf parsley

1 ripe tomato, seeded and chopped

⅓ cup finely chopped red onion

½ cup finely chopped scallions, white and green parts

2 tablespoons fresh lemon juice

1 tablespoon extra virgin olive oil

Salt and freshly ground pepper

⅓ cup chopped spearmint (optional)

side dish
Add crumbled feta cheese to make this a meatless meal.

cook smart
Dried black-eyed peas are clearly superior to canned in taste and texture. These quick-cooking beans, without soaking, are ready in 45 to 60 minutes and can be made up to 2 days ahead and then refrigerated.

If using canned black-eyed peas, skip this step: Place the dried beans in a medium saucepan with water to cover by 2 inches. Bring to a boil over medium-high heat. Reduce the heat and simmer, covered, until the beans are tender, about 45 minutes. Drain and set aside to cool to room temperature; there will be 2 cups of cooked beans.

In a mixing bowl, use a fork to combine the beans, parsley, tomato, onion, and scallions. Add the lemon juice and oil and toss to combine. Season to taste with salt and pepper. Top with the spearmint, if desired.

indian rice pilaf

Basmati rice puffs up into a fluffy pilaf to serve with My Mother's Gourmet Chicken Curry (page 90), Cantonese Flank Steak (page 74), or Shredded Orange Pork in Lettuce Cups (page 84) or to dress up a rotisserie chicken. Indians like chewing on whole spices, including cloves, but pick them out if you prefer.

Makes 4 servings

1 tablespoon canola oil

3 whole cloves

1 piece (2 inches) cinnamon stick

½ teaspoon black mustard seeds

½ teaspoon cumin seeds

1 cup basmati rice

1 teaspoon salt

Heat the oil in a wide, medium or large saucepan over medium-high heat. Add the cloves, cinnamon, mustard, and cumin and cook, lifting and swirling the pan occasionally, until the spices are fragrant and a popping noise starts, 1 to 2 minutes. Mix in the rice and cook, stirring, for 2 minutes. Pour in 2 cups of water and add the salt. When the water boils, reduce the heat to medium-low, cover tightly, and cook for 20 minutes. Fluff the rice with a fork and serve immediately.

▶ **can be doubled**

side dish
For Lemon Rice, add the juice of ½ lemon along with the water.

cook smart
If you double the recipe, the cooking times remain the same. Do not increase the size of the cinnamon stick.

cocoa-mashed sweet potatoes

▶ can be doubled

When roasted, the orange-fleshed sweet potatoes often called yams are so moist that mashing them with just a bit of butter turns them into a creamy puree. A touch of cocoa powder adds unexpected depth to their naturally sweet flavor. They are a perfect accompaniment to Pecan Chicken Paillards with Honey Mustard Cream (page 78) and to turn Moroccan Pork Satay (page 40) into a meal.

Makes 4 servings

1 ½ pounds Garnet, Jewel, or Beauregard sweet potatoes

1 tablespoon unsalted butter

1 tablespoon Demerara or firmly packed dark brown sugar

¼ teaspoon cocoa powder

Salt and freshly ground pepper

side dish

For variety, use ¼ teaspoon of ground cinnamon, cumin, pumpkin pie spice, or ground ancho chile in place of the cocoa powder.

cook smart

Coating the potatoes with oil seals the pores in their skins, making the roasted potatoes even creamier.

Line the bottom of the oven with aluminum foil. Preheat the oven to 400°F.

Rub the potatoes lightly with oil or nonstick spray. Bake the potatoes directly on the oven rack for 40 to 60 minutes, or until they are soft when squeezed.

Split the potatoes and scoop the flesh into a mixing bowl. Add the butter, sugar, and cocoa and mash vigorously with a fork until the potatoes are creamy, 2 minutes. If fibrous, the hot potatoes usually smooth out when mashed, but they can be pureed in a food processor, if desired. Season to taste with salt and pepper.

quinoa pilaf with garden vegetables

Popping transforms quinoa from a light grain into an ethereal pilaf. It also adds a nice, nutty flavor. The popped quinoa is also good without the vegetables, particularly when you cook it with broth. Serve with Salsa Fajitas (page 72) or Mole Chicken Enchiladas (page 106). It is also the filling for Baked Red Peppers with Quinoa and Feta (page 113).

Makes 6 servings

▶ **can be doubled**

1 cup white quinoa

2 cups chicken or vegetable broth, or water

2 tablespoons olive oil

1 carrot, finely chopped

1 celery rib, finely chopped

½ red bell pepper, seeded and finely chopped

½ green bell pepper, seeded and finely chopped

1 medium red onion, finely chopped

½ cup corn kernels, fresh or frozen

In a fine-mesh sieve, rinse the quinoa under cool water. Shake to remove as much water as possible.

In a medium, heavy saucepan over medium-high heat, roast the quinoa, stirring frequently with a wooden spatula. If the damp kernels stick to the pan, scrape firmly to keep them moving. After 5 to 6 minutes, the quinoa will make a crackling sound as the grains start popping. When the sound has almost stopped, after about 3 minutes, remove the pan from the heat.

Carefully add the broth or water, standing back to avoid being spattered. Cover the pan and return it to the burner, reduce the heat, and simmer for 10 minutes. Check the grain, adding additional broth or water if necessary. Continue cooking until the grain is translucent, tender, and fluffy, 2 to 5 minutes. Let sit covered for 10 minutes. Fluff the quinoa with a fork to separate the grains.

Meanwhile, heat the oil in a medium skillet. Add the carrot, celery, peppers, and onion and cook until the onion is soft, 5 minutes, stirring often. Add the vegetables to the quinoa. Add the corn and mix with a fork to combine. Serve hot or warm.

side dish

This pilaf becomes a salad if you toss it with the herbed lemon and olive oil dressing used with Baked Red Peppers with Quinoa and Feta (page 113).

cook smart

Any combination of vegetables works, so substitute zucchini, mushrooms, butternut squash, leek, even tomatoes, making sure the total amount measures 2½ cups of finely chopped vegetables.

baked polenta

Chicken Chili Verde (page 124), Sunday Red Sauce with Sausage, Meat, and Meatballs (page 131), Sake-Soy Short Ribs (page 145), and Beef Stew with Red Wine and Cinnamon (page 129) all partner well with polenta, so I make this often. It's easy because this hands-off method needs little tending and produces a firm polenta that's perfect for sopping up sauces. For a softer, creamy polenta, keep stirring the polenta in the pot, then mix in some butter or cheese.

Makes 6 servings

1 tablespoon olive oil	3 cups boiling water
¾ cup stone-ground yellow cornmeal or polenta (not instant)	1 teaspoon salt

side dish

Stone-ground yellow cornmeal is a whole grain because it includes the germ of the corn.

cook smart

If cooked polenta sticks to the baking dish, rather than using elbow grease to clean it, place the hot pan in the sink, fill with cold water, and let it soak. After an hour or two, you will find the polenta neatly released from the dish.

Preheat the oven to 350°F. Coat a 9-inch x 9-inch baking dish with nonstick spray.

In a heavy saucepan or medium skillet, heat the oil over medium-high heat. Mix in the cornmeal or polenta and cook, stirring with a wooden spoon until it is coated and the cornmeal is fragrant and hot to the touch, 3 to 4 minutes. Reduce the heat, if necessary, to avoid browning.

Off the heat, gradually pour in the boiling water, standing back as the mixture will spatter. Immediately whisk vigorously until the mixture is smooth. Stir in the salt and spread the polenta in the prepared baking dish in an even layer.

Bake the polenta, uncovered, for 45 minutes, or until it is thick and slightly grainy but tender to the bite. Serve immediately or set the polenta aside to cool. If desired, cover the cooled polenta and refrigerate for 2 to 3 days.

To serve, cut the polenta into squares. To reheat, wrap in foil and heat in a 350°F oven for 20 to 30 minutes, depending on the amount. Or in a nonstick skillet, heat 1 tablespoon of olive oil and cook until the polenta is crisp outside and heated through.

new england cornbread

Southerners like their cornbread sweet, while Yankees prefer it dense and with pronounced corn flavor. Assembling this baked side dish from scratch takes barely longer than if you added the milk and egg to a mix. Serve it with Chicken Chili Verde (page 124) or Mississippi Pepper Pot (page 54), or along with Sweet and Tangy Bison Balls (page 38) to turn them into a meal.

Makes 9 squares

3 tablespoons unsalted butter

¾ cup unbleached all-purpose flour

¾ cup stone-ground yellow cornmeal

3 tablespoons sugar

1 teaspoon baking powder

½ teaspoon salt

1 large egg

¾ cup milk

Preheat the oven to 325°F. Butter an 8-inch x 8-inch baking pan, preferably dark metal or ovenproof glass, and set aside.

Melt the butter and cool to room temperature.

In a bowl, whisk together the flour, cornmeal, sugar, baking powder, and salt. In a measuring cup, beat the egg with the milk, then mix in the cooled butter. Pour the wet ingredients into the dry and whisk just until they are blended. Spread the batter in the prepared pan.

Bake for 25 minutes, or until the cornbread is golden on top and the edges are lightly browned. A knife inserted into the center should come out clean. Cool the cornbread for 10 minutes on a wire rack. Cut into 9 pieces and serve warm.

▶ can be doubled

side dish
Use ¼ cup sugar if you want a sweeter cornbread, and only 2 tablespoons for an even more pronounced corn flavor.

cook smart
Stone-ground cornmeal is a whole grain. Indian Head Stone-Ground or Bob's Mill medium-grind cornmeal works best in this recipe.

20-minute tomato sauce

For tomato sauce in a hurry, I use this Neapolitan-style sauce to make Pizza Noodle Casserole (page 98), Baked Four-Cheese Ziti (page 108), or a lasagna at the last minute. Better tasting than anything out of a jar, its ingredients are nearly always in the pantry. As a meal-maker, it turns a defrosted chicken breast or baked eggplant slices plus a topping of melted mozzarella into a complete dish in just 20 minutes.

Makes 3 cups

2 tablespoons extra virgin olive oil

3 garlic cloves, peeled and halved

1 can (28 ounces) crushed tomatoes

1 can (8 ounces) tomato sauce or puree

1 teaspoon dried basil

1 teaspoon dried oregano

½ teaspoon sugar

Salt and freshly ground pepper

side dish

This full-bodied sauce is good on penne and other hearty pasta.

cook smart

A coating of nonstick spray inside plastic containers avoids staining from the tomatoes.

Heat the oil in a large, deep saucepan over medium-high heat. Add the garlic and cook until golden, 3 minutes, turning the pieces several times so they do not burn. Remove the garlic.

Add the crushed tomatoes and tomato sauce or puree, basil, oregano, and sugar. Reduce the heat and simmer, partially covered, for 15 minutes. Season to taste with salt and pepper.

This sauce keeps, covered, in the refrigerator for up to 5 days.

chapter 9

desserts

For desserts and sweet indulgences, your freezer can be a treasure chest. Besides keeping a supply of ready-to-bake cookie dough on hand for Cherry Chocolate Chippers, Butter Pecan Meltaways, and other cookie jar goodies, it keeps killer cheesecakes and Old-Fashioned Apple Pie with the flakiest crust ever beautifully. Stock it with Orange Blossom Cupcakes, ready to spread with their luscious, equally freezable cream cheese frosting, and a Double Chocolate Layer Cake with Fudge Buttercream Frosting, all ready to assemble, and you will always be ready to celebrate birthdays and other special occasions, too.

Another sweet benefit of freezing is being able to make a major dessert like Banana Coconut Bread Pudding or Sticky Toffee Pudding, serve part, and then freeze the rest for instant dessert another day. And when you need a treat right now, a Frozen Hot Fudge Sundae, Cookies and Cream Mini Tart, or nostalgic Almond Tortoni provides instant gratification. So do Freeze Please Fudge Brownies and spiced Mexican Chocolate Shortbread, so make a double batch and freeze one to hold in reserve.

To complete an elegant dinner, crêpes garnished with fresh berries are simple yet impressive. To make an evening romantic, sharing chocolate fondue works magic. Both freeze well and defrost in minutes.

Because some baked goods that are great fresh from the oven can turn dry in the freezer no matter how well they are wrapped, I replace some of the butter with oil, a technique that I learned from master baker Mani Niall. It helps retain moisture better, and the result is amazing.

- frozen hot fudge sundaes
- cookies and cream mini tarts
- cherry chocolate chippers
- peanut butter cookies, naturally
- butter pecan meltaways
- mexican chocolate shortbread
- red hot pinwheels
- banana coconut bread pudding
- sticky toffee pudding with caramel sauce
- crêpes with ginger apples and honey cream
- orange blossom cupcakes
- cream cheese frosting
- freeze please fudge brownies
- chocolate cream cheese frosting
- orange marmalade cream cheese frosting
- akasha's carrot cake
- double chocolate mini loaves
- chocolate chip pound cake
- deep dark chocolate fondue
- decadent after midnight cheesecake
- mocha chocolate cheesecake
- double chocolate layer cake with fudge buttercream frosting
- ginger peach crisp
- fresh blueberry crumble
- old-fashioned apple pie
- flaky pie crust
- spiced tea granita
- almond tortoni
- mango sherbet
- avocado sorbet

frozen hot fudge sundaes

▶ sundaes freeze
for up to 4 weeks,
hot fudge sauce
for up to 8 weeks

▶ can be doubled

▶ quick fix

Imagine having a sundae topped with dark, gooey-chewy fudge sauce anytime you crave it. Vanilla or coffee ice cream are my favorite flavors to use, though I sometimes use coconut sorbet to make these single-serve sundaes milk-free. As the thick, velvety sauce cools, it coats the ice cream like a soft shell. With this treat in your freezer, bliss is just a quick spoonful away.

Makes 4 servings

for the hot fudge sauce

½ cup boiling water

6 tablespoons unsalted butter, diced

½ cup unsweetened Dutch-process cocoa powder

1 cup superfine sugar

2 tablespoons light corn syrup

1 teaspoon vanilla extract

1 pint premium vanilla or coffee ice cream

side dish
Dairy-free frozen desserts made from soy or coconut milk make great sundaes.

cook smart
Since butter is mostly fat, people allergic to dairy may be able to tolerate it.

To make the fudge sauce, in a medium saucepan, place the water, butter, and cocoa and set over medium heat. Whisk until they are combined and smooth, 2 minutes. Add the sugar and corn syrup and bring to a gentle boil. Cook the sauce until it coats a spoon thickly, 3 minutes. Off the heat, mix in the vanilla. Cool the sauce to room temperature. Makes 1¾ cups.

Store Hot Fudge Sauce in a covered container in the refrigerator for up to 2 weeks.

for serving now To use, warm the fudge sauce in a microwaveable container until it flows enough to drizzle.

For each sundae, spoon 2 tablespoons of Hot Fudge Sauce into the bottom of a wide, shallow bowl; a stemmed dessert dish; or an old-fashioned glass. Add a ½-cup scoop of the ice cream, then 3 tablespoons more fudge sauce over the ice cream. Serve immediately.

to freeze To freeze Hot Fudge Sauce alone, once it has cooled to room temperature, pour it into plastic freezer jars or other freezer-safe plastic containers. Press plastic freezer wrap onto the surface of the sauce and seal the containers.

To assemble sundaes to freeze, the 9-ounce plastic glasses used at parties are perfect. Spoon 1 tablespoon of the sauce into the bottom of the glass. Using a shallow, wide soup spoon, scoop the ice cream horizontally from the container in a wide ¼-cup wedge and add it to the glass. Top with another 2 tablespoons of the sauce. Add the remaining ¼ cup ice cream, smoothing the top with the back of the spoon, then add another 2 tablespoons of fudge sauce. Press a square of plastic freezer wrap onto the sauce, then firmly press the corners of the wrap sticking up around the inner sides of the glass against the inside of the glass. Place each assembled sundae in the freezer before making the next one.

to defrost and serve Transfer the frozen sauce to the refrigerator to thaw for 6 to 10 hours, depending on the amount.

To serve assembled sundaes, let each sundae sit at room temperature for 5 minutes.

freezer note Freezing makes plastic glasses fragile. To protect the sundaes, place them in a wide, shallow plastic container and store where other packages of food will not touch them.

cookies and cream mini tarts

Miniature ice cream tarts with a crust made from crushed chocolate sandwich cookies are just enough to satisfy your sweet craving without regret. A drizzle of Hot Fudge Sauce over the petite tarts makes the perfect finishing touch (or use chocolate sprinkles). Gluten-free cookies work for making the crunchy shells.

Makes 6

16 chocolate sandwich cookies

2 tablespoons unsalted butter, softened

1 ½ cups premium vanilla ice cream or dairy-free coconut frozen dessert

Hot Fudge Sauce (opposite)

- ▶ freeze for up to 4 weeks
- ▶ can be doubled
- ▶ quick fix

In a food processor, grind the cookies into fine crumbs. Measure 1 ½ cups and reserve any extra for another use.

Place the crumbs in a mixing bowl, add the butter, and work the mixture with a fork until the crumbs are evenly dark and cling together when pressed between your fingers, 2 to 3 minutes.

Using the back of a tablespoon, spread 3 to 4 tablespoons of crumbs over the bottom and up the sides of each of 6 miniature tart shell pans, pressing lightly. Then go over the crumbs again, pressing more firmly and smoothing the crumbs as you work. Pay special attention where the bottom and sides meet to keep the crust thin. Use a spoon and your fingers to make a rim around the top of each pan.

side dish

Let your imagination be your guide in selecting ice cream flavors to use. I like chocolate sorbet or Chunky Monkey.

Preheat the oven to 350°F.

Bake the tart shells for 6 to 8 minutes, or until they smell fragrant, look darker, and feel dry to the touch. Cool completely on a wire rack; the tart shells become crisp as they cool.

for serving now If using freshly made tart shells, freeze them for 30 minutes to chill and firm the crust. Skip this step if using previously frozen shells.

Fill a tart shell with ¼ cup of the ice cream, spreading it with the back of a spoon and smoothing the top. Do not worry if the top is not completely even. Return the ice cream–filled tart to the freezer and fill the remaining tart shells, one at a time. When all of the tarts are filled, open-freeze until solid, 30 minutes.

Using a teaspoon, drizzle the fudge sauce in lines and zigzags over the top of each tart. Return the drizzled tarts to the freezer until the sauce is chewy, 15 minutes. Serve immediately.

to freeze Fill a tart shell using ¼ cup of the ice cream and hold in the freezer while filling the remaining tarts.

Wrap the filled tarts in plastic freezer wrap, pressing it firmly against the surface of the ice cream. Place 2 tarts together, tops facing, and wrap in heavy-duty foil. Return the wrapped tarts to the freezer, storing them in a resealable plastic freezer bag, if desired.

to defrost and serve Bring the Hot Fudge Sauce to room temperature.

Take the tarts from the freezer and drizzle the tops with Hot Fudge Sauce. The ice cream softens quickly, so by the time you have decorated the tarts and let them stand a few minutes for the sauce to firm up, they will be ready to serve.

cherry chocolate chippers

These buttery 2-bite treats cram in tart cherries, pecans, and chunks of chocolate. Bake them until crisp or keep your cookies chewy—baking times are given for both preferences. Easy to grab from a cookie jar, these chippers also ship well.

Makes 4½ dozen

2 cups unbleached all-purpose flour

¼ teaspoon baking soda

Pinch of salt

¾ cup (1½ sticks) unsalted butter, softened

½ cup packed light brown sugar

6 tablespoons granulated sugar

1 large egg

2 teaspoons vanilla extract

1 bag (16 ounces) Scharffen Berger chunks (62% cacao) or 1¼ cups semisweet chocolate chips

1 cup chopped pecans

¾ cup dried tart cherries

▶ freeze for up to 4 weeks

▶ can be doubled

▶ feeds a crowd

In a small bowl, combine the flour, baking soda, and salt. In a large bowl, use a handheld mixer on medium-high to beat the butter until it is fluffy, 3 minutes. Add the sugars and beat until well combined, 2 minutes. Mix in the egg and vanilla. Add the dry ingredients and mix on medium speed until just combined. By hand, fold in the chocolate, pecans, and cherries until they are evenly distributed in the batter.

To shape the cookies, roll walnut-size pieces of dough between your palms into balls.

for baking now Place racks in the upper and lower thirds of the oven. Preheat the oven to 375°F.

Flatten the dough balls slightly and place them 2 inches apart on ungreased light-colored baking sheets.

Bake the cookies for 8 minutes. Rotate the pans, reverse their position in the oven, and bake 3 to 4 minutes longer for chewy cookies, or 6 to 7 minutes longer, or until the cookies are golden on top and just starting to brown around the edge, for crisp ones. Transfer the cookies to a wire rack to cool.

These cookies keep in an airtight container for up to 10 days.

to freeze Open-freeze the balls of dough, about 1 hour. Store the unbaked balls of dough in a resealable 1-quart plastic freezer bag. Or vacuum seal the frozen dough in batches of 12.

side dish

Raisins can replace the dried cherries.

to defrost and bake Thaw the dough in the plastic bag in the refrigerator for 24 hours.

Bring the dough to room temperature. Flatten the balls of dough into 2-inch disks and place them 2 inches apart on an ungreased light-colored baking sheet.

Bake the cookies for 8 minutes. Rotate the pans, reverse their positions in the oven, and bake 3 to 4 minutes longer for chewy cookies, or 6 to 7 minutes longer, or until the cookies are golden on top and just starting to brown around the edge, for crisp ones. Transfer the cookies to a wire rack to cool.

peanut butter cookies, naturally

▶ freeze for up
  to 4 weeks

▶ can be doubled

▶ feeds a crowd

Using natural peanut butter is unusual in recipes for this classic cookie. The benefits include avoiding corn syrup and trans fats—plus it gives these cookies more intensely nutty flavor and crunchier texture. Their rustic edges announce they are different. Rich as shortbread and studded with roasted peanuts, these cookies ship well, too.

Makes 3 dozen

1 ¼ cups unbleached all-purpose flour

¾ teaspoon baking soda

¼ teaspoon salt

6 tablespoons (¾ stick) unsalted butter

¾ cup natural peanut butter (see Cook Smart)

¾ cup lightly packed dark brown sugar

¼ cup granulated sugar

1 large egg, at room temperature

1 teaspoon vanilla extract

½ cup dry-roasted peanuts, coarsely chopped

to bake

¼ cup granulated sugar

side dish
Two of these cookies plus a glass of milk makes a good snack.

cook smart
Natural peanut butter contains no trans fats, but some brands are sweetened. Unsweetened ones, such as Whole Foods 365 or Smuckers, or sweetened ones like Skippy Natural, all work in this recipe.

In a small bowl, combine the flour, baking soda, and salt and set aside.

In a mixing bowl, use a handheld mixer on medium speed to beat the butter until fluffy, 1 minute. Add the peanut butter and mix until combined. Mix in the sugars until well combined, 2 minutes. Mix in the egg and vanilla. Add the peanuts. With a rubber spatula, work in the dry ingredients and peanuts until a stiff dough holds together, with crumbly edges. Breaking off walnut-size pieces, roll the dough into 1-inch balls.

for baking now Preheat the oven to 350°F.

Place ¼ cup granulated sugar in a small bowl. Roll the balls of dough in the sugar, then set on an ungreased baking sheet, spaced 2 inches apart. Press with the tines of a fork to flatten the cookies into 1 ½-inch x ½-inch disks, then turn the fork 90 degrees and press again, making a grid pattern; the edges of the cookie will split in places as you press.

Bake for 6 to 8 minutes, or until the cookies are lightly colored. Using a metal spatula, transfer them to a wire rack to cool.

These cookies keep, sealed in an airtight container, for 2 weeks.

to freeze Open-freeze the unbaked dough balls, then store in resealable 1-quart plastic freezer bags. Or vacuum seal in batches of 12 and return the frozen cookie dough to the freezer.

to defrost and bake Thaw the dough in the refrigerator for 24 hours. Let it sit at room temperature until you can flatten the balls of dough into 1 ½-inch disks, 20 minutes. If the dough shatters when being shaped, squeeze it back together in your fist, and shape it again.

Place ¼ cup granulated sugar in a small bowl. Roll the disks of dough in the sugar, then set on an ungreased baking sheet, spaced 2 inches apart. Press with the tines of a fork to mark the cookies, then turn the fork 90 degrees and press again, making a grid pattern; the edges of the cookie will split in places as you press.

Bake for 6 to 8 minutes, or until the cookies are lightly colored. Using a metal spatula, transfer them to a wire rack to cool.

butter pecan meltaways

▶ freeze for up
  to 8 weeks

▶ can be doubled

▶ feeds a crowd

Everyone seems to treasure childhood memories of a buttery cookie rolled in confectioners' sugar that melts in your mouth. Most people coat these chubby crescents twice with sugar, but I prefer the way the flavor of the nuts comes forward when you coat them just once.

Makes 3½ dozen

1 cup (2 sticks) unsalted butter, softened

1 cup lightly packed ground pecans

1 teaspoon vanilla extract

2 cups confectioners' sugar

2 cups unbleached all-purpose flour

½ teaspoon salt

side dish

If you wish to sugar-coat the cookies a second time, place ¾ cup of confectioners' sugar in a shallow bowl and dredge the cookies, one at a time. Set the cookies on a wire rack over wax paper before storing to help the sugar set.

cook smart

These cookies are easy to overbake. To find the perfect baking time for your oven, bake a mini batch the first time you make them. (Overbaked, they are dry but still delicious.)

When making a double batch, I use a stand mixer.

To grind the pecans, pulse in a food processor using short bursts.

In a large mixing bowl, use a handheld mixer on medium speed to combine the butter and pecans, 2 minutes. Mix in the vanilla, then 1 cup of the sugar, and beat for 1 minute to blend well. With the mixer on low or using a rubber spatula, blend in the flour and salt until the mixture forms a silky, soft dough. Divide the dough into 3 parts, and shape each into an 8-inch x 1¾-inch log.

for baking now Wrap each log in plastic wrap. Refrigerate the dough until firm, 2 hours, or for up to 2 days.

Preheat the oven to 325°F. Let the chilled dough sit out for 15 minutes, then cut each log into ¾-inch slices. Roll the slices between your palms to form a 2-inch cylinder with pointed ends. Place on an ungreased baking sheet and bend into a U-shape. Space the cookies 2 inches apart, placing them in 3 long rows.

Bake for 12 minutes, or until the cookies are pale on top and lightly colored on the bottom. Let the cookies cool on the baking sheet for 2 minutes, then transfer to a wire rack set over wax paper. Immediately coat the hot cookies generously with the remaining 1 cup sugar, using a shaker or sieve (see Side Dish). The cooled cookies keep in an airtight container for up to 1 week.

to freeze Wrap the dough in plastic freezer wrap. Refrigerate for 2 hours. Seal the chilled dough in heavy-duty foil and freeze. Or open-freeze the dough, unwrapped, then vacuum seal and return to the freezer.

to defrost and bake Thaw the frozen dough in the refrigerator for 24 hours. Slice and bake as above.

mexican chocolate shortbread

▶ freeze for up
  to 6 weeks

▶ can be doubled

▶ elegant for
  entertaining

The aroma that fills your house when baking these spiced cookies invites you to relax with a cup of coffee and a long triangle of this shortbread. You can do it anytime when you keep a batch in the freezer. Also makes a lovely gift.

Makes 12 pieces

8 tablespoons (1 stick) unsalted butter

¾ cup unbleached all-purpose flour
  plus 1 tablespoon

3 tablespoons unsweetened Dutch-
  process cocoa powder

½–1 teaspoon ground cinnamon

¼ teaspoon salt

¼ cup superfine sugar

side dish
The British call these long, tapered wedges petticoat shortbread.

Preheat the oven to 375°F.

Cut the butter into small pieces and chill until it is hard, 15 to 20 minutes.

In the bowl, combine the flour, cocoa, cinnamon, and salt. In another bowl, use a wooden spoon to work the butter and sugar until well combined, 2 minutes. Sift in the dry ingredients and mix to form a soft dough, about 1 minute. Transfer the dough to an 8-inch round cake pan. With your fingers, working from the center out, pat the dough into an even layer in the pan, then use the back of a metal spoon to smooth it. Chill for 20 minutes.

With a sharp knife, score the chilled dough into quarters, then with the tines of a fork, pierce the shortbread in 2 rings, making the first 2 inches from the outer edge and the second one closer to the center of the pan.

Bake for 15 minutes, or until the center of the shortbread is dry to the touch and the edge is starting to darken. Cool in the pan on a wire rack for 10 minutes. Run a thin, sharp knife around the edge of the pan. Invert the pan and press gently to help unmold the shortbread. Flip the shortbread back to topside up. Using a long, sharp knife (not serrated), cut the shortbread into 12 wedges and cool completely on the rack. Store the shortbread in an airtight container or wrapped in foil. It keeps at room temperature for 1 week, tightly sealed.

for serving now If possible, let the baked shortbread sit for 24 hours.

to freeze Wrap the cooled shortbread in plastic freezer wrap, then heavy-duty foil, and freeze.

to defrost and serve Unwrap the frozen shortbread and let it sit at room temperature for 20 minutes before serving.

red hot pinwheels

▶ freeze for up
   to 4 weeks

▶ can be doubled

▶ feeds a crowd

First you taste the chocolate and the spice in the spiral filling, and then the chile heat in these icebox cookies hits you. The dough is made like pie crust, an idea inspired by Elinor Klivans, author of several freeze-and-serve dessert cookbooks. I find making it by hand produces a finer cookie, but use a food processor if you wish. Lining your baking sheets with foil buffers the heat to prevent the cookies from burning on the bottom.

Makes 3 dozen

¼ cup sugar

2 teaspoons unsweetened Dutch-process cocoa powder, preferably Guittard Cocoa Rouge

1 teaspoon ground ancho chile

¼ teaspoon ground cloves

1 cup unbleached all-purpose flour

⅛ teaspoon salt

8 tablespoons (1 stick) unsalted butter, cut into small cubes and chilled

3 tablespoons ice water

cook smart

As with pie crust, the colder the ingredients and the less they are handled, the better the cookie.

In a small bowl, combine the sugar, cocoa, ground chile, and cloves. Set aside 1 tablespoon for another use, such as to sprinkle on oatmeal or warm toast.

By hand: Combine the flour and salt in a mixing bowl. Add the chilled butter and toss to coat the cubes with the flour. Using a pastry cutter or 2 knives, work the butter and flour together until the mixture looks like lumpy sand, 4 minutes. Starting with 2 tablespoons, sprinkle the cold water over the dough and work until the dough starts coming together, adding more water if needed, then switch to using your fingertips and press the dough into a rough ball.

In a food processor: Place the flour, salt, and butter in the bowl of a food processor and toss to coat the butter with the flour. Pulse until the mixture looks like lumpy sand, with some loose flour. Gradually add the water, sprinkling 1 tablespoon over the mixture and pulsing to blend before making the next addition, until the dough just comes away from the sides of the bowl.

Turn the dough out onto a floured surface and shape into a 4-inch square. Wrap the dough in plastic wrap and refrigerate for 15 minutes, or until firm.

On a lightly floured surface, roll the dough into a 9-inch x 12-inch rectangle that is ¼ inch thick, with the narrow end towards you. Sprinkle the spice mixture over the dough, leaving a ¼-inch border along the sides and top. Starting at the bottom, roll the dough up tightly. Press to seal the ends and press firmly along the seam to seal. Wrap the dough in plastic wrap.

for baking now Refrigerate the log of dough until thoroughly chilled, 1 hour.

Preheat the oven to 375°F. Cover 2 baking sheets with foil.

Using a serrated or very sharp knife, cut the log crosswise into ¼-inch slices. Space the cookies 1 inch apart on the prepared baking sheets. Bake until the cookies are golden on top and lightly browned on the bottom, 11 to 12 minutes, reversing and rotating the baking sheets halfway through. Let the cookies sit on the baking sheets for 2 minutes, then transfer to a wire rack and cool completely. These cookies keep in an airtight tin for 5 days.

to freeze Open-freeze the log of rolled dough until firm, 1 hour. Wrap in plastic wrap, then heavy-duty foil, and return to the freezer.

to defrost and bake Thaw the dough in the refrigerator for 24 hours. Slice the cold dough crosswise into ¼-inch slices using a serrated or very sharp knife. Bake the cookies as above.

banana coconut bread pudding

The firm crust of golden semolina bread makes it an interesting choice for bread pudding. Combined with rum-soaked raisins, banana, and coconut milk, the result is a pleasing combination of exceptionally creamy pudding studded with chewy bits and a lush harmony of tropical banana, coconut, and rum flavors.

Makes 6 to 8 servings

¾ cup raisins

½ cup rum (preferably dark) or orange juice

2 large ripe bananas

1 can (15 ounces) unsweetened coconut milk, regular or light

1 cup heavy cream, at room temperature

3 large eggs, at room temperature

1 cup sugar

⅛ teaspoon salt

1 ½ teaspoons ground cinnamon

1 teaspoon vanilla extract

1 loaf (12 ounces) Italian semolina bread

2 teaspoons unsalted butter

1 tablespoon raw sugar

▶ freeze for up to 8 weeks

▶ can be doubled

▶ feeds a crowd

▶ elegant for entertaining

To plump the raisins, soak with the rum in a small bowl for 15 to 30 minutes. Drain them well.

In a blender, whirl the bananas with the coconut milk, cream, eggs, sugar, salt, cinnamon, and vanilla until smooth. Cut the bread into 1-inch slices, then into 1-inch chunks. In a large mixing bowl, combine the bread with the banana mixture until the bread is well saturated, 2 minutes. Cover with plastic wrap and refrigerate for 2 hours.

Preheat the oven to 350°F. Coat a 9-inch x 9-inch baking pan or ovenproof dish with the butter.

Scoop the pudding into the prepared pan, pressing with the back of a large spoon to eliminate any air pockets. Sprinkle the sugar over the top of the pudding.

Bake for 40 minutes, or until the pudding is golden brown on top and moist but not liquid in the center when a knife is inserted. Set the pudding on a wire rack and cool to room temperature.

for serving now Cut the pudding into 6 or 8 pieces and serve on dessert plates, drizzled with Caramel Sauce (page 208) or Hot Fudge Sauce (page 194).

to freeze Refrigerate the cooled pudding in the pan until chilled, 3 to 4 hours. Cut into portions and wrap individually in plastic freezer wrap, then heavy-duty foil. Freeze the chilled pudding on a baking sheet.

to defrost and serve Remove the foil and thaw the portions of pudding on a plate in the refrigerator for 6 to 8 hours.

Preheat the oven to 350°F.

Remove the plastic wrap from the pudding and then wrap 1 or 2 portions together in foil. Place the packages on a baking sheet and warm in the oven until the pudding is heated through, 35 to 45 minutes. Serve drizzled with Caramel or Hot Fudge Sauce.

freezer note Freezing makes this bread pudding even creamier.

sticky toffee pudding with caramel sauce

When I first swooned over this cozy English dessert, America had yet to discover the seduction of what looks like a failed bran muffin. Happily, the chef at Gilpin Lodge, a country hotel in the Lake District, where I was staying, shared his recipes for both the pudding and its exquisite sauce.

Makes 8 servings

3 tablespoons unsalted butter plus 2 teaspoons

1 cup chopped pitted dates

1 teaspoon vanilla extract

½ teaspoon baking soda

½ teaspoon cinnamon

¼ teaspoon ground ginger

¼ teaspoon ground allspice

⅛ teaspoon ground cardamom

⅔ cup unbleached all-purpose flour

1 teaspoon baking powder

¼ teaspoon salt

⅔ cup sugar

1 egg, lightly beaten

Caramel Sauce (page 208)

- freeze for up to 8 weeks
- can be doubled
- feeds a crowd
- elegant for entertaining

Preheat the oven to 350°F. Using 2 teaspoons of the butter, grease a muffin tin with eight 3-inch cups.

In a small bowl, combine the dates, vanilla, baking soda, cinnamon, ginger, allspice, and cardamom and set aside. Sift the flour with the baking powder and salt onto wax paper.

Use a wooden spoon to cream the remaining 3 tablespoons butter in a large mixing bowl until soft, 2 minutes. Add the sugar and stir vigorously until the mixture is light and fluffy, 1 minute. Mix in the date mixture and the egg. Fold in the flour mixture with a rubber spatula just until blended. Fill the cups of the prepared muffin tin two-thirds full.

Bake for 15 to 18 minutes, or until the tops of the puddings feel springy when lightly pressed in the center. Cool in the tin for 5 minutes, then run a thin knife around the edges and turn the puddings out onto a wire rack.

for serving now Place the warm puddings on individual dessert plates. Spoon a pool of warm Caramel Sauce around each pudding and serve.

to freeze Cool the puddings to room temperature. Wrap individually in plastic freezer wrap, then heavy-duty foil. Refrigerate to chill, 3 to 4 hours, and then place the puddings on a baking sheet and freeze. Store the frozen puddings together in a resealable plastic freezer bag.

cook smart
If your muffin tin has 12 cups, fill the unused cavities halfway with water to protect them from burning.

to defrost and serve Remove the foil and defrost the puddings on a plate in the refrigerator for 6 to 8 hours.

Preheat the oven to 350°F.

Remove the plastic wrap from the puddings. Wrap the puddings, singly or in pairs, in foil and heat on a baking sheet for 25 to 30 minutes, or until warm, not hot. Serve with Caramel Sauce.

caramel sauce

▶ **freeze for up to 8 weeks**

▶ **can be doubled**

Almost maple in flavor, this sauce goes well over Sticky Toffee Pudding (page 207), Banana Coconut Bread Pudding (page 205), and Johnny Appleseed French Toast (page 251). Spooned over vanilla or coffee ice cream, it makes a easy, blissful dessert.

Makes 1 cup

1 cup firmly packed dark brown sugar

6 tablespoons heavy cream

1 cup coarsely chopped pecan halves (optional)

In a small, heavy saucepan, cook the sugar and cream over low heat without stirring until the sugar has dissolved and the sauce boils. Remove from the heat and stir in the pecans, if using. Cool to lukewarm before using. This sauce keeps, covered in the refrigerator, for 5 days.

to freeze Pour the hot sauce into a plastic freezer container and cool to room temperature. Cover tightly and refrigerate to chill. Freeze the chilled sauce.

to defrost and serve Defrost the sauce in the refrigerator for 6 hours. Heat the chilled sauce in a bowl in the microwave at 50 percent power for 1 minute, or in a small saucepan over medium heat for 8 minutes, stirring occasionally.

crêpes with ginger apples and honey cream

Crêpes offer multiple ways to make desserts that are cozy yet have a touch of elegance. Besides filling the crêpes with warm spiced apples, you can fold them over sliced fresh strawberries or drizzle them with Hot Fudge Sauce (page 194). Unless you make crêpes often, expect to toss out the first 2 or 3—even chefs do. Once you get the wrist motion going and the pan heated right, though, turning out a stack of crêpes is easy.

Makes 8 servings

2 tablespoons unsalted butter

½ cup milk plus 2 tablespoons

½ cup unbleached all-purpose flour

1 large egg

½ teaspoon vanilla extract

Pinch of salt

1 tablespoon sugar

to serve

2 tablespoons unsalted butter

▶ crêpes freeze for up to 6 weeks

▶ can be doubled

▶ feeds a crowd

▶ elegant for entertaining

Melt 1 tablespoon of the butter in a small bowl in the microwave and cool slightly.

In a blender, whirl ½ cup of the milk with the flour, egg, melted butter, vanilla, salt, and sugar for 10 seconds, making a smooth batter with the consistency of heavy cream. Cover and refrigerate the batter for 2 hours or up to 3 days.

Preheat the oven to 200°F.

Heat a 6- or 7-inch nonstick heavy skillet over medium-high heat until water flicked into it balls up and dances. If the batter has separated, whirl it in the blender, adding milk by the tablespoon if it has thickened.

Using ½ teaspoon of the remaining butter and a paper towel, coat the hot pan very lightly. Holding the pan in 1 hand, pour in about 3 tablespoons of batter, tilting and rotating the pan to coat the bottom. Cook until the crêpe looks dull on top and the bottom is browned, 60 to 90 seconds. Loosen with a spatula and flip the crêpe. Cook the second side for 15 seconds. Flip the crêpe onto a plate. Wipe the pan lightly with more butter, add the batter, and repeat. Keep thinning the batter as needed. Wrap the stacked crêpes in foil and hold in the oven while making the filling.

ginger apples

▶ can be doubled

Use 1 or more kinds of apples, from a sweet Golden variety to tart Granny Smith, to make this filling for crêpes.

Ready in 10 minutes, these buttery apples are also good as a side dish with pork chops or roast turkey.

Makes 8 servings

> 1 ½ pounds apples, such as Golden Delicious, Ginger Gold, or Fuji
>
> 2 tablespoons unsalted butter
>
> 1 tablespoon fresh lemon juice
>
> 2–3 tablespoons sugar
>
> 1 teaspoon grated fresh ginger or ½ teaspoon ground

Peel, quarter, and core the apples, then slice thinly.

Melt the butter in a medium skillet over medium heat. Add the apples and lemon juice and increase the heat to medium-high. Cook the apples for 3 minutes, stirring occasionally. Sprinkle the sugar and ginger over the apples and cook until they soften and the thinnest slices are translucent, 3 to 4 minutes. Scoop the apples into a bowl. Wipe out the pan and set aside.

honey cream

▶ quick fix

▶ elegant for
  entertaining

Egg whites normally turn watery when frozen, and whipped cream, icy but here, honey makes them both freeze nicely for up to 3 days. It gives a definite flavor to this light topping, something to keep in mind when selecting the honey you use. Also dollop Honey Cream on fresh berries or a baked apple.

Makes 1 cup

> ½ cup heavy cream, chilled
>
> 1 tablespoon honey
>
> 1 large egg white, at room temperature
>
> 1 tablespoon confectioners' sugar

COOK & FREEZE

Whip the cream in a chilled mixing bowl. Mix in the honey and set aside.

In another bowl, beat the egg white until soft peaks form. Sprinkle on the confectioners' sugar and use a rubber spatula to fold in. Add the beaten egg white to the whipped cream and fold gently to combine.

If not serving immediately, cover the surface of Honey Cream with plastic freezer wrap and refrigerate for 24 hours, or freeze in a plastic freezer container and use within 3 days. After that, it starts to separate. Transfer the frozen cream to the refrigerator until it softens, 1 hour.

for serving filled crêpes now For each crêpe, melt 1 teaspoon of butter in a pan over medium heat. Add the crêpe and cook for 30 seconds. Turn and cook until the crêpe is warm and pliable, 30 to 60 seconds, then use a wide spatula to transfer it to a dessert plate. Spoon a scant ½ cup of warm Ginger Apples onto half of the warm crêpe and fold it over, enclosing them. Add a dollop of Honey Cream and serve. Repeat to make as many servings as desired.

to freeze Cool the crêpes to room temperature, then separate with wax paper. Wrap in plastic freezer wrap, then foil. Refrigerate to chill. Transfer the packet of chilled crêpes to the freezer.

to defrost and serve Thaw the wrapped crêpes in the refrigerator for 4 to 6 hours. Remove the foil and set out at room temperature until the crêpes will separate without cracking, 20 minutes.

Warm the crêpes in butter and fill, as For Serving Filled Crêpes Now, above.

side dish
As an alternative, fold crêpes over ¼ cup sliced, lightly sweetened strawberries. Or, in the style of crêpes suzette, warm the crêpes in butter, fold in half, then in half again, and serve in pairs, drizzled with Hot Fudge Sauce (page 194).

cook smart
Eggology's pasteurized egg whites whip well and let you avoid raw eggs. Many other brands do no whip.

orange blossom cupcakes

▶ freeze for up
  to 8 weeks

▶ can be doubled

▶ feeds a crowd

Marmalade-flavored cream cheese frosting adds the perfect finishing touch to these golden cupcakes with a moist, fluffy crumb. The surprise of marmalade inside is optional but nice when serving these sunny cupcakes fresh from the oven.

Makes 12 cupcakes

1 ¼ cups unbleached all-purpose flour

1 ¼ teaspoons baking powder

¼ teaspoon salt

½ cup (1 stick) unsalted butter, at room temperature

¾ cup sugar

2 large eggs, at room temperature

½ teaspoon vanilla extract

½ cup milk, at room temperature

¼ cup marmalade (optional)

Orange Marmalade Cream Cheese Frosting (page 215)

side dish

Chocolate Cream Cheese Frosting (page 215) or Fudge Butter-cream Frosting (page 228) is also good on these cupcakes.

Preheat the oven to 350°F. Line the cups of a muffin tin with 12 foil liners.

In a small mixing bowl, whisk together the flour, baking powder, and salt. In another bowl, use a handheld mixer on medium to beat the butter until fluffy, 2 minutes. Add the sugar and beat until the mixture looks like whipped cream cheese, 2 minutes. Add the eggs, one at a time, blending well after each one. Add the vanilla. Add the dry ingredients in 3 parts and the milk in 2, starting and ending with the dry ingredients. When just blended, spoon the batter into the prepared muffin tin and smooth the tops with the back of a spoon. If desired, when the cups are half-filled, drop 1 teaspoon marmalade in the center of the batter, then cover with the remaining batter.

Bake for 20 to 25 minutes, or until the tops are golden and spring back when pressed with your finger. Cool the cupcakes in the muffin tin on a wire rack for 5 minutes. Turn them out onto the rack and cool completely. Wrapped in plastic, these cupcakes keep at room temperature for 24 hours.

for serving now Frost and serve the baked cupcakes on the same day.

to freeze Wrap the individual cupcakes in plastic freezer wrap. Freeze, then store the wrapped cupcakes together in a resealable plastic freezer bag.

to defrost and serve Thaw the plastic-wrapped cupcakes at room temperature, about 30 minutes.

cream cheese frosting

▶ freeze for up
  to 8 weeks

▶ quick fix

This is the frosting Akasha uses to top her carrot cake. It is less sweet than most, with good cream cheese flavor. I also use it as the base for Chocolate Cream Cheese Frosting for Double Chocolate Mini Loaves (page 218) and for the Orange Marmalade Cream Cheese Frosting on Orange Blossom Cupcakes (page 212).

Makes 1 ½ cups

- 1 package (8 ounces) cream cheese, at room temperature
- 2 tablespoons nonhydrogenated vegetable shortening
- 2 tablespoons unsalted butter, softened
- 2 cups confectioners' sugar
- ½ teaspoon vanilla extract

cook smart
The shortening helps this frosting freeze nicely and spread well when thawed.

In a mixing bowl, beat the cream cheese, shortening, and butter with a handheld mixer on medium speed until combined and soft. Add the sugar and beat until the icing is smooth. Mix in the vanilla.

chocolate cream cheese frosting
Mix 2 ounces of melted semisweet chocolate into the frosting together with the vanilla.

orange marmalade cream cheese frosting
Omit the vanilla and mix in 2 tablespoons of orange marmalade. Use a fine-cut orange marmalade.

freeze please fudge brownies

When you take these brownies from the oven, a cracked top and crusty sides surround their soft fudge center. After freezing, though, these ultra chocolate brownies become more evenly creamy and chewy. Eat them slightly thawed, about 15 minutes out of the freezer.

▶ freeze for up to 6 weeks

▶ can be doubled

Makes 16 brownies

2 tablespoons unsalted butter

2 tablespoons canola oil

5 ounces bittersweet chocolate (70–72% cacao), chopped

1 ¼ cups unbleached all-purpose flour plus 1 tablespoon

1 teaspoon baking powder

¼ teaspoon salt

3 large eggs, at room temperature

1 cup sugar

1 teaspoon vanilla extract

½ cup chopped walnuts (optional)

Preheat the oven to 350°F. Coat an 8-inch x 8-inch baking pan with butter or nonstick spray and flour lightly.

In a small bowl, combine the butter, oil, and chocolate and melt in a microwave for 1 minute at 50 percent power, or over hot water. Cool to room temperature.

Sift the flour, baking powder, and salt together onto wax paper.

In a mixing bowl, using a handheld mixer on medium speed, beat the eggs lightly. Add the sugar and vanilla and beat until thick, 3 minutes. Blend in the chocolate mixture. Sprinkle the dry ingredients over the wet and use a rubber spatula to blend just until the batter is mixed. Spread the batter in the prepared pan. Sprinkle the walnuts over the top, if using.

Bake for 25 minutes, or until the top is hard and shiny and a knife inserted into the center is almost clean. Cool the brownies in the pan for 4 hours. Unmold and store, wrapped in foil, overnight and ideally for 24 hours, before cutting.

for serving now Cut as many brownies as you will serve, keeping the rest wrapped in foil at room temperature for up to 5 days.

to freeze Cut the cooled brownies into 4 quarters. Wrap each quarter in plastic freezer wrap, then heavy-duty foil, and freeze.

to defrost and serve Unwrap the quarters and let stand at room temperature for 15 minutes. Cut each section into 4 pieces and serve while still cold.

cook smart
Use a fruity chocolate such as Guittard or Trader Joe's One-Pounder rather than one that tastes acidic.

An ovenproof glass baking dish is ideal for getting these brownies crusty outside and creamy in the center.

akasha's carrot cake

▸ freeze for up
  to 8 weeks

▸ can be doubled

▸ feeds a crowd

This moist, spicy cake gets rave reviews from everyone, including top celebrities at Restaurant Akasha in Los Angeles. It is so good that you can simply dust it lightly with confectioners' sugar if you don't feel like making the cream cheese frosting.

Makes one 8-inch square cake, 9 servings

1 ½ cups unbleached all-purpose flour

1 ½ teaspoons baking soda

½ teaspoon baking powder

½ teaspoon salt

2 teaspoons ground cinnamon

1 teaspoon ground ginger

¼ teaspoon freshly grated nutmeg

½ cup canola oil

1 cup granulated sugar

2 tablespoons packed light brown sugar

¾ cup buttermilk

1 ½ teaspoons vanilla extract

1 ½ teaspoons grated orange zest

1 tablespoon orange juice

2 cups shredded carrots (about 2 large)

¾ cup canned crushed pineapple, well drained

½ cup shredded unsweetened dried coconut

½ cup chopped walnuts

Cream Cheese Frosting (page 215) (optional)

side dish

For a layer cake, double the recipe and bake in two 10-inch round pans. To assemble, use a double batch of Cream Cheese Frosting to fill between layers and over the top of the cake.

cook smart

Replace the buttermilk with soymilk for the best vegan cake ever.

Preheat the oven to 350°F. Coat an 8-inch x 8-inch baking pan with nonstick spray and dust with flour, tapping out the excess. Set aside.

Into a large mixing bowl, sift the flour, baking soda, baking powder, salt, cinnamon, ginger, and nutmeg. In a medium bowl, whisk the oil and sugars together until well combined, 1 minute. Add the buttermilk, vanilla, and orange zest and juice and whisk until the mixture is cloudy and well combined, 1 minute. Pour the wet ingredients into the dry, stirring with a rubber spatula just to combine; do not overmix. Fold in the carrots, pineapple, coconut, and walnuts just until combined. Spread the batter in the prepared pan, smoothing it to the edges.

Bake for 35 to 40 minutes, or until the cake springs back when pressed lightly in the center and a toothpick inserted into the middle comes out clean. Cool the cake completely in the pan on a wire rack before unmolding.

for serving now If desired, spread Cream Cheese Frosting over the top of the cooled cake. Refrigerate for 1 to 2 hours to set the frosting.

to freeze Wrap the cooled cake, whole or cut into squares, in plastic freezer wrap, then heavy-duty foil, and freeze. Do not freeze the frosted cake, as the frosting will make the cake soggy.

to defrost and serve Unwrap and thaw the cake on a plate at room temperature, 4 hours for the whole cake, 1 hour for individual servings. Frost as For Serving Now on page 216, if desired.

freezer note Defrosted, this carrot cake is even moister than when just baked.

double chocolate mini loaves

▶ freeze for up to 8 weeks

▶ can be doubled

When a friend stops by, sharing one of these loaves is just right. Sour cream gives them a fine, velvety crumb and keeps them moist before and after freezing. Chocolate Cream Cheese Frosting (page 214) may be gilding the lily, but with chocolate, is there really too much of a good thing?

Makes 3 loaves, each serving 3 to 4

4 ounces bittersweet chocolate (70–72% cacao)

1 ¼ cups unbleached all-purpose flour

2 tablespoons unsweetened natural cocoa powder

1 ½ teaspoons baking powder

½ teaspoon baking soda

⅛ teaspoon salt

10 tablespoons (1 ¼ sticks) unsalted butter, softened

1 cup sugar

3 large eggs, at room temperature

½ cup sour cream

½ teaspoon vanilla extract

Chocolate Cream Cheese Frosting (page 215) or confectioners' sugar

side dish
Baked in foil pans, these cakes make a welcome gift.

cook smart
To soften butter, let it sit at room temperature for 20 to 30 minutes; it should yield when pressed gently.

Melt the chocolate in a microwave at 50 percent power, stirring every 30 seconds. Cool the chocolate to room temperature.

Preheat the oven to 350°F. Coat three 5-inch x 3¼-inch x 2-inch mini-loaf baking pans with nonstick spray and set aside (see Side Dish).

Sift the flour, cocoa, baking powder, baking soda, and salt together onto a sheet of wax paper. In a large bowl, using a handheld mixer on medium-high speed, beat the butter and sugar until fluffy and pale, 3 minutes. Blend in the chocolate. Add the eggs, one at a time, mixing well after each addition. Mix in the sour cream and vanilla. Add the dry ingredients and mix with a rubber spatula just until combined. Divide the batter among the 3 prepared pans.

Bake for 25 minutes, or until a knife inserted into the center of a cake comes out clean. Cool in the pan on a wire rack for 5 minutes. Run a knife around the sides of each pan, then turn the cakes out and cool completely on a wire rack. They taste best wrapped in foil and allowed to mellow for 24 hours at room temperature unless being frozen.

for serving now Frost with Chocolate Cream Cheese Frosting or serve dusted with confectioners' sugar.

to freeze Wrap the cooled cakes individually in plastic freezer wrap, then heavy-duty foil, and freeze.

to defrost and serve Remove the foil and thaw the plastic-wrapped cakes at room temperature for 6 to 8 hours. Frost the tops, then refrigerate for 1 hour to set the frosting. Let the frosted cakes sit at room temperature for 20 minutes before serving. Or serve dusted with confectioners' sugar.

chocolate chip pound cake

▶ freeze for up
to 4 weeks

▶ feeds a crowd

Pound cake is buttery and rich but looks plain, so I add mini chocolate chips to dress it up. Because it is so simple, the flavor of this classic cake benefits when you use the best butter and eggs fresh from the farmers' market.

Makes 8 servings

2 cups unbleached all-purpose flour

1 teaspoon baking powder

¼ teaspoon salt

4 large eggs

2 tablespoons heavy cream

1 cup sugar

1 cup (2 sticks) unsalted butter, at room temperature, plus extra for the pan

1 teaspoon vanilla extract

1 cup mini chocolate chips

cook smart

Heavy cream makes this pound cake lighter and helps keep it moist when you freeze it.

If you wrap the cooled cake in plastic wrap and allow it to ripen overnight on the counter, it will taste even better.

Preheat the oven to 325°F. Butter a 9-inch x 5-inch loaf pan and place the pan on an air-cushioned baking sheet or 2 regular baking sheets stacked on top of each other.

In a mixing bowl, whisk the flour, baking powder, and salt. In another bowl, beat 1 of the eggs with the cream and set aside.

In a large mixing bowl, use a handheld mixer on high to whip the sugar and butter for 5 minutes; they will be very pale and fluffy. Add the eggs, one at a time, beating for 1 minute after each addition, and adding the egg with cream last. Scrape down the sides of the bowl as needed. Mix in the vanilla. By hand, use a rubber spatula to fold in the dry ingredients until just blended; do not overmix. Fold in the chocolate chips. The batter will be thick. Spread the batter in the prepared pan, smoothing the top.

Bake for 65 to 70 minutes, or until the cake feels springy to the touch and a knife inserted into the center comes out clean. Cool the cake in the pan on a wire rack for 30 minutes, then run a knife around the sides of the pan and turn the cake out onto the rack. Cool completely.

for serving now Slice and serve.

to freeze Wrap the cooled cake tightly in plastic freezer wrap, then heavy-duty foil, and freeze.

to defrost and serve Remove the foil and defrost the cake on a wire rack until it is room temperature all the way through, 3 to 4 hours. Slice and serve.

deep dark chocolate fondue

At parties, serving this fondue is a great icebreaker. It is also deliciously romantic when shared by 2. The better the chocolate used, the more luxurious your fondue will taste.

Makes 8 servings

1 ½ cups semisweet chocolate chips, such as Guittard Extra Dark Chocolate Chips (63% cacao)

¼ cup heavy cream

2 tablespoons light corn syrup

⅛ teaspoon salt

3 tablespoons unsalted butter

to serve

1 ½ teaspoons liqueur, such as Bailey's or Frangelico, or vanilla extract

for dipping

Long-stemmed strawberries

Clementine sections

Bing cherries with stems

Dried apricots

Candied ginger chunks

Cubed Chocolate Chip Pound Cake (opposite)

Marshmallows

▶ **freeze for up to 3 months**

▶ **can be doubled**

▶ **feeds a crowd**

▶ **quick fix**

In a medium, heavy saucepan over medium-low heat, melt the chocolate with the cream, corn syrup, salt, and butter. Cook, stirring with a wooden spoon, until the chocolate melts and the fondue is silken, 8 to 10 minutes.

for serving now Mix in the liqueur or vanilla. Pour the warm fondue into a ceramic fondue dish or prewarmed heavy ceramic bowl. Serve immediately, on a large platter surrounded by your choice of dippers.

to freeze Pour the warm fondue into a resealable 1 quart plastic freezer bag and smooth into a thin, even layer. Seal and cool to room temperature. Freeze the fondue flat on a baking sheet lined with wax paper.

to defrost and serve Slit the bag and chop the fondue into chunks. Place in a small, heavy saucepan and warm over medium-low heat, stirring with a wooden spoon or microwave at 50 percent power, stirring every 30 seconds. Mix in the liqueur or vanilla. If the fondue is too thick, add cream by the tablespoon until it has the right consistency, then transfer the fondue to a fondue dish and keep warm.

If vacuum sealed, the fondue can be melted right in the bag in a large pot of warm water, then poured into a fondue pot and flavored with the liqueur or vanilla.

side dish

This is a great dish to share at a potluck. To transport it, simply pack up the frozen fondue, a fondue pot, and dippers, and then warm the fondue at the party.

cook smart

The organic corn syrup made by Wholesome Sweeteners is not high fructose.

decadent after midnight cheesecake

▶ freeze for up
  to 6 weeks

▶ can be doubled

▶ feeds a crowd

Rumor has it that Sara Lee cheesecake eaten directly out of its foil pan after midnight while standing in front of the open freezer contains no calories. What I really want in that pan, though, is this New York–style cheesecake made by Joe Nipitella. Bake this super-creamy cake in an 8-inch square foil pan, Sara Lee–style, or a round springform one. Having all of the key ingredients at room temperature is essential.

Makes 12 to 16 servings

½ cup graham cracker crumbs

1 cup plus 2 teaspoons sugar

1 teaspoon cold unsalted butter

2 packages (8 ounces each) cream cheese, at room temperature

3 large eggs, at room temperature

1 cup sour cream, at room temperature

1 teaspoon vanilla extract

cook smart

To reduce the amount of air bubbles in the finished cake, keep your mixer at medium-low speed.

Place a rack in the center of the oven. Preheat the oven to 375°F. If using a springform pan, wrap the outside with foil to make it waterproof.

For the crust, in a small bowl, combine the crumbs, 2 teaspoons sugar, and butter, working them between your fingertips until the crumbs hold together when pressed between your fingers. Spread over the bottom of the prepared springform pan or an 8-inch square foil pan, press firmly into an even layer, and set aside.

In a deep mixing bowl, use a handheld mixer on medium-low to blend the cream cheese and 1 cup sugar together until well combined, 2 minutes. Add the eggs, one at a time, mixing well after each one. Add the sour cream and vanilla and mix until well blended. Pour the mixture into the prepared pan and rap it sharply on the counter several times to knock out air bubbles.

Set a roasting pan large enough to hold the cheesecake pan comfortably onto the oven rack and place the cheesecake in the center. Carefully add boiling water to the roasting pan to ½ inch below the rim of the cheesecake pan.

Bake the cheesecake for 40 minutes. Turn off the oven and let the cheesecake remain in the oven for 50 minutes without opening the door.

Cool the cheesecake completely on a wire rack. Cover the pan with foil and refrigerate the cheesecake for 24 hours.

for serving now Let the cake sit out for 20 minutes. Cut a square cheesecake into 12 or 16 pieces, a round cake into 12 wedges. Use a knife dipped in hot water to cut the cake. Keep wiping and warming the blade for clean cuts.

to freeze Open-freeze the chilled cake. (Remove the collar from the pan if baked in a springform pan.) Wrap in plastic freezer wrap, then heavy-duty foil, and return the cake to the freezer.

to defrost and serve Thaw the frozen cake in the refrigerator until it can be cut, 6 to 10 hours. Serve chilled.

mocha chocolate cheesecake

▶ **freeze for up to 8 weeks**

▶ **feeds a crowd**

Dense and voluptuous, this is the ultimate chocolate lover's cheesecake. To complement the tang of the cream cheese, I like using a fruity chocolate such as Guittard semisweet chocolate (61% cacao) and mocha-java coffee.

Makes one 8-inch cake, 8 to 12 servings

¼ cup hot strong coffee

8 ounces semisweet chocolate chips or wafers (61–63% cacao)

1 cup Chocolate Cookie Crust Crumbs (page 195)

2 8-ounce packages cream cheese

1 cup sugar

4 large eggs

2 teaspoons vanilla extract

¼ teaspoon salt

cook smart

Setting a pan of water on the floor of the oven keeps the cheesecake moist and helps prevent cracking.

Place a rack in the center of the oven. Preheat the oven to 325°F.

In a deep microwaveable bowl, pour the hot coffee over the chocolate and let sit for 2 minutes, then stir for 2 minutes. If the chocolate is not completely melted, microwave briefly and stir again. Cool the melted chocolate to room temperature.

For the crust, spread the cookie crumbs over the bottom of an 8-inch springform pan and pressing firmly, 1 inch up the sides.

In a deep mixing bowl, using a handheld mixer on medium-low, beat the cream cheese until fluffy, 2 to 3 minutes. Mix in the sugar a little at a time, stopping to scrape down the sides of the bowl several times. One at a time, add the eggs, mixing well after each one. Using a rubber spatula, mix in the melted chocolate, vanilla, and salt. Pour the mixture into the prepared pan. Rap the pan sharply on the counter several times to knock out air bubbles.

Set the cheesecake on the oven rack. Fill a 9-inch pan with boiling water and place on the floor of the oven. Bake until the center of the cake wobbles like custard, 50 to 60 minutes. Turn off the oven and leave the cake in it with the oven door open for 15 minutes. Place the cake on a wire rack and gently work a knife around the edges to loosen it. Cool the cake completely.

for serving now Cover the cooled cake with foil and refrigerate for 24 hours.

Let the cake sit out for 20 minutes. Cut the cake into 8 to 12 pieces, using a knife dipped in hot water. Keep wiping and warming the blade to make clean cuts.

to freeze Refrigerate the cake to chill, 8 hours.

Remove the pan collar from the cooled cake. Open-freeze the cake. Wrap in plastic freezer wrap, then heavy-duty foil, and return the cake to the freezer.

Note: I often freeze this cake in 2 halves because it is so rich, only a large group can finish it.

to defrost and serve Unwrap the frozen cake, then replace the foil only. Thaw the cake in the refrigerator for 12 to 18 hours.

freezer note This cake gets even denser in the freezer, becoming almost as intense as creamy fudge.

double chocolate layer cake
with fudge buttercream frosting

▸ freeze cake
  layers for up
  to 4 weeks

▸ feeds a crowd

▸ elegant for
  entertaining

A layer cake is perhaps the ultimate American special occasion dessert. This one features tender chocolate layers swathed with creamy, dark fudge frosting. It is over the top when you want to celebrate a birthday or wow your favorite chocolate lover. Assembling it takes less than 30 minutes once its layers and frosting are thawed.

Makes one 9-inch cake, 10 to 12 servings

2–4 ounces semisweet chocolate
  (60–62% cacao)

½ cup unsweetened Dutch-process
  cocoa powder

2 cups unbleached all-purpose flour

¾ teaspoon baking powder

½ teaspoon baking soda

½ teaspoon salt

10 tablespoons (1 ¼ sticks) unsalted
  butter, at room temperature, plus
  extra for pans

⅓ cup canola oil

1 ½ cups sugar

3 large eggs

1 teaspoon vanilla extract

1 cup buttermilk

1 recipe Fudge Buttercream Frosting
  (page 228)

cook smart

For me, less is more, so I serve this cake simply enrobed in its deep dark frosting. To dress it up, you can sprinkle grated chocolate on top.

Melt the chocolate in the microwave at 50 percent power, stirring every 30 seconds, and cool to room temperature.

Preheat the oven to 350°F. Butter and flour two 9-inch x 2-inch round baking pans. Cut 2 parchment circles to fit the bottoms of the pans and butter and flour the parchment.

Sift the cocoa into a mixing bowl. Add the flour, baking powder, baking soda, and salt and whisk to combine. Set aside.

In a large mixing bowl, use a handheld mixer on high to whip the butter until fluffy, 1 minute. Add the oil and beat until the mixture resembles mayonnaise, 1 minute. Add the sugar and beat until the mixture is pale and thick, 2 minutes. One at a time, add the eggs, beating for 1 minute after each addition and scraping down the sides of the bowl as needed. Mix in the vanilla. Add the dry ingredients in thirds, alternating with the buttermilk in 2 additions, starting and ending with the dry ingredients. Using a mixer on low speed or working by hand with a rubber spatula, mix only until each addition is blended in. Fold in the melted chocolate. The batter will be thick. Divide the batter between the 2 pans, smoothing the tops.

Set the pans on a dark-colored baking sheet and bake for 26 to 28 minutes, or until the cake feels springy in the center and is pulling away from the sides of the pan. Cool the layers in the pans for 5 minutes, then run a knife around the sides of the pans and turn the layers out onto wire racks. Remove the parchment, and using another rack, flip the layers back to top side up. Cool completely.

for serving now Wrap the cooled layers in plastic wrap and allow to sit at room temperature for 24 hours to let the flavors meld. Fill and frost with Fudge Buttercream Frosting. Refrigerate for 2 hours to set the frosting. The frosted cake can be covered with foil and refrigerated for 24 hours. Let stand at room temperature for 30 minutes before serving.

to freeze Wrap the cooled layers tightly in a double layer of plastic freezer wrap. Stack and wrap the layers in heavy-duty foil, then freeze.

to defrost and serve Remove the foil and defrost the layers on a wire rack at room temperature. Frost and serve as above.

fudge buttercream frosting

▶ freeze for up
to 8 weeks

▶ can be doubled

▶ quick fix

Creamy and forgiving, this intensely chocolate frosting spreads easily. Chilling sets it, making the cake easy to transport. At room temperature, it returns to being soft and shiny. One batch will fill and frost two 9-inch layers generously, or several dozen cupcakes.

Makes 3½ cups

6 ounces bittersweet (70–72%) chocolate
1 cup (2 sticks) unsalted butter, at room temperature
3 cups confectioners' sugar
½ cup sour cream

side dish
When frosting a yellow, white, or devil's food cake, sweeter, 60 to 62% chocolate will taste better than using 70% in the frosting.

Melt the chocolate in the microwave at 50 percent power, stirring every 30 seconds, or over medium-low heat in a double-boiler. Cool the chocolate to room temperature.

In a large mixing bowl, use a handheld mixer on medium speed or a wooden spoon to beat the butter until fluffy, 1 minute. Mix in half the sugar. Blend in the melted chocolate, then the remaining sugar. Mix in the sour cream. This frosting keeps, tightly covered, in the refrigerator for up to 1 week.

to freeze Scoop the frosting into a plastic freezer container. Cover the top with plastic freezer wrap, then cover tightly with the lid. Refrigerate the frosting to chill, then transfer it to the freezer.

to defrost and serve Defrost the frosting at room temperature. Stir well to be sure the frosting is evenly creamy.

ginger peach crisp

Local tree-ripened peaches make the most delectable crisp, but their season is short. The rest of the year, this dessert is better made with frozen sliced peaches than unripe fresh ones. If planning to freeze, please read this recipe all the way through before starting so you use the correct method, based on whether you're using fresh or frozen peaches.

▶ **freeze for up to 4 weeks**

▶ **can be doubled**

Makes 4 to 6 servings

5 large ripe peaches, peeled and cut into 1-inch slices, 5–6 cups fruit, or sliced frozen peaches, defrosted according to package directions

½ cup peach jam

2 tablespoons finely chopped preserved ginger (see Cook Smart)

⅓ cup sugar

1 teaspoon ground cinnamon

⅛ teaspoon salt

4 tablespoons (½ stick) cold unsalted butter, cut into small pieces

¼ cup sliced almonds

topping

1 cup old-fashioned rolled oats

¼ cup all-purpose flour

Preheat the oven to 375°F. Coat an 8-inch x 8-inch baking dish with nonstick spray and set aside.

In a mixing bowl, use a fork to combine the peaches, jam, and ginger. Spread the filling in the prepared baking dish in an even layer. In another bowl, combine the oats, flour, sugar, cinnamon, and salt. Using a pastry cutter or your fingertips, work the butter into the topping. When the mixture starts to clump, add the

Using a serrated swivel-blade peeler zips the skin off fresh peaches without bruising their flesh.

Preserved ginger not coated in crystallized sugar is ideal.

almonds. With your fingertips, continue working the mixture until it resembles moist clumps of sand. A handful at a time, sprinkle the topping loosely over the fruit in an even layer.

for serving now Bake the crisp until the topping is lightly browned and the juices bubble around the edge of the pan, 30 to 35 minutes. Let the crisp stand for 30 minutes, or until nearly room temperature, before serving.

Divide the crisp among 4 to 6 wide, shallow bowls and serve immediately.

to freeze *If using fresh peaches:* Bake the crisp for 20 minutes, or until the fruit has softened but the juices are not bubbling. Cool to room temperature, then refrigerate to chill.

If using defrosted peaches: Skip the above steps.

Open-freeze the chilled crisp, then cover with plastic freezer wrap, pressing it against the surface of the topping. Wrap in heavy-duty foil and return to the freezer.

to defrost and serve Unwrap and defrost in the refrigerator for 8 to 12 hours.

Preheat the oven to 375°F.

Bake the chilled crisp until the topping is lightly browned and the juices bubble around the edge of the pan, 30 minutes. Let the crisp stand for 30 minutes, or until nearly room temperature, before serving.

Divide the crisp among 4 to 6 wide, shallow bowls and serve immediately.

fresh blueberry crumble

❯ freeze for up
  to 6 weeks

❯ can be doubled

Even though this is a casual dessert, it still deserves the best ingredients. To me, this means using fresh fruit. Happily, blueberries from Chile, available much of the time they are out of season in the United States, let you enjoy this quickly assembled, much-loved crumble almost anytime. I also keep one in the freezer to bridge the time when there are no fresh berries in the market.

Makes 6 servings

6 cups fresh blueberries

1 tablespoon fresh lemon juice

½–¾ cup granulated sugar

1 tablespoon tapioca starch

1 tablespoon grated lemon zest
   (optional)

⅓ cup firmly packed brown sugar

⅛ teaspoon salt

6 tablespoons (¾ stick) cold unsalted
   butter, thinly sliced

1 egg yolk

topping

½ cup unbleached all-purpose flour

¼ cup whole-wheat pastry flour

Coat a deep 6-cup or 8-inch x 8-inch baking dish with nonstick spray and set aside.

In a large saucepan, combine the berries and lemon juice.

In a small bowl, combine the granulated sugar with the tapioca starch and add to the blueberries. Cook over medium-high heat, stirring occasionally, until the sugar has dissolved and the berries are just starting to get tender. Spread the filling in the prepared baking dish. Sprinkle on the zest, if using. Let sit until the filling is at room temperature before adding the topping.

To make the topping: In a mixing bowl, combine the flours, brown sugar, and salt, using your fingers to combine well. Scatter the butter over the dry ingredients, and use a pastry cutter or fork to blend the mixture until it resembles crumbly sand, 4 minutes. Beat the yolk lightly in a small bowl and add half to the topping; discard the remaining yolk. Blend with a pastry cutter until the topping forms large, soft clumps, 1 minute. Sprinkle the topping evenly over the filling.

for serving now Preheat the oven to 375°F. Bake the crumble until the juices are bubbly and the topping is golden brown, 45 minutes. Let the crumble stand for 20 minutes, then divide it among 6 to 8 dessert bowls and serve warm.

to freeze Open-freeze, then wrap the crisp in plastic wrap and heavy-duty foil. Return to the freezer.

to defrost and serve Remove the foil and thaw the crumble in the refrigerator for 12 hours.

Preheat the oven to 375°F and bake as For Serving Now, allowing an extra 5 to 10 minutes, if necessary. Let the crumble stand for 20 minutes, then divide it among 6 to 8 dessert bowls and serve warm.

old-fashioned apple pie

▶ freeze for up
to 4 weeks

▶ can be doubled

▶ freeze now,
cook later

▶ feeds a crowd

Follow every step of this recipe, particularly for the crust, which I learned from the extraordinary Carole Walters, and I promise the best pie you have ever made. Even if you have never made a pie, it is a primer for success. Using a partially cooked filling reduces shrinkage and the hollow space under the top crust that plagues pie-makers.

Makes one 9-inch pie, 8 servings

3 pounds apples, such as Granny Smith, Jonagold, Rome, and Golden Delicious

1 tablespoon fresh lemon juice

3 tablespoons unsalted butter plus 1 teaspoon

½ cup lightly packed brown sugar

¼ cup granulated sugar

1 teaspoon ground cinnamon

¼ teaspoon ground cloves

1 recipe Flaky Pie Crust (page 236)

Peel, quarter, core, and cut the apples into ¼-inch slices. In a large bowl, toss the sliced apples with the lemon juice and set aside.

Melt 3 tablespoons of the butter in a large skillet over medium heat. Add the apples, stirring to coat with the butter, and cook for 3 minutes, stirring often. Combine the sugars, cinnamon, and cloves in a small bowl and sprinkle over the apples. Cook until the apples are crisp-tender, 3 to 4 minutes. Using a slotted spoon, spread the apples on a platter or 13-inch x 9-inch baking dish to cool. There will be 5 to 6 cups. Reserve the pan juices to add to applesauce or butternut squash soup, or just drink it.

Coat a 9-inch pie plate with butter and set aside. Following the directions on page 237, roll out the dough for the bottom and top crusts. Spoon the cooled apples into the prepared bottom crust, using a slotted spoon to leave any liquid behind.

Drape the top crust over the filled pie. With your hands, push the crust gently up and towards the center from the outer edge of the pie to ease it over the filling. Use a scissors to trim the overhang, leaving 1 ¼ inches all around. Fold the crusts under and press them together to seal. Crimp around the rim with the tines of a fork, or press the crust into a decorative pattern with your fingers.

for serving now Brush the top of the pie with egg white. Refrigerate the assembled pie for 20 minutes.

Preheat the oven to 400°F.

Place the pie on a dark-colored baking sheet. Using a small, sharp knife, cut out a 1-inch circle in the center of the top crust and make 4 pairs of cuts around the circle.

Bake the pie for 30 minutes. Cover the edges of the crust with strips of foil to prevent them from burning, and bake for 30 to 40 minutes longer, or until the crust is golden brown. Cool the pie on a wire rack. Serve lukewarm or at room temperature.

to freeze Open-freeze the unbaked pie in the pan until solid, 4 hours. If you wish, unmold the frozen pie. Wrap the frozen pie in plastic freezer wrap, then heavy-duty foil, and return the pie to the freezer.

to defrost and serve Unwrap and, if necessary, drop the frozen pie back into the original pie plate. Cover with plastic wrap and defrost the pie in the refrigerator for 12 hours. Thawed, the pie will keep up to 24 hours before baking.

Preheat the oven to 400°F. Bake the pie as For Serving Now on page 234.

flaky pie crust

▶ **freeze for up to 8 weeks**

▶ **freeze now, cook later**

Chilling is key to making flaky pie crust, so refrigerate all of the ingredients before combining them. Using a pastry cutter or 2 round-bladed dinner knives produces a more tender crust than using a food processor. If you choose to use a processor, chill the bowl and blade as well as the flour and fats. Always pulse to blend in the fats and liquid. Some bakers even chill the bottom crust, then let it become pliable again, before fitting it into the pie plate.

Makes 1 double crust for a 9-inch pie, or 2 single crusts

½ cup (1 stick) unsalted butter

5⅓ tablespoons (⅓ cup) nonhydrogenated vegetable shortening (stick form)

3 cups unbleached all-purpose flour

3 tablespoons sugar

½ teaspoon salt

7–8 tablespoons ice water

Cut the butter and shortening into ½-inch cubes. In a large bowl, combine the flour, sugar, and salt. Refrigerate the butter, shortening, and flour mixture for 30 to 60 minutes, or until well chilled.

Add the cubed butter and shortening to the flour mixture and toss to coat completely. Using a pastry cutter or 2 knives, work the fat into the flour until the mixture looks sandy, about 5 minutes. Sprinkle 4 tablespoons of cold water, one at a time, over the mixture, and keep cutting until clumps of powdery dough form, adding water by the tablespoon and then the teaspoon until the dough holds together when you press a bit of it between your fingers. Lightly press the dough into a large ball and cut it in half. Shape each half into a 5-inch disk.

to use now Wrap each disk in plastic wrap and let the dough rest in the refrigerator for at least 30 minutes and up to 24 hours before rolling out.

Let the dough sit at room temperature until it resists slightly when pressed with a finger, 15 to 60 minutes. Follow the directions in To Roll Out Pie Crust, below.

to freeze Wrap the disks in plastic freezer wrap, then heavy-duty foil, and freeze.

to defrost and use Thaw the wrapped dough in the refrigerator for 24 hours.

to roll out pie crust

1 egg white
Flour for coating work surface

Center a disk of dough on a lightly floured work surface. Working always from the center out, push a rolling pin towards the top, then the bottom, then either side. Rotate the dough 90 degrees and repeat, always easing up on the rolling pin as you near the edge. Do not flip the dough over.

When the dough is a 13-inch disk, fit it into the pie plate, easing it down the sides. With a scissors, trim away the overhang, leaving 1 inch all around. Whisk the egg white in a small dish with 1 tablespoon of water and brush the bottom of the crust to coat. Chill the crust while the egg white dries, 20 minutes. Prick the bottom and sides of the crust with a fork.

For a double-crust pie, use the same method to roll out the second disk to 13 inches and slide it onto a parchment-covered baking sheet.

Chill both crusts, uncovered, while making your pie filling.

side dish
This crust is good for all fruit pies, including cherry, peach, and blueberry.

cook smart
Covering your work surface with freezer paper makes rolling out the crust easier as well as speeding cleanup.

spiced tea granita

▶ freeze for up
  to 5 days

▶ can be doubled

Black tea steeped with spices gives this icy dessert intense flavor. To avoid bitterness and let the spices dominate, be sure to remove the tea bags promptly. A dark metal pan is ideal for freezing the granita, as it holds the cold best.

Makes 4 servings

1 piece (4 inches) cinnamon stick	½ teaspoon coriander seeds
4 cloves	¾ cup sugar
3 cardamom pods, cracked	2 black tea bags, preferably Constant Comment
1 piece (1 ½ inches) fresh ginger, peeled and thinly sliced	

side dish

For summer refreshment, reduce the sugar to ½ cup and heap the granita into 2 tall glasses, add straws, and serve as a reviving slush.

Place an 8-inch x 8-inch metal pan in the freezer.

In a medium saucepan, combine the cinnamon, cloves, cardamom, ginger, and coriander with 2 cups of water. Mix in the sugar. Bring to a boil over medium-high heat, cover, reduce the heat, and simmer for 3 minutes. Off the heat, add the tea bags and steep for 3 minutes. Remove the tea bags, squeezing them over the pot. Cover and set aside for 30 minutes.

Strain the spiced tea into the chilled pan and let sit until at room temperature. Set the pan in the freezer until ice crystals form around the edges of the pan, 30 to 40 minutes. Using a fork, scrape the crystals into the center of the pan and return to the freezer for 30 minutes. Repeat scraping and freezing at least 3 more times, until the granita is completely frozen.

for serving now Scrape the granita with a fork; using the side of the fork makes a finer, snowier granita, while using the tines produces a chunkier texture.

Spoon the granita into 4 dessert dishes or wine glasses. Serve immediately.

for serving later The granita can be covered with plastic freezer wrap and held for up to 5 days in the freezer. If it freezes too solidly, defrost slightly before scraping. Serve as above.

freezer note When multiplying the recipe, increase the size of the pan so the liquid is never more than ¾ inch deep in the pan. If necessary, use more than 1 pan.

almond tortoni

Every Italian-American restaurant used to serve this almond-flavored frozen dessert in a pleated paper cup. Reading a history of frozen desserts, I discovered that making it is incredibly simple. And if you set the tortoni in the freezer before you make dinner, it will be frozen by the time you are ready for dessert. Just sweet enough to be satisfying, it fits today's desire for small treats.

Makes 8 servings

¼ cup slivered almonds

1 cup heavy cream

¼ cup confectioners' sugar

½ teaspoon vanilla extract

¼ teaspoon natural almond flavoring

1 large egg white, at room temperature

Pinch of salt

⅓ cup crushed amaretti cookies, about 8

▶ freeze for up to 8 weeks

▶ quick fix

▶ feeds a crowd

Preheat the oven to 350°F. Spread the almonds on a baking sheet in 1 layer. Bake until the nuts are lightly browned, 8 minutes, stirring twice. Transfer to a plate and cool to room temperature. Finely chop the nuts and set aside.

Line 8 cups of a muffin tin with liners, preferably foil, and set aside. In a mixing bowl, place the cream, sugar, vanilla, and almond flavoring. Using a handheld mixer on high or a whisk, beat the cream until stiff. In a second bowl, whip the egg white with the salt until soft peaks form. Scoop the whites into the whipped cream, add ¼ cup of the crushed amaretti, and fold with a rubber spatula to combine.

Spoon the tortoni into the muffin cups, overfilling them slightly. In a small bowl, combine the roasted chopped almonds with the remaining amaretti crumbs. Sprinkle the mixture over the tortoni, just covering the tops and pressing lightly.

Open-freeze the tortoni until firm, about 1 hour.

for serving now Serve the frozen tortoni directly from the freezer.

to freeze and serve If not serving immediately, wrap the frozen tortoni individually in plastic freezer wrap. Store the wrapped tortoni in resealable 1-quart plastic freezer bags.

Do not defrost. Serve the tortoni directly from the freezer.

side dish

Whipped egg white lightens this dessert. Eggcology's pasteurized whites are ideal if you prefer to avoid raw eggs.

mango sherbet

▶ freeze for up
   to 1 week

▶ elegant for
   entertaining

Pureed fresh mango makes this an exceptionally creamy sherbet. The best kinds to use for fiber-free flesh and lush flavor are the flat, oval ataulfo variety, also called Champagne mangoes, or large, green Keitt mangoes from California and Mexico. You will need 2 or 3 smaller mangoes or one Keitt. This recipe requires an ice cream maker.

Makes 6 servings

2 cups diced mango flesh

¼ cup buttermilk

¼ cup light corn syrup

2 tablespoons fresh lime juice

⅛ teaspoon salt

Fresh blueberries or raspberries
   (optional, for garnish)

Mint sprigs (optional, for garnish)

Whirl the mango in a food processor until pureed. If the puree contains fibers, pass it through a strainer and return to the food processor. Add the buttermilk, corn syrup, lime juice, and salt and whirl until the mixture is a creamy, smooth puree.

Pour the mango mixture into an ice cream maker and freeze according to the manufacturer's directions. Pack the sherbet into a plastic container just large enough to hold it and smooth plastic wrap over the top. Seal and freeze the sherbet for 3 to 6 hours to ripen.

for serving now Scoop the sherbet into small dessert bowls or martini glasses and garnish with fresh berries and a mint sprig, if desired.

to freeze Mango Sherbet is smoothest when served within 1 to 2 days.

to defrost and serve For the creamiest texture, let the frozen sherbet sit for 15 minutes before scooping.

side dish

Sherbet usually contains milk or egg white, while sorbets are dairy-free and vegan.

cook smart

The organic corn syrup made by Wholesome Sweeteners is not high fructose and is made from non-GMO corn. Along with the buttermilk, it helps keep this frozen dessert creamy for up to a week. Multiplying this recipe depends on the capacity of your ice cream maker. If it is a 1-quart size with a chilled sleeve, you need to refreeze the sleeve for each batch.

avocado sorbet

▶ freeze for up
to 2 weeks

On hot summer days, I could live on this refreshing, tangy frozen dessert. Hass avocados make it smooth as silk and give it a beautiful soft green color. This recipe can be made with or without an ice cream maker.

Makes 3 cups

2 medium-size ripe avocados,
  1¾–2 cups flesh
1 pint good-quality lemon sorbet

¼ cup confectioners' sugar
2 tablespoons fresh lemon juice

side dish
When it melts, this frozen dessert becomes like a light, almost whipped pudding that is so good you may even want to serve it this way deliberately.

cook smart
Good-quality lemon sorbet does not have the bitter aftertaste lemon oil gives lesser ones.

Multiplying this recipe depends on the capacity of your ice cream maker. If it is a 1-quart size with a chilled sleeve, you need to refreeze the sleeve for each batch.

Puree the avocados in a blender. Add the sorbet, sugar, and lemon juice and whirl to combine.

If the avocado and lemon sorbet mixture is still chilled, scoop the mixture into an ice cream maker and freeze according to the manufacturer's directions. Otherwise, transfer the mixture to a container, cover, and chill well, 3 to 5 hours, then freeze.

Transfer the fresh sorbet to a container with a tight-fitting cover. Press plastic wrap onto the surface, then cover the container. Freeze for 8 to 24 hours before serving.

for serving now The color of this unexpected dessert almost demands serving it in clear glass. Stemmed wine or martini glasses are particularly nice.

to freeze and serve The fat in the avocado helps keep this sorbet smooth for 3 to 4 days. After that, it still tastes wonderful, but small ice crystals will gradually make it less creamy.

To serve, let the sorbet sit out just until it is soft enough to scoop, 5 to 10 minutes.

chapter 10

breakfast and brunch

Appealing breakfasts that are ready quickly—your freezer can shine in providing them. Reach in and select from Ricotta Pancakes, Chocolate Pancakes, crisp waffles, or crunchy cinnamon toast to pop into the toaster oven. By the time coffee is brewed, they will be waiting for you. So make a double batch on Sunday and store some in the freezer to enjoy during the coming weeks.

Having guests for brunch also becomes easier when you can pull a Red Pepper and Leek Quiche, Spinach and Chorizo Strata, or a pan of baked French toast out of the freezer instead of having to get up early to prepare them.

Other ways to start weekdays better include portable breakfasts like a microwaveable whole-grain burrito stuffed with beans, sausage, and cheese; a zucchini muffin; or whole-grain Oatmeal Banana Bread.

- cinnamon breakfast bruschetta
- chocolate pancakes
- ricotta pancakes
- toaster waffles
- fully loaded breakfast burrito
- johnny appleseed french toast
- cinnamon zucchini muffins
- oatmeal banana bread
- red pepper and leek quiche
- spinach and chorizo strata
- wild blueberry sauce
- freezer strawberry preserves

cinnamon breakfast bruschetta

▶ freeze for 4 weeks

▶ can be doubled

▶ quick fix

Warm cinnamon toast topped with creamy cheese makes an irresistible quick breakfast, freshly made or taken from the freezer. Enjoy it, at home or on the go. Using melted butter raises this above ordinary cinnamon toast as it helps the cinnamon sugar soak deep into the bread and turn it as crisp as bruschetta. Let the toast cool slightly before serving, especially for children, as the melted sugar makes these slices very hot.

Makes 4 servings

2 tablespoons unsalted butter, melted

2 tablespoons sugar

1 teaspoon ground cinnamon

4 slices firm white bread

to serve

½ cup ricotta or cottage cheese

side dish
These bruschetta are also a good afternoon snack.

cook smart
A silicone pastry brush is ideal for spreading the thick, sticky cinnamon butter.

Whole-grain bread is fine when serving the bruschetta freshly made. When frozen, however, the defrosted bread is too moist to crisp when toasted.

In a small bowl, melt the butter in the microwave. Add the sugar and cinnamon and whisk to combine.

Using a silicone pastry brush, brush one-fourth of the melted butter and cinnamon mixture over each bread slice, covering the bread on 1 side.

for serving now In a toaster oven, toast the bread until the spread is bubbling and the bread is lightly toasted, 2 to 4 minutes. Use tongs to transfer the hot toast to a plate, taking care as the sugar topping gets very hot. Spread 2 tablespoons of the cheese over each slice of toasted bread, which gets crisper as it cools slightly. Serve warm.

to freeze Open-freeze the bruschetta for 1 hour. Wrap slices individually in plastic freezer wrap, then stack 2 to 4 slices and seal them together in heavy-duty foil. Return to the freezer.

to defrost and serve Unwrap the frozen bruschetta and bake in a toaster oven at 350°F until the spread is bubbling and the bread is lightly toasted, about 4 minutes. Use tongs to transfer the hot toast to a plate, taking care as the sugar topping gets very hot. Spread 2 tablespoons of the cheese over each bruschetta, which will get crisper as it cools slightly, and serve.

chocolate pancakes

I created these intensely chocolate pancakes as a birthday gift for a friend who loves choc-olate. (For a dairy-free version of this recipe, using soymilk and soy flour, see *12 Best Foods Cookbook*.) To blend well, make sure all of the ingredients are at room temperature.

Makes 4 servings

1 ¼ cups unbleached all-purpose flour

¾ cup unsweetened Dutch-process cocoa powder

2 teaspoons baking powder

2 tablespoons sugar

3 large eggs

3 tablespoons unsalted butter, melted, or canola oil

1 ½ cups milk

Pinch of salt

to serve

Maple syrup or confectioners' sugar

1 pint fresh strawberries, hulled and sliced (optional)

▶ **freeze for up to 8 weeks**

▶ **can be doubled**

▶ **quick fix**

▶ **elegant for entertaining**

Into a medium bowl, sift the flour, cocoa, and baking powder. Mix in the sugar.

In another bowl, beat the eggs. Whisk in the butter or oil, milk, and salt until well combined. Add the wet ingredients to the dry, mixing just until blended. The mixture should be slightly lumpy and have the consistency of cake batter.

Spray a medium, cast-iron skillet with nonstick spray or use a nonstick pan. Place the pan over medium-high heat. Ladle the batter into the pan by scant quarter cups. Cook until bubbles form on the surface and the edges darken, about 2 min-utes. Turn and cook until the pancakes resist lightly when gently pressed in the center with your finger, about 2 minutes. Repeat until all the batter is used up.

for serving now Hold the pancakes, covered loosely with foil, on a plate in a 200°F oven until the entire batch is ready to serve. Serve, accompanied by either maple syrup or a sprinkling of confectioners' sugar, and sliced strawberries, if desired.

to freeze Cool the pancakes on a wire rack. Using parchment or wax paper squares to separate the pancakes, wrap tightly in plastic freezer wrap, then heavy-duty foil. Freeze the pancakes on a baking sheet. Store the wrapped pancakes in a resealable 1-quart plastic freezer bag, if desired.

to defrost and serve Unwrap the pancakes and let sit at room temperature until flexible enough to separate easily. Heat the partially thawed pancakes directly on the rack in a toaster oven at 350°F until heated through, about 6 minutes.

side dish

This batter also makes crisp waffles. Serve warmed pancakes for dessert, topped with a scoop of vanilla ice cream and drizzled with warm Hot Fudge Sauce (page 194).

cook smart

For freezing, using a combination of 1 ½ tablespoons of butter and 1 ½ tablespoons of oil makes pancakes that are more tender when defrosted.

ricotta pancakes

▶ freeze for up to
8 weeks

▶ can be doubled

▶ quick fix

▶ elegant for
entertaining

On the griddle, these golden pancakes puff up light as a cloud. They freeze beautifully, and when warmed in a toaster oven, are nearly as tender as when first made. These petite pancakes serve well with Wild Blueberry Sauce (page 259).

Makes 3 servings

1 cup ricotta cheese

3 large eggs, well beaten

¼ cup (½ stick) unsalted butter, melted and cooled to room temperature

½ teaspoon vanilla extract

¼ teaspoon salt

¼ cup unbleached all-purpose flour

to serve

Maple syrup, Wild Blueberry Sauce (page 259), or confectioners' sugar

side dish
Reheated, these pancakes are tasty enough to eat like a slice of toast. You can even take the frozen pancakes to the office to reheat in a toaster oven there.

cook smart
Using reduced-fat ricotta cheese is fine when serving the pancakes freshly made, but they will be tougher and drier when defrosted.

In a mixing bowl, whisk the cheese and eggs together until well combined. Whisk in the butter, vanilla, and salt. Add the flour and whisk until the batter is well blended.

Heat a griddle or large skillet over high heat until water flicked on the surface balls up and dances. Reduce the heat to medium-high. Lightly butter or oil the surface of the griddle or pan. If serving right away, preheat the oven to 200°F.

For each pancake, spoon 2 generous tablespoons of batter onto the griddle or pan, allowing plenty of room for spreading. When some bubbles appear and the tops look dry, carefully slide a wide spatula under the pancakes and gently flip them. Cook until the second side is lightly browned.

for serving now Serve immediately, or hold the finished pancakes on a platter in the oven until the entire batch is ready.

Place 3 pancakes on each plate. Pass a pitcher of warm syrup, or sprinkle the pancakes lightly with confectioners' sugar.

to freeze Cool the pancakes to room temperature on a wire rack. Using parchment or wax paper squares to separate the pancakes, stack 3 and wrap tightly in plastic freezer wrap, then heavy-duty foil. Freeze the packets of pancakes on a baking sheet. Store wrapped pancakes together in a resealable 1-quart plastic freezer bag, if desired.

to defrost and serve Thaw unwrapped pancakes at room temperature until flexible enough to separate easily. Heat the partially thawed pancakes in a 350°F toaster oven until heated through, about 10 minutes.

toaster waffles

▶ freeze for up to
4 weeks

▶ can be doubled

Homemade waffles have become a rare treat. But in about 10 minutes, you can enjoy them whenever. Grabbing them from the freezer, you can use them as a warm platform for fruit preserves or drizzled them with Hot Fudge Sauce (page 194).

Makes 4 servings

2 cups unbleached all-purpose flour

2 tablespoons sugar

1 tablespoon baking powder

½ teaspoon salt

2 large eggs

1 ½ cups milk

3 tablespoons unsalted butter, melted, at room temperature

1 tablespoon canola oil

to serve

Wild Blueberry Sauce (page 259), maple syrup, or confectioners' sugar

In a mixing bowl, combine the flour, sugar, baking powder, and salt. In a large measuring cup, whisk the eggs with the milk and add to the flour mixture. Add the butter and oil and whisk to make a smooth batter.

Coat a waffle iron with nonstick spray and heat it. Ladle in batter to fill three-quarters of the waffle iron and spread it evenly. Bake until waffles are crisp on both sides, 3 to 5 minutes, depending on your waffle iron.

for serving now Serve the hot waffles immediately, accompanied by Wild Blueberry Sauce or maple syrup or dusted with confectioners' sugar.

to freeze Cool to room temperature and separate along the grooves between the waffles. Open-freeze the waffles on a baking sheet lined with wax paper, 1 hour. Using parchment or wax paper squares to separate the waffles, stack them in pairs and wrap tightly in plastic freezer wrap, then heavy-duty foil. Store the packages of waffles in a resealable 1-gallon plastic freezer bag, if desired.

to defrost and serve Unwrap the frozen waffles and heat in a toaster oven until crisp, about 5 minutes. Or pop them into the toaster. Do not defrost the waffles before heating.

Serve the hot waffles immediately, accompanied by Wild Blueberry Sauce or maple syrup or dusted with confectioners' sugar.

freezer note Reheated, the waffles are drier and crunchier outside, not as chewy-crisp as when freshly made.

fully loaded breakfast burrito

▶ freeze for up to 4 weeks

▶ can be doubled

For a sustaining breakfast that includes whole grain, protein, and plenty of fiber (plus eye-opening heat, if you wish), this is one of the best dishes to keep in your freezer. These burritos defrost beautifully and almost instantly in the microwave, so you can take them to work, frozen, and zap them there. Vegetarians can omit the chorizo or replace it with a meat alternative.

Makes 4

¼ cup brown basmati rice

2 tablespoons canola oil

4 whole-wheat tortillas (7- or 8-inch diameter)

6 ounces fresh chorizo sausage

1 can (15 ounces) pinto beans, rinsed and drained

3 tablespoons prepared salsa

Salt and freshly ground pepper

½ cup (2 ounces) shredded Monterey Jack, Jalapeño Jack, or mild Cheddar cheese

side dish

Eggs, usually included in a breakfast burrito, turn grainy when frozen. If you really want one included, snuggle a scrambled egg into the warmed burrito just before serving.

cook smart

By brand, tortillas vary in thickness and size. You want the thinnest, most flexible whole-wheat tortillas. Choose those measuring 7 or 8 inches across; they may be labeled for tacos or fajitas. I find Maria and Ricardo's Tortilla Factory Soft Taco-Size organic whole-wheat tortillas from Trader Joe's are just right.

In a small saucepan, combine the rice with ¾ cup of water. Bring to a boil and add 1 tablespoon of the oil. Reduce the heat, cover, and cook until the rice is tender, 30 to 40 minutes. Set aside, covered.

Preheat the oven to 350°F.

Wrap the tortillas in foil and place in the oven to warm, 8 minutes. Set the wrapped warm tortillas aside.

Heat the remaining 1 tablespoon oil in a medium skillet over medium-high heat. Add the chorizo and cook, breaking it into small bits. Transfer the cooked chorizo to a mixing bowl, using a slotted spoon to drain it. Pour all but 1 tablespoon of the fat from the pan and return the pan to the heat.

Add the beans to the skillet. Using a fork, mash the beans coarsely, leaving some whole. Mix in the salsa and season the beans to taste with salt and pepper. When the mixture is heated through, add it to the cooked chorizo. Measure ½ cup of the warm rice and add it to the filling, saving the remaining rice for another use.

Add the cheese and use a fork to mix the filling until combined.

Place a warm tortilla on a work surface. Spoon one-fourth of the burrito filling horizontally across the center of the burrito. With the back of the spoon, shape the filling into a long, flat rectangle, leaving 1 inch at either edge of the tortilla. Lift up the edge of the tortilla towards you and roll to enclose filling, folding in the sides after the first turn. Repeat to make 3 more tortillas.

for serving now Wrap the burritos in foil and warm on a baking sheet in the oven until heated through, 15 to 20 minutes. Serve immediately.

to freeze Wrap the filled burritos individually in plastic freezer wrap and cool to room temperature. Wrap in heavy-duty foil and freeze.

to defrost and serve Unwrap a frozen burrito and wrap loosely in a paper towel. Heat in the microwave at full power for 1 minute 45 seconds. Turn the burrito over and microwave 1 minute 30 seconds longer. Serve immediately.

johnny appleseed french toast

Staying at a bed-and-breakfast in Vermont during fall foliage season, I was treated to this golden baked French toast studded with apples and raisins. Moist and creamy, it was essentially bread pudding for breakfast. The secrets to making it are using a tender egg bread, such as challah, and blending the eggs with cream cheese. Served just from the oven, it makes a glorious brunch. Freezing a second pan will let you enjoy it effortlessly another time, too.

▶ freeze for up to 6 weeks

▶ can be doubled

Makes 4 to 6 servings

⅓ cup golden raisins

½ cup apple cider or unfiltered apple juice

12 lightly packed cups challah or other egg bread, cut into 1-inch pieces

1 medium Golden Delicious apple, peeled, cored, and finely chopped

1½ cups milk

2 ounces cream cheese, diced

4 large eggs

1½ teaspoons vanilla extract

⅛ teaspoon salt

⅛ teaspoon freshly grated nutmeg

1 tablespoon sugar

¼ teaspoon ground cinnamon

to serve

Maple syrup

In a small bowl, soak the raisins in the cider or juice until plump, 20 to 30 minutes. Drain, discarding the liquid, and set aside.

Coat an 8-inch x 8-inch baking dish with butter or nonstick spray and set aside.

In a large mixing bowl, combine the bread, apple, and plumped raisins. In a blender, whirl the milk, cream cheese, eggs, vanilla, salt, and nutmeg until blended and pour over the bread. Toss, using a fork or your hands, until the bread is thoroughly soaked. Pack the soaked bread into the prepared dish and set aside for 30 minutes, or cover with plastic wrap and refrigerate overnight.

Preheat the oven to 350°F. If refrigerated, let the French toast sit at room temperature for 30 minutes. In a small bowl, combine the sugar and cinnamon and sprinkle over the top of the French toast.

Bake for 35 minutes, or until the top is golden brown and a knife inserted into the center feels hot.

for serving now Let the baked French toast sit for 10 minutes. Cut into 4 or 6 pieces and serve. Pass warmed maple syrup separately.

to freeze Cool the French toast in the dish. Cover with foil and refrigerate until cold. Unmold the French toast, cut into portions, and wrap individually in plastic freezer wrap, then heavy-duty foil. Freeze the chilled French toast.

to defrost and serve Thaw the French toast in the refrigerator for 6 to 12 hours, depending on the portion size. Remove the plastic wrap and reuse the foil to wrap the French toast.

Preheat the oven to 350°F.

Heat the foil-wrapped portions of French toast for 25 to 45 minutes, or until heated through. Serve with maple syrup.

cinnamon zucchini muffins

These special muffins and helps them go particularly well with a steaming cup of hot chocolate or coffee. Baking with oil can produce a heavy result, but not with my method of combining cold egg and oil. This technique instead helps create a fluffy, light crumb.

Makes 12

1½ cups finely grated zucchini

2 cups unbleached all-purpose flour

1½ teaspoons ground cinnamon

¾ teaspoon baking soda

¼ teaspoon baking powder

½ teaspoon salt

1 large egg, cold

1 cup sugar

½ cup canola oil, chilled

½ cup cold water

1 teaspoon vanilla extract

½ cup chopped walnuts

½ cup golden raisins

▶ freeze for up to 4 weeks

▶ can be doubled

▶ feeds a crowd

Preheat the oven to 400°F. Coat 12 cups of a muffin tin with nonstick spray and set aside.

Line a baking sheet with a double layer of paper towels. Spread the shredded zucchini in a thin layer on the towels and set aside for 20 minutes to drain.

In a medium bowl, whisk together the flour, cinnamon, baking soda, baking powder, and salt. In another bowl, beat the egg. Add the sugar and beat with a handheld mixer on medium-high until thick and lemon colored, 3 to 4 minutes. Add the oil, water, and vanilla and beat until the mixture resembles mayonnaise. Add the egg mixture to the dry ingredients, using a few swift strokes of a rubber spatula to combine them. Before they are completely mixed, fold in the zucchini, walnuts, and raisins. Spoon the batter into the prepared muffin tin, filling the cups almost to the top.

Bake for 20 to 25 minutes, or until a knife inserted in the center of a muffin comes out clean. Set the pan on a wire rack and cool the muffins for 10 minutes. Turn them out onto the rack.

for serving now Serve the muffins warm.

to freeze Cool the muffins completely. Wrap them individually in plastic freezer wrap, then heavy-duty foil. Store together in a resealable 1-gallon plastic freezer bag.

to defrost and serve Remove the foil and thaw the plastic-wrapped muffins on a wire rack on the counter. If desired, place the thawed muffins on a baking sheet in a 350°F oven for 10 to 15 minutes, just until warm.

cook smart
If the squash is very moist, wring it in cheesecloth to avoid making the muffins soggy.

oatmeal banana bread

▶ freeze for up to
   8 weeks

▶ can be doubled

▶ feeds a crowd

I serve this quick bread for breakfast since oats and buttermilk make it a complete meal. Try toasting a generous slice and topping it with apple butter.

Makes 8 servings

1 cup quick-cooking oats (not instant)

1 cup buttermilk

1 ½ cups unbleached all-purpose flour

1 teaspoon baking powder

1 teaspoon baking soda

1 ½ teaspoons ground cinnamon

¼ teaspoon salt

1 cup mashed ripe bananas, about
   2 large

1 cup sugar

2 large eggs

⅓ cup canola oil

½ cup chopped walnuts (optional)

side dish

For a snack, top a toasted slice of the bread with cottage cheese.

cook smart

Use bananas whose skins are turning black.

In a mixing bowl, combine the oats and buttermilk and set aside for 1 hour.

Preheat the oven to 350°F. Coat a 9-inch x 5-inch baking pan with nonstick spray and set aside.

In a small bowl, combine the flour, baking powder, baking soda, cinnamon, and salt. Mix the bananas and sugar into the softened oats. Break the eggs into a bowl and tilt it to 1 side. With a fork, lightly beat the eggs, and then mix them into the banana batter. Mix in the oil. Add the dry ingredients and mix with a rubber spatula. Spread the batter in the prepared pan. Sprinkle the nuts over the top, if using.

Bake until a knife inserted into the middle of the bread comes out clean, 65 to 75 minutes. The bread will be very dark. If it browns too quickly, tent foil loosely over the top. Cool the bread in the pan for 10 minutes, run a knife around the sides of the pan, and turn the bread out onto a wire rack to cool completely.

for serving now Wrap the cooled bread in plastic wrap and allow it to mellow at room temperature for 8 to 24 hours. Cut into 1-inch slices using a serrated knife. This bread keeps, wrapped in plastic, for up to 3 days at room temperature.

to freeze Wrap the cooled loaf in plastic freezer wrap, then heavy-duty foil, and freeze.

to defrost and serve Unwrap the frozen loaf and thaw on a plate at room temperature for 6 to 8 hours. Slice and serve.

freezer note Freezing actually makes this bread even moister.

red pepper and leek quiche

Creamy and rich, this golden quiche will remind you why no one cares if this dish is a cliché. Cream in the filling eliminates weeping when the frozen quiche is reheated. Sealing the crust with egg white helps it stay crisp, too. If you use a foil pie plate, the quiche can be frozen in its pan, ready to thaw and pop in the oven.

Makes 8 servings

- 1 single pie crust (9 inches), unbaked Flaky Pie Crust (page 236), or store-bought pie crust
- 3 large eggs, at room temperature
- 1 tablespoon unsalted butter
- 1 medium red bell pepper, seeded and chopped
- 1 medium leek, white and 2 inches of the pale green part, thinly sliced

- 1 cup heavy cream, at room temperature
- ¼ cup grated Asiago cheese (optional)
- ½ teaspoon dried thyme
- ½ teaspoon salt
- ⅛ teaspoon freshly ground pepper
- 4 deli-size slices Swiss cheese

- freeze for up to 8 weeks
- can be doubled
- feeds a crowd
- elegant for entertaining

Preheat the oven to 375°F. Place the chilled unbaked crust on a dark-colored baking sheet.

Break the eggs into a mixing bowl, but do not beat them. Dipping a pastry brush into the egg white, use it to coat the bottom and sides of the pie crust.

Bake the empty pie crust for 5 minutes, until it looks and feels dry. Set the partially baked crust aside, still on the baking sheet, leaving the oven on.

In a medium skillet, melt the butter over medium-high heat. Add the bell pepper and leek and cook until soft, 8 minutes, stirring often. Cool the vegetables for 5 minutes.

Meanwhile, whisk the eggs well. Add the cooked vegetables, cream, Asiago, thyme, salt, and pepper and whisk to combine. Arrange the cheese slices to cover the bottom of the cooled, partially baked crust. Set the baking sheet on the oven rack and pour the filling into the crust.

Bake the quiche for 35 to 40 minutes, or until the filling looks golden and no longer jiggles, and a knife inserted into the center comes out clean.

for serving now Cool the quiche on the baking sheet for 10 minutes. Cut it into wedges and serve.

side dish
Including some green from the leek boosts the flavor of the filling.

cook smart
Prepared frozen pie crust is an exception to the rule that you should avoid freezing foods twice.

Deli-size cheese slices are just the right size to line the crust.

Baking the quiche on a dark baking sheet helps avoid a soggy bottom crust.

to freeze Transfer the quiche to a wire rack and cool to room temperature. If storing the frozen quiche in its pie plate, wrap it in plastic freezer wrap, pressing the wrap against the surface of the filling. Wrap the quiche in foil. Refrigerate to chill, then freeze. To unmold and store the quiche without the pie plate, open-freeze until solid, about 6 hours. Unmold the frozen quiche onto plastic freezer wrap, wrap tightly, and then wrap in heavy-duty foil. Return the wrapped quiche to the freezer.

to defrost and serve If necessary, unwrap and drop the frozen quiche back into the original pie plate. Re-cover with plastic wrap, and thaw the quiche on a wire rack in the refrigerator for 12 to 18 hours.

Preheat the oven to 350°F.

Unwrap the thawed quiche and place on a dark baking sheet. Let it sit at room temperature while the oven heats.

Bake for 20 to 30 minutes, or until a knife inserted into the center feels hot to the touch. After 20 minutes, if the crust is deep gold, wrap foil around the edge to keep it from burning. Let the hot quiche sit for 5 minutes before cutting.

spinach and chorizo strata

A cross between baked French toast and a savory pudding, this strata is perfect for brunch. You can assemble 1 or 2 well ahead, then refrigerate 1 for up to 12 hours before baking and freeze the second to serve another time. Thanks to spicy chorizo, this dish packs lots of flavor.

▶ freeze for up to 4 weeks

▶ freeze now, cook later

Makes 4 servings

8 ounces fresh chorizo	2 cups milk, at room temperature
1 small onion, finely chopped	1 teaspoon salt
1 garlic clove, finely chopped	Freshly ground pepper
1 package (10 ounces) frozen chopped spinach, defrosted and squeezed dry	8 slices dense white bread
	2 cups (8 ounces) shredded Monterey Jack cheese
5 large eggs, at room temperature	

Set a medium skillet over medium-high heat. Squeeze the chorizo from its casing into the pan, breaking it up with a wooden spoon, when cooked through, 8 minutes.

If you cannot find fresh
chorizo, use the dried
kind, finely chopped and
cooked with 2 table-
spoons of canola oil.
Choose either spicy or
mild chorizo, according
to your taste.

Use a slotted spoon to scoop the chorizo into a mixing bowl, leaving its fat in the pan. Add the onion and garlic to the pan and cook until the onion is soft, 5 minutes, stirring often. Add the onion and garlic to the chorizo. Separate the spinach clumps with your fingers, add it to the mixing bowl, and mix with a fork to combine.

In another bowl, whisk the eggs lightly. Add the milk, salt, and 3 or 4 grinds of pepper and whisk to combine.

Coat a 9-inch x 9-inch baking dish with nonstick spray. Arrange 4 slices of the bread to cover the bottom of the dish; there may be some small spaces. Spread the spinach mixture to cover the bread in an even layer. Sprinkle on half of the cheese. Cover with the remaining bread. Pour the egg mixture over the strata, then sprinkle on the remaining cheese.

for serving now Let the strata stand at room temperature while heating the oven to 350°F.

Bake, uncovered, until the strata is puffy and browned on top or 45 minutes. Let sit for 10 minutes before serving.

to freeze Open-freeze the strata until solid, about 8 hours. Turn the frozen strata out onto plastic freezer wrap and wrap tightly. Wrap in heavy-duty foil and return the strata to the freezer.

to defrost and serve Unwrap the frozen strata and drop it back into the original baking dish. Cover the top with plastic wrap and thaw in the refrigerator for 18 to 24 hours.

Preheat the oven to 350°F. Let the strata sit at room temperature while the oven heats.

Bake until the strata is puffy and browned on top, 45 minutes. Let sit for 10 minutes, then serve.

wild blueberry sauce

Blueberries taste so good and are so magnificently healthy that I look for ways to eat them every day. This spiced syrup is one of my favorites. In addition to benefiting from using antioxidant-supercharged wild blueberries, you get to enjoy the pleasure of maple syrup, too.

Makes 2 cups

½ cup blueberry juice

¼ cup maple syrup, preferably Grade B

1 stick (2 inches) Mexican cinnamon (see Cook Smart)

2 cups frozen wild blueberries

▶ freeze for up to 4 weeks

▶ can be doubled

▶ feeds a crowd

In a medium saucepan, combine the juice, maple syrup, and cinnamon stick. Bring to a gentle boil over medium heat, cover, and remove from the heat to steep for 20 to 30 minutes. Remove and discard the cinnamon stick.

for serving now Add the blueberries and cook the syrup over medium heat just until they are defrosted and the syrup is warm; do not boil, which toughens the berries. Pour the syrup into a pitcher and serve. Unused syrup keeps, covered in the refrigerator, for 2 weeks.

to freeze Cool the spiced syrup to room temperature. Stir in the frozen blueberries. Freeze the syrup in a resealable 1-quart plastic freezer bag or divide it between 2 plastic freezer containers. Refrigerate to chill, then freeze.

to defrost and serve Defrost the syrup in the refrigerator. Or thaw the syrup in a large bowl of cold water, changing the water every 15 minutes and breaking the syrup into chunks as it defrosts. Pour the defrosted syrup into a saucepan, add 1 tablespoon of maple syrup, and set over medium heat just until warmed.

freezer note The maple syrup flavor fades in the freezer. Adding a tablespoon of maple syrup before serving brings it back.

cook smart

Use Mexican cinnamon, or canela, which tastes sweet and spicy (plus it is inexpensive). Cassia from Vietnam or China, often sold as cinnamon, is a good alternative.

freezer strawberry preserves

▶ freeze for up to
6 weeks

▶ elegant for
entertaining

Imagine making homemade preserves in minutes and using only 1 cup of sugar for 4 jars of preserves. Using no-cook freezer jam pectin (see Side Dish) lets you do both. Jam made with pectin has a less luxurious texture, but you get sparkling, uncooked preserves with all the sun-ripe flavor and nutrition of the fresh fruit. Be sure to select intensely red, fully ripe, unblemished strawberries.

Makes 4 cups

3 pounds ripe strawberries, at room temperature

3 tablespoons fresh lemon juice

Fruit pectin (see Side Dish)

1 cup sugar

side dish

The 1-cup plastic freezer jars made by Ball, available at www. freshpreserving.com and www.amazon.com, are the perfect containers for freezer preserves. Ball also sells freezer jam pectin, although I prefer Pomona's Universal Pectin, which is made from citrus and is preservative-free. Natural food markets, www.amazon.com, and www.pomonapectin. com sell it.

cook smart

Local strawberries can be sublimely good. But if the weather is rainy, they will be watery. They can also be sharply acidic. Driscoll strawberries, grown in California and Florida, lack locavore allure, but they have reliable flavor and toothsome flesh that makes good preserves.

Rinse and hull the berries. Cut the fruit into ¾-inch pieces, removing any blemished areas, and place in a wide, shallow bowl. Crush the berries, using a potato masher or sturdy fork, until they are moist and juicy but still chunky. Measure 4 cups, reserving any extra for another use.

Mix the lemon juice with the berries and let sit for 30 minutes to draw out more juice.

Following the package directions, prepare the pectin and calcium mixture provided with it. Add ½ cup of the pectin to the strawberries and mix well. Mix in the sugar until very well combined. Add the calcium water as directed and mix well.

Spoon the preserves into four 1-cup plastic freezer jars or other immaculately clean containers that seal tightly. Let the preserves sit at room temperature for 2 hours to set.

for serving now These preserves can be served as soon as they have set. Refrigerated, they keep for 2 weeks.

to freeze Chill the preserves in the refrigerator, then freeze. While at their best for 6 weeks, frozen preserves, I find, do keep reasonable flavor for up to 3 months.

to defrost and serve Thaw frozen preserves in the refrigerator, about 6 hours.

cooking to fill your freezer

British royalty believe in producing an heir and a spare. To stock the freezer, the equivalent by cooking double recipes and making multiple dishes in one cooking session. Do this twice a week for a month, stowing the extra servings of soups, casseroles, meatloaf, and other dishes in the freezer, and you will quickly build up a nice selection of instant meals.

A good way to accomplish this is to dedicate a Sunday afternoon or weekday evening to making two or three dishes. The secret here is picking recipes where the work fits together. Looking through the chapters, here are examples of dishes that are easy to make in one kitchen session. Once you experience the efficiency of this method, you may schedule a regular "freezer night" on your calendar.

This grouped cooking is particularly useful when a key ingredient, such as ground beef or chicken breasts, is on special or you plan to shop at a club super-store. Given today's food costs, it can save you a bundle.

Secrets for success in grouped cooking include:

- Read through all of the recipes and make a careful shopping list.

- Keep a photocopy of all the recipes handy while shopping, as well as in the kitchen.

- Before going into the kitchen, write out a master list of all the preparation needed for all the recipes so you can see how to group the work. Use this as a guide to keep the steps in order when in the kitchen.

- Complete as many preparation steps as possible before you start to cook. For example, chop all of the onions and other chopped ingredients called for, and measure the flour and other dry ingredients for all the recipes.

- Label the containers holding the individual ingredients for each dish, then group them together.
- Put on music you like. Cook with a friend and share what you make together, or enjoy this as "me" time. Most of all, have fun.

souper sunday

Spiced Butternut Squash and Carrot Soup (page 60)

Easy Split Pea Soup (page 50)

Zucchini Vichyssoise (page 42)

To make this trio of meatless soups, set three pots on the stove, add the chopped veggies called for, simmer until done, and then puree each soup.

mad for meatballs

Sweet and Tangy Bison Balls (page 38)

Frankie's Meatballs (page 134)

Italian Wedding Soup (page 66)

For two of these recipes, you bake the meatballs. For the third, simmer them in 20-Minute Tomato Sauce (page 192), roll up your sleeves and go for making Sunday Red Sauce (page 131), or simply use prepared tomato sauce.

viva vegetarian

Best Ever Lentil Chili (page 135)

Persian Red Lentil and Beet Soup (page 56)

Maple Baked Beans (page 160)

These three protein-rich legume dishes include two that can simmer on the stove at the same time and cook in less than an hour. The baked beans, made in a slow cooker, are a set-it-and-forget-it dish.

grind it out

Always Good Meat Loaf (page 121)

Turkish Ground Beef Kebabs (page 76)

Pizza Noodle Casserole (page 98)

When ground beef is on special or you shop at a superstore, grouping these recipes lets you enjoy substantial savings. Making a pair of meatloaves (baked in separate pans) and either two casseroles or a double recipe of the kebabs requires 6 pounds of ground meat. The result is five meals that each feed from four to eight.

crazy for cookies

Cherry Chocolate Chippers (page 197)

Peanut Butter Cookies, Naturally (page 198)

Red Hot Pinwheels (page 204)

Assembling the dough for these three treats, even when doubling the recipes, takes about 2 hours and ensures a rich future for your cookie jar. If you decide to bake up a batch or two, you will need another hour, with the dividend of fresh-baked cookies to enjoy.

a chocolate orgy

Hot Fudge Sauce (see Frozen Hot Fudge Sundaes, page 194)

Deep Dark Chocolate Fondue (page 221)

Mexican Chocolate Shortbread (page 202)

Freeze Please Fudge Brownies (page 215)

Chocoholics, go for it! In half an hour you can make glorious fudge sauce and mix up a sinful fondue. Then put your oven to work for buttery shortbread and brownies. Your reward will be a stash of heavenly chocolate treats and the aroma of chocolate perfuming the house.

acknowledgments

Creating recipes and writing are journeys of discovery. Thank you to everyone along the way who supported and contributed to the process of arriving at the best recipes, techniques, and text. Here are shout-outs I need to share.

As experts who guided me and provided essential information: Akasha Richmond, Mani Niall, Eileen Guastella, Jessica Meyer at King Arthur Flour, and Patricia Schweitzer at Reynolds Consumer Products. And to Rose Levy Beranbaum, Dorrie Greenspan, and Carole Walters for expertise shared ex libris.

For finding ingredients with flavors that are just right, both before and after freezing: the folks at Driscoll Berries, Guittard chocolate, Melissa's, PomWonderful, and Wholesome Sweeteners.

Recipe testing required a team of assistants, road testers, and tasters. Thank you Lorri Allen, Sydney Fox, Ann Smith, Barney Stein, and Christina Zavala, plus Marsha, Mariebelle, the Volpis, Mario, Manny, and everyone else at 460 East; Mildred and all the Millers and Tessorieros; Lucy, Mark, and Shandi at Dr. T's; and Dr. Goss, the dentist with a sweet tooth. Also to Amanda Bosca, Hilary Maler, and Meryl Rosofsky for helpful observations, and to Laura Weiss for the good times and family cookie recipe shared in your cozy kitchen.

When my freezer overflowed, thank you Amanda, Nadine, Susi, and Mike for providing backup space. Mike, the cheesecake was a fair price to pay.

Thanks to Lani Bloom for your unflagging help in turning thoughts into perfected recipes, recipes into accurate text, and text into a neatly organized manuscript. And to Jay for eating above and beyond the call of duty.

To Pam Krauss: Without your vision and editing, this book would not be, or be nearly as good. Thank you for initiating and guiding the stimulating journey. Thank you also to Amy King at Rodale for a handsome book, and to Meghan Shlow and Deborah William for beautiful food, perfectly presented, and to Kate Mathis for mouthwatering photos.

Angela Miller, my agent, thank you for always turning proposals into reality, and to Thad Rutkowski and The Writers' Voice group for insights that made the words work better.

For escapes that cleared my head, thanks to everyone at the oldest established permanent floating mah-jongg game on the West Side, and to the bookshop at the New York Public Library's Webster Branch, an endless source of vintage murder mysteries and sociable chat.

Finally, to the family and friends who listen and endure—Muriel, Barney, Nadine, and Pam. And to Joan, for eating, observing, and for your unstinting support.

Index

Underscored page references indicate side bar text. **Boldfaced** page references indicate photographs.